Ethnologist and adventurer THOR HEYERDAHL became known to the world when he organized and led the famous Kon-Tiki (1947) and Ra (1969–70) transoceanic scientific expeditions. Both were intended to prove the possibility of ancient transoceanic contacts among distant civilizations and cultures.

In the 1947 voyage of the primitive raft *Kon-Tiki*, Heyerdahl and a small crew sailed from the Pacific coast of South America to Polynesia, demonstrating the possibility that the Polynesians may have originated in South America. The story of the voyage was related in KON-TIKI and in a documentary motion picture of the same name.

Heyerdahl's accounts of his other incredible expeditions include *Aku-Aku: The Secret of Easter Island* (1958); *Fatu-Hiva: Back to Nature* (1974); and *Early Man and the Ocean: A Search for the Beginnings of Navigation and Seaborne Civilizations* (1979).

TITLES AVAILABLE IN THE ENRICHED CLASSICS SERIES

OTHER CLASSICS

Thor Heyerdahl

Kon-Tiki

ACROSS THE PACIFIC BY RAFT

Translated by
F. H. LYON

SIMON & SCHUSTER PAPERBACKS
NEW YORK LONDON TORONTO SYDNEY

Simon & Schuster Paperbacks
A Division of Simon & Schuster, Inc.
1230 Avenue of the Americas
New York, NY 10020

Supplementary materials copyright © 1973 by Simon & Schuster, Inc.

This Simon & Schuster paperback edition May 2013

SIMON & SCHUSTER PAPERBACKS and colophon are registered trademarks of Simon & Schuster, Inc.

For information regarding special discounts for bulk purchases, please contact Simon & Schuster Special Sales at 1-866-506-1949 or business@simonandschuster.com.

The Simon & Schuster Speakers Bureau can bring authors to your live event. For more information or to book an event, contact the Simon & Schuster Speakers Bureau at 1-866-248-3049 or visit our website at www.simonspeakers.com.

COVER ARTWORK © 2013 THE WEINSTEIN COMPANY

Manufactured in the United States of America

10 9 8 7 6 5 4 3 2

ISBN 978-1-4767-5337-9
ISBN 978-1-4516-8592-3 (ebook)

CONTENTS

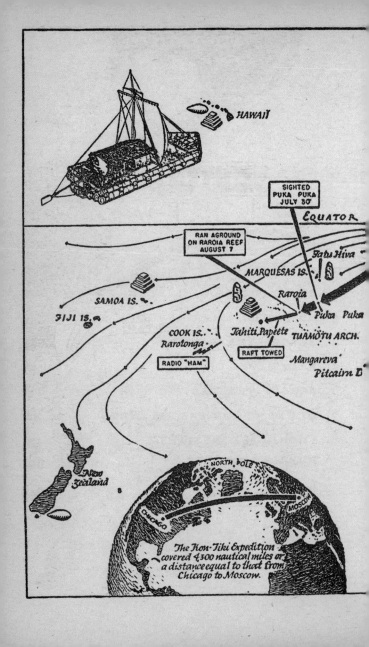

HAWAII

SIGHTED
PUKA PUKA
JULY 30°

EQUATOR

RAN AGROUND
ON RAROIA REEF
AUGUST 7

Fatu Hiva

MARQUESAS IS.

Raroia

SAMOA IS.

FIJI IS.

Puka Puka

COOK IS.
Rarotonga

Tahiti, Papeete

TUAMOTU ARCH.

RAFT TOWED

RADIO "HAM"

Mangareva

Pitcairn I.

New
Zealand

NORTH POLE

MOSCOW

CHICAGO

The Kon-Tiki Expedition
covered 4300 nautical miles or
a distance equal to that from
Chicago to Moscow.

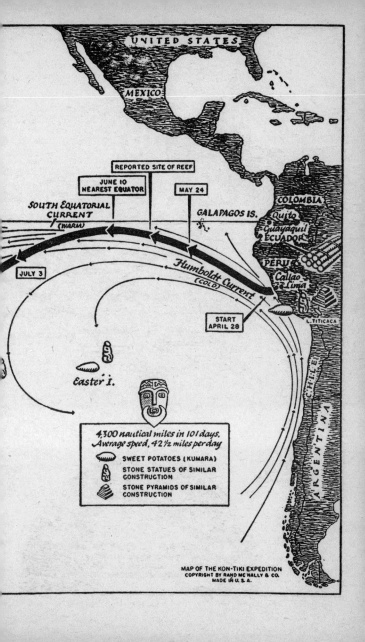

UNITED STATES

MEXICO

REPORTED SITE OF REEF

JUNE 10
NEAREST EQUATOR

MAY 24

SOUTH EQUATORIAL
CURRENT
(WARM)

GALAPAGOS IS.

COLOMBIA
Quito
Guayaquil
ECUADOR

PERU
Callao
Lima

JULY 3

Humboldt Current
(COLD)

START
APRIL 28

L. TITICACA

Easter I.

CHILE

4,300 nautical miles in 101 days.
Average speed, 42½ miles per day

SWEET POTATOES (KUMARA)

STONE STATUES OF SIMILAR
CONSTRUCTION

STONE PYRAMIDS OF SIMILAR
CONSTRUCTION

ARGENTINA

MAP OF THE KON-TIKI EXPEDITION
COPYRIGHT BY RAND MC NALLY & CO.
MADE IN U.S.A.

Kon-Tiki

Foreword to the 35th Anniversary Edition

SOME PEOPLE BELIEVE IN FATE, OTHERS DON'T. I DO, and I don't. It may seem at times as if invisible fingers move us about like puppets on strings. But for sure, we are not born to be dragged along. We can grab the strings ourselves and adjust our course at every crossroad, or take off at any little trail into the unknown.

The pages that follow recount the story of a young man pulled up against the wall until he grasped the strings of destiny. When today I read this story which once I wrote myself, I recall the most decisive moment in my life, when I, a sworn landlubber with a fear of water deeper than to my neck, cut all ties to the land and steered out into the largest and deepest body of water on earth, into a strange adventure and an unknown future. From then till the present day, my life has been filled with adventures linked together like pearls on a thread. Pearls rarely turn up in oysters served to you on a plate; you have to dive for them. Adventure for adventure's sake has never appealed to me. But I do not shun adventure if it comes my way.

I grew up as an overprotected boy. A dreamer. My university years were split between studies of man and beast. I was formally educated as a zoologist at Oslo University, but my heart was with my studies of Pacific peoples at the Kroepelien Polynesian Library in the same city, the world's largest private library on Polynesia (it has since been incorporated in the Kon-Tiki Museum Library, Oslo). And as a bookworm unable to swim, I went in 1937 to Polynesia to live for a year on the jungle island Fatu Hiva, severed from contact with the outside world.

I went to Polynesia to study how *animals* had reached
oceanic islands, carried by winds and currents. I came home
with a controversial theory of how *man* had reached these
islands in prehistoric times. Scholars had invariably assumed that all early voyagers into the Pacific had sailed and
paddled straight from Southeast Asia. I disagreed. Prevailing winds and currents would prevent their traveling directly
eastward from Asia. Yet there were two feasible sea routes
to Polynesia: One was a circuitous route from Southeast
Asia by way of Northwest America to Hawaii, and the other
from South America directly to eastern Polynesia.

This book tells the story of how six young men proved
that a prehistoric voyage from South America was possible,
contrary to the predictions of scientists and sailors. The
South American balsa raft, which scholars had claimed
would sink if it were not regularly dried out ashore, stayed
buoyant as a cork. And Polynesia, held to be inaccessible for
a watercraft from ancient America, proved to be well within
the range of aboriginal voyagers from Peru.

How did science react to being proved wrong? Among the
first to yield was the world's leading authority on prehistoric
watercraft in Peru, Dr. S. K. Lothrop of Harvard University, the very scholar whose judgment about balsa rafts we
had disproven. But the worldwide publicity given the *Kon-
Tiki* voyage was considered a slap in the face by other
scientists who had quoted Lothrop and based their own
work and teachings on the assumption that balsa rafts would
sink. From all over the world, scholars hit back, accusing us
of a stunt without scientific merit. Public interest increased
with the polemics. The book on the *Kon-Tiki* expedition
became a best-seller, eventually translated into 65 languages, and our film of the voyage was awarded an Oscar as
best documentary feature for 1951.

Years of controversy followed, during which scholars
everywhere initially refused to even listen to the arguments
behind the "Kon-Tiki theory." The first formal challenge
came from the Royal Swedish Society for Anthropology and
Geography, which asked me in 1950 to defend my views and
as a result awarded me my first scientific medal. Other
awards followed, in Scotland, then France. In 1952, five
years after the raft voyage, I was able to publish for the first

time my 800-page volume *American Indians in the Pacific: The Theory Behind the Kon-Tiki Expedition*. The same year, I accepted an invitation to deliver three lectures at the 30th International Americanist Congress at Cambridge University; when the congress next assembled, in Brazil, I attended as an honorary vice-president.

Nonetheless, the polemics continued. The Galapagos Islands were said to disprove the Kon-Tiki theory. They lie closer to South America than any of the Polynesian islands. If South American voyagers dared to sail all the way to Polynesia, why had they not settled the Galapagos as well? A new challenge. New library studies.

Numerous scholars had been to the Galapagos since Darwin's visit in 1835. Zoologists, botanists, geologists—but not a single archaeologist. None had come to look for early human traces that far from the mainland. The visitors all quoted one another to the effect that no human eye had seen these islands before the Europeans arrived in 1535. Having discovered that Inca balsa rafts were entirely capable of reaching the Galapagos, I brought the first two archaeologists to investigate the islands in 1953. We searched in the few level places where early rafts could have landed between the rugged lava cliffs and rocks. Four prehistoric campsites were located on three of these arid islands. From the barren soil, the trowels of the scientists scraped up large quantities of potsherds and other artifacts, many of them identified as pre-Inca by the U.S. National Museum. This proved that numerous voyagers from Peru and Ecuador had visited the island group in pre-Columbian times. Permanent settlement had been prevented by only seasonal access to drinking water.

The nearest inhabitable island out at sea was Easter Island, halfway between South America and the rest of Polynesia. The colossal statues and stone walls of unknown origins that dotted the landscape were said by the Polynesian population to be the remains from an earlier people. Because this island lay farthest from Asia, most scholars believed it was the last to have been reached by aboriginal man. How then, I wondered, could the Easter Islanders have had time to develop and later forget this amazing prehistoric culture, which furthermore had surprised scholars by closely resem-

bling pre-Inca remains? Dr. H. Lavachery, the only profes-
sional archaeologist to have visited Easter Island, admitted
that he had never attempted excavations because the soil
seemed shallow and human settlement was thought to be
late.

In 1955–56, I chartered an expedition ship for a one-year
survey of Easter Island and eastern Polynesia with a
multinational team including five archaeologists. Excavations revealed that the famous giant heads were actually
statues buried to their necks, with huge bodies and arms
below ground. One clan on the island, claiming descent from
the statuemakers, demonstrated how the colossal stone figures were quarried, transported, and raised on end. The
archaeologists uncovered previously unknown types of
statues and stone houses that followed prototypes from pre-
Inca South America. Carbon dating showed that the island
had been inhabited at least a thousand years earlier than
hitherto assumed.

A turning point in the still heated discussions came in
1961, when some 3,000 specialists assembled at the Tenth
Pacific Science Congress in Honolulu. Our Galapagos and
Easter Island expeditions were discussed in the sessions for
archaeology, physical anthropology, and botany, and in a
special symposium on the Galapagos group. A resolution
unanimously passed at the congress stated that Southeast
Asia with adjacent islands and South America constituted
the main source areas of Pacific island peoples and cultures.

The fierce fighting on all fronts now petered out to occasional sniping. No tempest at sea is harder on a man than to
stand alone encircled by a firing squad of international
authorities. A firm conviction of being in the right becomes
your only armor against the barrage of assaults that can
often be both personal and unfair. Yet dissidence and controversy are what bring science forward. Agreement and ac-
ceptance rarely stimulate experiments and progress. By this
time, invitations from universities and scientific academies
allowed me to present and defend my case widely. Honorary
professorates and doctor's degrees, scientific medals, and
fellowship in academies of science from New York to Moscow reflected that the tide had turned.

I now felt free to turn to the ocean on the opposite side of

America. The trade winds and currents of the tropical Atlantic pushed constantly from Africa to America on the same course and with the same strength as they left America's Pacific side for Polynesia. Planked ships were unknown in America until Columbus arrived, but reed ships were typical for great pre-Columbian civilizations on either side of the Atlantic. On Easter Island, we had found outlines of reed ships incised on the chests of statues, and small reed boats still made by the islanders were the same as those used in the former Inca empire. They in turn were amazingly like the oldest form of ship among the great Old World civilizations in Egypt, Mesopotamia, and the Indus Valley.

Like the balsa raft, reed ships were assumed incapable of long sea voyages because of waterlogging. In 1970, seven of us from seven nations succeeded in sailing our reed ship *Ra II* from Morocco in Africa to Barbados in America at our second attempt at crossing the Atlantic in an Egyptian type vessel of papyrus reeds. In 1977–78, eleven of us from different nations spent five months on the *Tigris*, a Sumerian type reed ship, navigating from Iraq to Oman, the Indus Valley, and Africa.

With crews as unfamiliar with reed bundle boats and balsa log rafts as myself, I had found it possible in my lifetime to sail such vessels from Mesopotamia to the Indus Valley, from Asia to Africa, from Africa to America, and from America to Polynesia. Why could not the intrepid inventors of these seaworthy sailing craft, who built pyramids, have managed the same in the course of centuries?

Unlike pyramids, old boats sink or rot. With our ocean crossings, we had proved prehistoric seafaring possible, but the old wakes were gone. There were still those who insisted that, although the vessels were proven seaworthy, pre-European voyagers might nonetheless have preferred to sail within sight of land. The proof to the contrary came in 1982, when I went for the first time to explore the tiny Maldive Islands, far out in the Indian Ocean off the southern tip of India. During the last decade, airborne mass tourism has invaded this archipelago, which lies too far from any continent to have attracted modern archaeologists.

Maldive history began in A.D. 1153 with the arrival of Moslem Arabs, over three centuries before Columbus's time. Moslem religion rigidly forbids human illustrations of any kind, so it was a startling discovery when some islanders found a big stone statue with long ears emerging from the ground. Because of our reed ship voyage in the Indian Ocean, I was informed in 1982 by the Maldive authorities about this statue. I rushed to the spot to find that all but the head had been smashed by religious fanatics. It was a large and beautiful Buddha head, and showed that Buddhists had been there before the Arabs came in 1153.

Asked by the president of the young Republic of Maldives to start the first local excavations, I returned with archaeologists from Oslo University in 1983. The Maldives proved to be an undisturbed archaeological paradise. Stone stele with multiple heads of the grinning Hindu demon-god Shiva and a stone mask of the trunk-nosed sea monster Makara lay hidden in the ground. The Hindus must have been there even before the prehistoric Buddhists. On Gaaf-Gan, an uninhabited jungle island right on the equator, we found a square pyramidal temple still standing 30 feet above the ground. Richly decorated with sun symbols and astronomically oriented to the sun, it had been raised by ancient sun worshippers and was approached by ramps on all four sides. The decor included lion sculptures and the high relief of an ox. We could never have asked for more concrete proof of prehistoric seafaring.

The *Kon-Tiki* expedition opened my eyes to what the ocean really is. It is a conveyor and not an isolator. The ocean has been man's highway from the days he built the first buoyant ships, long before he tamed the horse, invented wheels, and cut roads through the virgin jungles.

THOR HEYERDAHL

May 1984

Kon-Tiki

1 A THEORY

*Retrospect—The Old Man on Fatu Hiva—Wind and Current
—Hunting for Tiki—Who Peopled Polynesia?—Riddle of
the South Seas—Theories and Facts—Legend of Kon-Tiki
and the Mysterious White Men—War comes*

ONCE IN A WHILE YOU FIND YOURSELF IN AN
odd situation. You get into it by degrees and in the most
natural way but, when you are right in the midst of it, you
are suddenly astonished and ask yourself how in the world
it all came about.

If, for example, you put to sea on a wooden raft with a
parrot and five companions, it is inevitable that sooner or
later you will wake up one morning out at sea, perhaps a
little better rested than ordinarily, and begin to think about it.

On one such morning I sat writing in a dew-drenched logbook:

—*May 17. Norwegian Independence Day. Heavy sea. Fair
wind. I am cook today and found seven flying fish on deck,
one squid on the cabin roof, and one unknown fish in Torstein's sleeping bag. . . .*

Here the pencil stopped, and the same thought interjected
itself: This is really a queer seventeenth of May—indeed,
taken all round, a most peculiar existence. How did it all
begin?

If I turned left, I had an unimpeded view of a vast blue sea
with hissing waves, rolling by close at hand in an endless
pursuit of an ever retreating horizon. If I turned right, I saw

the inside of a shadowy cabin in which a bearded individual
was lying on his back reading Goethe with his bare toes carefully dug into the latticework in the low bamboo roof of the
crazy little cabin that was our common home.

"Bengt," I said, pushing away the green parrot that wanted
to perch on the logbook, "can you tell me how the hell we
came to be doing this?"

Goethe sank down under the red-gold beard.

"The devil I do; you know best yourself. It was your
damned idea, but I think it's grand."

He moved his toes three bars up and went on reading
Goethe unperturbed. Outside the cabin three other fellows
were working in the roasting sun on the bamboo deck. They
were half-naked, brown-skinned, and bearded, with stripes of
salt down their backs and looking as if they had never done
anything else than float wooden rafts westward across the
Pacific. Erik came crawling in through the opening with his
sextant and a pile of papers.

"98° 46′ west by 8° 2′ south—a good day's run since yesterday, chaps!"

He took my pencil and drew a tiny circle on a chart which
hung on the bamboo wall—a tiny circle at the end of a chain
of nineteen circles that curved across from the port of Callao
on the coast of Peru. Herman, Knut, and Torstein too came
eagerly crowding in to see the new little circle that placed us
a good 40 sea miles nearer the South Sea islands than the last
in the chain.

"Do you see, boys?" said Herman proudly. "That means
we're 850 sea miles from the coast of Peru."

"And we've got another 3,500 to go to get to the nearest
islands," Knut added cautiously.

"And to be quite precise," said Torstein, "we're 15,000 feet
above the bottom of the sea and a few fathoms below the
moon."

So now we all knew exactly where we were, and I could go
on speculating as to why. The parrot did not care; he only
wanted to tug at the log. And the sea was just as round, just
as sky-encircled, blue upon blue.

Perhaps the whole thing had begun the winter before, in

the office of a New York museum. Or perhaps it had already begun ten years earlier, on a little island in the Marquesas group in the middle of the Pacific. Maybe we would land on the same island now, unless the northeast wind sent us farther south in the direction of Tahiti and the Tuamotu group. I could see the little island clearly in my mind's eye, with its jagged rust-red mountains, the green jungle which flowed down their slopes toward the sea, and the slender palms that waited and waved along the shore. The island was called Fatu Hiva; there was no land between it and us where we lay drifting, but nevertheless it was thousands of sea miles away. I saw the narrow Ouia Valley, where it opened out toward the sea, and remembered so well how we sat there on the lonely beach and looked out over this same endless sea, evening after evening. I was accompanied by my wife then, not by bearded pirates as now. We were collecting all kinds of live creatures, and images and other relics of a dead culture.

I remembered very well one particular evening. The civilized world seemed incomprehensibly remote and unreal. We had lived on the island for nearly a year, the only white people there; we had of our own will forsaken the good things of civilization along with its evils. We lived in a hut we had built for ourselves, on piles under the palms down by the shore, and ate what the tropical woods and the Pacific had to offer us.

On that particular evening we sat, as so often before, down on the beach in the moonlight, with the sea in front of us. Wide awake and filled with the romance that surrounded us, we let no impression escape us. We filled our nostrils with an aroma of rank jungle and salt sea and heard the wind's rustle in leaves and palm tops. At regular intervals all other noises were drowned by the great breakers that rolled straight in from the sea and rushed in foaming over the land till they were broken up into circles of froth among the shore boulders. There was a roaring and rustling and rumbling among millions of glistening stones, till all grew quiet again when the sea water had withdrawn to gather strength for a new attack on the invincible coast.

"It's queer," said my wife, "but there are never breakers like this on the other side of the island."

"No," said I, "but this is the windward side; there's always a sea running on this side."

We kept on sitting there and admiring the sea which, it seemed, was loath to give up demonstrating that here it came rolling in from eastward, eastward, eastward. It was the eternal east wind, the trade wind, which had disturbed the sea's surface, dug it up, and rolled it forward, up over the eastern horizon and over here to the islands. Here the unbroken advance of the sea was finally shattered against cliffs and reefs, while the east wind simply rose above coast and woods and mountains and continued westward unhindered, from island to island, toward the sunset.

So had the ocean swells and the lofty clouds above them rolled up over the same eastern horizon since the morning of time. The first natives who reached these islands knew well enough that this was so, and so did the present islanders. The long-range ocean birds kept to the eastward on their daily fishing trips to be able to return with the eastern wind at night when the belly was full and the wings tired. Even trees and flowers were wholly dependent on the rain produced by the eastern winds, and all the vegetation grew accordingly. And we knew by ourselves, as we sat there, that far, far below that eastern horizon, where the clouds came up, lay the open coast of South America. There was nothing but 4,000 miles of open sea between.

We gazed at the driving clouds and the heaving moonlit sea, and we listened to an old man who squatted half-naked before us and stared down into the dying glow from a little smoldering fire.

"Tiki," the old man said quietly, "he was both god and chief. It was Tiki who brought my ancestors to these islands where we live now. Before that we lived in a big country beyond the sea."

He poked the coals with a stick to keep them from going out. The old man sat thinking. He lived for ancient times and was firmly fettered to them. He worshiped his forefathers and their deeds in an unbroken line back to the time of the

gods. And he looked forward to being reunited with them.
Old Tei Tetua was the sole survivor of all the extinct tribes
on the east coast of Fatu Hiva. How old he was he did not
know, but his wrinkled, bark-brown, leathery skin looked as
if it had been dried in sun and wind for a hundred years.
He was one of the few on these islands that still remembered
and believed in his father's and his grandfather's legendary
stories of the great Polynesian chief-god Tiki, son of the sun.

When we crept to bed that night in our little pile hut, old
Tei Tetua's stories of Tiki and the islanders' old home beyond the sea continued to haunt my brain, accompanied by
the muffled roar of the surf in the distance. It sounded like a
voice from far-off times, which, it seemed, had something it
wanted to tell, out there in the night. I could not sleep. It was
as though time no longer existed, and Tiki and his seafarers
were just landing in the surf on the beach below. A thought
suddenly struck me and I said to my wife: "Have you noticed
that the huge stone figures of Tiki in the jungle are remarkably like the monoliths left by extinct civilizations in South
America?"

I felt sure that a roar of agreement came from the breakers.
And then they slowly subsided while I slept.

*   *   *

So, perhaps, the whole thing began. So began, in any case,
a whole series of events which finally landed the six of us and
a green parrot on board a raft off the coast of South America.

I remember how I shocked my father and amazed my
mother and my friends when I came back to Norway and
handed over my glass jars of beetles and fish from Fatu Hiva
to the University Zoological Museum. I wanted to give up animal studies and tackle primitive peoples. The unsolved
mysteries of the South Seas had fascinated me. There must
be a rational solution of them, and I had made my objective
the identification of the legendary hero Tiki.

In the years that followed, breakers and jungle ruins were a
kind of remote, unreal dream which formed the background
and accompaniment to my studies of the Pacific peoples. Al-

though the thoughts and inclinations of primitive man can never be rightly judged by an armchair student, yet he can, in his library bookshelves, travel wider beyond time and horizons than can any modern outdoor explorer. Scientific works, journals from the time of the earliest explorations, and endless collections in museums in Europe and America offered a wealth of material for use in the puzzle I wanted to try to put together. Since our own race first reached the Pacific islands after the discovery of South America, investigators in all branches of science have collected an almost bottomless store of information about the inhabitants of the South Seas and all the peoples living round about them. But there has never been any agreement as to the origin of this isolated island people, or the reason why this type is only found scattered over all the solitary islands in the eastern part of the Pacific.

When the first Europeans at last ventured to cross this greatest of all oceans, they discovered to their amazement that right out in the midst of it lay a number of small mountainous islands and flat coral reefs, isolated from each other and from the world in general by vast areas of sea. And every single one of these islands was already inhabited by people who had come there before them—tall, handsome people who met them on the beach with dogs and pigs and fowl. Where had they come from? They talked a language which no other tribe knew. And the men of our race, who boldly called themselves the discoverers of the islands, found cultivated fields and villages with temples and huts on every single habitable island. On some islands, indeed, they found old pyramids, paved roads, and carven stone statues as high as a four-story house. But the explanation of the whole mystery was lacking. Who were these people, and where had they come from?

One can safely say that the answers to these riddles have been nearly as many in number as the works which have treated of them. Specialists in different fields have put forward quite different solutions, but their affirmations have always been disproved later by logical arguments from experts who have worked along other lines. Malaya, India, China, Japan, Arabia, Egypt, the Caucasus, Atlantis, even Germany and Norway, have been seriously championed as the Polynesians' homeland. But every time some obstacle of a decisive character has appeared and put the whole problem into the melting pot again.

And where science stopped, imagination began. The mysterious monoliths on Easter Island, and all the other relics of unknown origin on this tiny island, lying in complete solitude halfway between the easternmost Pacific islands and the coast of South America, gave rise to all sorts of speculations. Many observed that the finds on Easter Island recalled in many ways the relics of the prehistoric civilizations of South America. Perhaps there had once been a bridge of land over the sea, and this had sunk? Perhaps Easter Island, and all the other South Sea islands which had monuments of the same kind, were remains of a sunken continent left exposed above the sea?

This has been a popular theory and an acceptable explanation among laymen, but geologists and other scientists do not favor it. Zoologists, moreover, prove quite simply, from the study of insects and snails on the South Sea islands, that throughout the history of mankind these islands have been completely isolated from one another and from the continents round them, exactly as they are today.

We know, therefore, with absolute certainty that the original Polynesian race must at some time, willingly or unwillingly, have come drifting or sailing to these remote islands. And a closer look at the inhabitants of the South Seas shows that it cannot have been very many centuries since they came. For, even if the Polynesians live scattered over an area of sea four times as large as the whole of Europe, nevertheless they have not managed to develop different languages in the different islands. It is thousands of sea miles from Hawaii in the north to New Zealand in the south, from Samoa in the west to Easter Island in the east, yet all these isolated tribes speak dialects of a common language which we have called Polynesian.

Writing was unknown in all the islands, except for a few wooden tablets bearing incomprehensible hieroglyphs which the natives preserved on Easter Island, though neither they

themselves nor anyone else could read them. But they had
schools, and the poetical teaching of history was their most
important function, for in Polynesia history was the same as
religion. The people were ancestor-worshipers; they worshiped their dead chiefs all the way back to Tiki's time, and
of Tiki himself it was said that he was son of the sun.

On almost every island learned men could enumerate the
names of all the island's chiefs back to the time when it was
first peopled. To assist their memories they often used a com-
plicated system of knots on twisted strings, as the Inca Indians
did in Peru. Modern scientists have collected all these local
genealogies from the different islands and found that they
agree with one another with astonishing exactness, both in
names and number of generations. It has been discovered in
this way, by taking an average Polynesian generation to rep-
resent twenty-five years, that the South Sea islands were not
peopled before about 500 A.D. A new cultural wave with a
new string of chiefs shows that another and still later migration reached the same islands as late as about 1100 A.D.

Where could such late migrations have come from? Very
few investigators seem to have taken into consideration the
decisive factor that the people which came to the islands at
so late a date was a pure Stone Age people. Despite their
intelligence and, in all other respects, astonishingly high culture, these seafarers brought with them a certain type of stone
ax and a quantity of other characteristic Stone Age tools and
spread these over all the islands to which they came. We must
not forget that, apart from single isolated peoples, inhabiting
primeval forests, and certain backward races, there were no
cultures in the world of any reproductive capacity which were
still at the Stone Age level in 500 or 1100 A.D., except in the
New World. There even the highest Indian civilizations were
totally ignorant at least of the uses of iron, and used stone
axes and tools of the same type as those used in the South
Sea islands right up to the time of the explorations.

These numerous Indian civilizations were the Polynesians'
nearest neighbors to the east. To westward there lived only
the black-skinned primitive peoples of Australia and Melane-
sia, distant relations of the Negroes, and beyond them again

were Indonesia and the coast of Asia, where the Stone Age lay farther back in time, perhaps, than anywhere else in the world.

Thus both my suspicions and my attention were turned more and more away from the Old World, where so many had searched and none had found, and over to the known and unknown Indian civilizations of America, which no one hitherto had taken into consideration. And on the nearest coast due east, where today the South American republic of Peru stretches from the Pacific up into the mountains, there was no lack of traces if one only looked for them. Here an unknown people had once lived and established one of the world's strangest civilizations, till suddenly, long ago, they had vanished as though swept away from the earth's surface. They left behind them enormous stone statues carved in the image of human beings, which recalled those on Pitcairn, the Marquesas, and Easter Island, and huge pyramids built in steps like those on Tahiti and Samoa. They hewed out of the mountains, with stone axes, stone blocks as large as railway cars and heavier than elephants, transported them for miles about the countryside, and set them up on end or placed them on top of one another to form gateways, huge walls, and terraces, exactly as we find them on some of the islands in the Pacific.

The Inca Indians had their great empire in this mountain country when the first Spaniards came to Peru. They told the Spaniards that the colossal monuments that stood deserted about the landscape were erected by a race of white gods which had lived there before the Incas themselves became rulers. These vanished architects were described as wise, peaceful instructors, who had originally come from the north, long ago in the morning of time, and had taught the Incas' primitive forefathers architecture and agriculture as well as manners and customs. They were unlike other Indians in having white skins and long beards; they were also taller than the Incas. Finally they left Peru as suddenly as they had come; the Incas themselves took over power in the country, and the white teachers vanished forever from the coast of South America and fled westward across the Pacific.

Now it happened that, when the Europeans came to the Pacific islands, they were quite astonished to find that many of the natives had almost white skins and were bearded. On many of the islands there were whole families conspicuous for their remarkably pale skins, hair varying from reddish to blonde, blue-gray eyes, and almost Semitic, hook-nosed faces. In contrast to these the genuine Polynesians had golden-brown skins, raven hair, and rather flat, pulpy noses. The red-haired individuals called themselves *urukehu* and said that they were directly descended from the first chiefs on the islands, who were still white gods, such as Tangaroa, Kane, and Tiki. Legends of mysterious white men, from whom the islanders were originally descended, were current all over Polynesia. When Roggeveen discovered Easter Island in 1722, he noticed to his surprise what he termed "white men" among those on shore. And the people of Easter Island could themselves count up those of their ancestors who were white-skinned right back to the time of Tiki and Hotu Matua, when they first came sailing across the sea "from a mountainous land in the east which was scorched by the sun."

As I pursued my search, I found in Peru surprising traces in culture, mythology, and language which impelled me to go on digging ever deeper and with greater concentration in my attempt to identify the place of origin of the Polynesian tribal god Tiki.

And I found what I hoped for. I was sitting reading the Inca legends of the sun-king Virakocha, who was the supreme head of the mythical white people in Peru. I read:

. . . . Virakocha is an Inca (Ketchua) name and consequently of fairly recent date. The original name of the sun-god Virakocha, which seems to have been more used in Peru in old times, was Kon-Tiki or Illa-Tiki, which means Sun-Tiki or Fire-Tiki. Kon-Tiki was high priest and sun-king of the Incas' legendary 'white men' who had left the enormous ruins on the shores of Lake Titicaca. The legend runs that the mysterious white men with beards were attacked by a chief named Cari who came from the Coquimbo Valley. In a battle on an island in Lake Titicaca the fair race was massacred, but Kon-Tiki himself and his closest companions escaped and later came down to the Pacific coast, whence they finally disappeared oversea to the westward. . . .

I was no longer in doubt that the white chief-god Sun-Tiki, whom the Incas declared that their forefathers had driven out of Peru on to the Pacific, was identical with the white chief-god Tiki, son of the sun, whom the inhabitants of all the eastern Pacific islands hailed as the original founder of their race. And the details of Sun-Tiki's life in Peru, with the ancient names of places round Lake Titicaca, cropped up again in historic legends current among the natives of the Pacific islands.

But all over Polynesia I found indications that Kon-Tiki's peaceable race had not been able to hold the islands alone for long. Indications that seagoing war canoes, as large as Viking ships and lashed together two and two, had brought Northwest Indians from the New World across the sea to Hawaii and farther south to all the other islands. They had mingled their blood with that of Kon-Tiki's race and brought a new civilization to the island kingdom. This was the second Stone Age people that came to Polynesia, without metals, without the potter's art, without wheel or loom or cereal cultivation, about 1100 A.D.

So it came about that I was excavating rock carvings in the ancient Polynesian style among the Northwest Coast Indians in British Columbia when the Germans burst into Norway in 1940.

*   *   *

Right face, left face, about face. Washing barracks stairs, polishing boots, radio school, parachute—and at last a Murmansk convoy to Finnmark, where the war-god of technique reigned in the sun-god's absence all the dark winter through.

Peace came. And one day my theory was complete. I must go to America and put it forward.

2 AN EXPEDITION IS BORN

So IT HAD BEGUN, BY A FIRE ON A SOUTH SEA
island, where an old native sat telling legends and stories of
his tribe. Many years later I sat with another old man, this
time in a dark office on one of the upper floors of a big
museum in New York.

Round us, in well-arranged glass cases, lay pottery frag-
ments from the past, traces leading into the mists of antiquity.
The walls were lined with books. Some of them one man had
written and hardly ten men had read. The old man, who
had read all these books and written some of them, sat
behind his worktable, white-haired and good-humored. But
now, for sure, I had trodden on his toes, for he gripped the
arms of his chair uneasily and looked as if I had interrupted
him in a game of solitaire.

"No!" he said. "Never!"

I imagine that Santa Claus would have looked as he did
then if someone had dared to affirm that next year Christmas
would be on Midsummer Day.

"You're wrong, absolutely wrong," he said and shook his head indignantly to drive out the idea.

"But you haven't read my arguments yet," I urged, nodding hopefully toward the manuscript which lay on the table.

"Arguments!" he repeated. "You can't treat ethnographic problems as a sort of detective mystery!"

"Why not?" I said. "I've based all the conclusions on my own observations and the facts that science has recorded."

"The task of science is investigation pure and simple," he said quietly. "Not to try to prove this or that."

He pushed the unopened manuscript carefully to one side and leaned over the table.

"It's quite true that South America was the home of some of the most curious civilizations of antiquity, and that we know neither who they were nor where they vanished when the Incas came into power. But one thing we do know for certain —that none of the peoples of South America got over to the islands in the Pacific."

He looked at me searchingly and continued:

"Do you know why? The answer's simple enough. They couldn't get there. They had no boats!"

"They had rafts," I objected hesitatingly. "You know, balsa-wood rafts."

The old man smiled and said calmly:

"Well, you can try a trip from Peru to the Pacific islands on a balsa-wood raft."

I could find nothing to say. It was getting late. We both rose. The old scientist patted me kindly on the shoulder, as he saw me out, and said that if I wanted help I had only to come to him. But I must in future specialize on Polynesia *or* America and not mix up two separate anthropological areas. He reached back over the table.

"You've forgotten this," he said and handed back my manuscript. I glanced at the title, "Polynesia and America; A Study of Prehistoric Relations." I stuck the manuscript under my arm and clattered down the stairs out into the crowds in the street.

That evening I went down and knocked on the door of an old flat in an out-of-the-way corner of Greenwich Village. I liked bringing my little problems down here when I felt they had made life a bit tangled.

A sparse little man with a long nose opened the door a crack before he threw it wide open with a broad smile and pulled me in. He took me straight into the little kitchen, where he set me to work carrying plates and forks while he himself doubled the quantity of the indefinable but savory-smelling concoction he was heating over the gas.

"Nice of you to come," he said. "How goes it?"

"Rottenly," I replied. "No one will read the manuscript." He filled the plates and we attacked the contents.

"It's like this," he said. "All the people you've been to see think it's just a passing idea you've got. You know, here in America, people turn up with so many queer ideas."

"And there's another thing," I went on.

"Yes," said he. "Your way of approaching the problem. They're specialists, the whole lot of them, and they don't believe in a method of work which cuts into every field of science from botany to archaeology. They limit their own scope in order to be able to dig in the depths with more concentration for details. Modern research demands that every special branch shall dig in its own hole. It's not usual for anyone to sort out what comes up out of the holes and try to put it all together."

He rose and reached for a heavy manuscript.

"Look here," he said. "My last work on bird designs in Chinese peasant embroidery. Took me seven years, but it was accepted for publication at once. They want specialized research nowadays."

Carl was right. But to solve the problems of the Pacific without throwing light on them from all sides was, it seemed to me, like doing a puzzle and only using the pieces of one color.

We cleared the table, and I helped him wash and dry the dishes.

"Nothing new from the university in Chicago?"

"No."

"But what did your old friend at the museum say today?"

"He wasn't interested, either," I muttered. "He said that,

as long as the Indians had only open rafts, it was futile to consider the possibility of their having discovered the Pacific islands."

The little man suddenly began to dry his plate furiously.

"Yes," he said at last. "To tell the truth, to me too that seems a practical objection to your theory."

I looked gloomily at the little ethnologist whom I had thought to be a sworn ally.

"But don't misunderstand me," he hastened to say. "In one way I think you're right, but in another way it's so incomprehensible. My work on designs supports your theory."

"Carl," I said. "I'm so sure the Indians crossed the Pacific on their rafts that I'm willing to build a raft of the same kind myself and cross the sea just to prove that it's possible."

"You're mad!"

My friend took it for a joke and laughed, half-scared at the thought.

"You're mad! A raft?"

He did not know what to say and only stared at me with a queer expression, as though waiting for a smile to show that I *was* joking.

He did not get one. I saw now that in practice no one would accept my theory because of the apparently endless stretch of sea between Peru and Polynesia, which I was trying to bridge with no other aid than a prehistoric raft.

Carl looked at me uncertainly. "Now we'll go out and have a drink," he said. We went out and had four.

*   *   *

My rent became due that week. At the same time a letter from the Bank of Norway informed me that I could have no more dollars. Currency restrictions. I picked up my trunk and took the subway out to Brooklyn. Here I was taken in at the Norwegian Sailors' Home, where the food was good and sustaining and the prices suited my wallet. I got a little room a floor or two up but had my meals with all the seamen in a big dining room downstairs.

Seamen came and seamen went. They varied in type, di-

mensions, and degrees of sobriety but they all had one thing
in common—when they talked about the sea, they knew what
they were talking about. I learned that waves and rough sea
did not increase with the depth of the sea or distance from
land. On the contrary, squalls were often more treacherous
along the coast than in the open sea. Shoal water, backwash
along the coast, or ocean currents penned in close to the land
could throw up a rougher sea than was usual far out. A vessel
which could hold her own along an open coast could hold her
own farther out. I also learned that, in a high sea, big ships
were inclined to plunge bow or stern into the waves, so that
tons of water would rush on board and twist steel tubes like
wire, while a small boat, in the same sea, often made good
weather because she could find room between the lines of
waves and dance freely over them like a gull. I talked to
sailors who had got safely away in boats after the seas had
made their ship founder.

But the men knew little about rafts. A raft—that wasn't a
ship; it had no keel or bulwarks. It was just something floating
on which to save oneself in an emergency, until one was
picked up by a boat of some kind. One of the men, nevertheless, had great respect for rafts in the open sea; he had drifted
about on one for three weeks when a German torpedo sank
his ship in mid-Atlantic.

"But you can't navigate a raft," he added. "It goes sideways
and backward and round as the wind takes it."

In the library I dug out records left by the first Europeans
who had reached the Pacific coast of South America. There
was no lack of sketches or descriptions of the Indians' big
balsa-wood rafts. They had a square sail and centerboard and
a long steering oar astern. So they could be maneuvered.

Weeks passed at the Sailors' Home. No reply from Chicago
or the other cities to which I had sent copies of my theory.
No one had read it.

Then, one Saturday, I pulled myself together and marched
into a ship chandler's shop down in Water Street. There I
was politely addressed as "Captain" when I bought a pilot
chart of the Pacific. With the chart rolled up under my arm
I took the suburban train out to Ossining, where I was a

regular week-end guest of a young Norwegian married couple who had a charming place in the country. My host had been a sea captain and was now office manager for the Fred Olsen Line in New York.

After a refreshing plunge in the swimming pool city life was completely forgotten for the rest of the week end, and when Ambjörg brought the cocktail tray, we sat down on the lawn in the hot sun. I could contain myself no longer but spread the chart out on the grass and asked Wilhelm if he thought a raft could carry men alive from Peru to the South Sea islands.

He looked at me rather than at the chart, half taken aback, but replied at once in the affirmative. I felt as much lightened as if I had released a balloon inside my shirt, for I knew that to Wilhelm everything that had to do with navigation and sailing was both job and hobby. He was initiated into my plans at once. To my astonishment he then declared that the idea was sheer madness.

"But you said just now that you thought it was possible," I interrupted.

"Quite right," he admitted. "But the chances of its going wrong are just as great. You yourself have never been on a balsa raft, and all of a sudden you're imagining yourself across the Pacific on one. Perhaps it'll come off, perhaps it won't. The old Indians in Peru had generations of experience to build upon. Perhaps ten rafts went to the bottom for every one that got across—or perhaps hundreds in the course of centuries. As you say, the Incas navigated in the open sea with whole flotillas of these balsa rafts. Then, if anything went wrong, they could be picked up by the nearest raft. But who's going to pick you up, out in mid-ocean? Even if you take a radio for use in an emergency, don't think it's going to be easy for a little raft to be located down among the waves thousands of miles from land. In a storm you can be washed off the raft and drowned many times over before anyone gets to you. You'd better wait quietly here till someone has had time to read your manuscript. Write again and stir them up; it's no good if you don't."

"I can't wait any longer now; I shan't have a cent left soon."

"Then you can come and stay with us. For that matter, how can you think of starting an expedition from South America without money?"

"It's easier to interest people in an expedition than in an unread manuscript."

"But what can you gain by it?"

"Destroy one of the weightiest arguments against the theory, quite apart from the fact that science will pay some attention to the affair."

"But if things go wrong?"

"Then I shan't have proved anything."

"Then you'd ruin your own theory in the eyes of everyone, wouldn't you?"

"Perhaps, but all the same one in ten might have got through before us, as you said."

The children came out to play croquet, and we did not discuss the matter any more that day.

The next week end I was back at Ossining with the chart under my arm. And, when I left, there was a long pencil line from the coast of Peru to the Tuamotu islands in the Pacific. My friend, the captain, had given up hope of making me drop the idea, and we had sat together for hours working out the raft's probable speed.

"Ninety-seven days," said Wilhelm, "but remember that's only in theoretically ideal conditions, with a fair wind all the time and assuming that the raft can really sail as you think it can. You must definitely allow at least four months for the trip and be prepared for a good deal more."

"All right," I said optimistically, "let us allow at least four months, but do it in ninety-seven days."

The little room at the Sailors' Home seemed twice as cozy as usual when I came home that evening and sat down on the edge of the bed with the chart. I paced out the floor as exactly as the bed and chest of drawers gave me room to do. Oh, yes, the raft would be much larger than this. I leaned out of the window to get a glimpse of the great city's remote starry sky, only visible right overhead between the high yard walls. If there was little room on board the raft, anyhow there would be room for the sky and all its stars above us.

On West Seventy-Second Street, near Central Park, is one of the most exclusive clubs in New York. There is nothing more than a brightly polished little brass plate with "Explorers Club" on it to tell passers-by that there is anything out of the ordinary inside the doors. But, once inside, one might have made a parachute jump into a strange world, thousands of miles from New York's lines of motorcars flanked by skyscrapers. When the door to New York is shut behind one, one is swallowed up in an atmosphere of lion-hunting, mountaineering, and polar life. Trophies of hippopotamus and deer, big-game rifles, tusks, war drums and spears, Indian carpets, idols and model ships, flags, photographs and maps, surround the members of the club when they assemble for a dinner or to hear lecturers from distant countries.

After my journey to the Marquesas Islands I had been elected an active member of the club, and as junior member I had seldom missed a meeting when I was in town. So, when I now entered the club on a rainy November evening, I was not a little surprised to find the place in an unusual state. In the middle of the floor lay an inflated rubber raft with boat rations and accessories, while parachutes, rubber overalls, safety jackets, and polar equipment covered walls and tables, together with balloons for water distillation, and other curious inventions. A newly elected member of the club, Colonel Haskin, of the equipment laboratory of the Air Material Command, was to give a lecture and demonstrate a number of new military inventions which, he thought, would in the future be of use to scientific expeditions in both north and south.

After the lecture there was a vigorous discussion. The well-known Danish polar explorer Peter Freuchen, tall and bulky, rose with a skeptical shake of his huge beard. He had no faith in such new-fangled patents. He himself had once used a rubber boat and bag tent on one of his Greenland expeditions instead of an Eskimo kayak and igloo, and it had all but cost him his life. First he had nearly been frozen to death in a snowstorm because the zipper fastening of the tent had frozen up so that he could not even get in. And after that he had been out fishing when the hook caught in the inflated rubber boat, and the boat was punctured and sank under him like a bit of rag. He and an Eskimo friend had managed to get ashore that time in a kayak which came to their help. He was sure no clever modern inventor could sit in his laboratory and think out anything better than what the experience of thousands of years had taught the Eskimos to use in their own regions.

The discussion ended with a surprising offer from Colonel Haskin. Active members of the club could, on their next expeditions, select any they liked of the new inventions he had demonstrated, on the sole condition that they should let his laboratory know what they thought of the things when they came back.

That was that. I was the last to leave the clubrooms that evening. I had to go over every minute detail of all this brand-new equipment which had so suddenly tumbled into my hands and which was at my disposal for the asking. It was exactly what I wanted—equipment with which we could try to save our lives if, contrary to expectation, our wooden raft should show signs of breaking up and we had no other rafts near by.

All this equipment was still occupying my thoughts at the breakfast table in the Sailors' Home next morning when a well-dressed young man of athletic build came along with his breakfast tray and sat down at the same table as myself. We began to chat, and it appeared that he too was not a seaman but a university-trained engineer from Trondheim, who was in America to buy machinery parts and obtain experience in refrigerating technique. He was living not far away and often had meals at the Sailors' Home because of the good Norwegian cooking there.

He asked me what I was doing, and I then gave him a short account of my plans. I said that, if I did not get a definite answer about my manuscript before the end of the week, I should get under way with the starting of the raft expedition. My table companion did not say much but listened with great interest.

Four days later we ran across each other again in the same dining room.

"Have you decided whether you're going on your trip or not?" he asked.

"Yes," I said. "I'm going."

"When?"

"As soon as possible. If I hang about much longer now, the gales will be coming up from the Antarctic and it will be hurricane season in the islands, too. I must leave Peru in a very few months, but I must get money first and get the whole business organized."

"How many men will there be?"

"I've thought of having six men in all; that'll give some change of society on board the raft and is the right number for four hours' steering in every twenty-four hours."

He stood for a moment or two, as though chewing over a thought, then burst out emphatically:

"The devil, but how I'd like to be in it! I could undertake technical measurements and tests. Of course, you'll have to support your experiment with accurate measurements of winds and currents and waves. Remember that you're going to cross vast spaces of sea which are practically unknown because they lie outside all shipping routes. An expedition like yours can make interesting hydrographic and meteorological investigations; I could make good use of my thermodynamics."

I knew nothing about the man beyond what an open face can say. It may say a good deal.

"All right," I said. "We'll go together."

His name was Herman Watzinger; he was as much of a landlubber as myself.

A few days later I took Herman as my guest to the Explorers Club. Here we ran straight into the polar explorer Peter Freuchen. Freuchen has the blessed quality of never disappearing in a crowd. As big as a barn door and bristling with beard, he looks like a messenger from the open tundra. A special atmosphere surrounds him—it is as though he were going about with a grizzly bear on a lead.

We took him over to a big map on the wall and told him about our plan of crossing the Pacific on an Indian raft. His boyish blue eyes grew as large as saucers as he listened. Then he stamped his wooden leg on the floor and tightened his belt several holes.

"Damn it, boys! I should like to go with you!"

The old Greenland traveler filled our beer mugs and began to tell us of his confidence in primitive peoples' watercraft and these peoples' ability to make their way by accommodating themselves to nature both on land and at sea. He himself had traveled by raft down the great rivers of Siberia and towed natives on rafts astern of his ship along the coast of the Arctic. As he talked, he tugged at his beard and said we were certainly going to have a great time.

Through Freuchen's eager support of our plan the wheels began to turn at a dangerous speed, and they soon ran right into the printers' ink of the *Scandinavian Press*. The very next morning there came a violent knocking on my door in the Sailors' Home; I was wanted on the telephone in the passage downstairs. The result of the conversation was that Herman and I, the same evening, rang the doorbell of an apartment in a fashionable quarter of the city. We were received by a well-dressed young man in patent-leather slippers, wearing a silk dressing gown over a blue suit. He made an impression almost of softness and apologized for having a cold with a scented handkerchief held under his nose. Nonetheless we knew that this fellow had made a name in America by his exploits as an airman in the war. Besides our apparently delicate host two energetic young journalists, simply bursting with activity and ideas, were present. We knew one of them as an able correspondent.

Our host explained over a bottle of good whisky that he was interested in our expedition. He offered to raise the necessary capital if we would undertake to write newspaper articles and go on lecture tours after our return. We came to an agreement at last and drank to successful co-operation between the backers of the expedition and those taking part in it. From now on all our economic problems would be solved; they were taken over by our backers and would not trouble us. Herman and I were at once to set about raising a crew and equipment, build a raft, and get off before the hurricane season began.

Next day Herman resigned his post, and we set about our task seriously. I had already obtained a promise from the research laboratory of the Air Material Command to send everything I asked for and more through the Explorers Club; they said that an expedition such as ours was ideal for testing their equipment. This was a good start. Our most important tasks were now, first of all, to find four suitable men who were willing to go with us on the raft and to obtain supplies for the journey.

A party of men who were to put out to sea together on board a raft must be chosen with care. Otherwise there would be trouble and mutiny after a month's isolation at sea. I did not want to man the raft with sailors; they knew hardly any more about managing a raft than we did ourselves, and I did not want to have it argued afterward, when we had completed the voyage, that we made it because we were better seamen than the old raft-builders in Peru. Nevertheless, we wanted one man on board who at any rate could use a sextant and mark our course on a chart as a basis for all our scientific reports.

"I know a good fellow, a painter," I said to Herman. "He's a big hefty chap who can play the guitar and is full of fun. He went through navigation school and sailed round the world several times before he settled down at home with brush and palette. I've known him since we were boys and have often been on camping tours with him in the mountains at home. I'll write and ask him; I'm sure he'll come."

"He sounds all right," Herman nodded, "and then we want someone who can manage the radio."

"Radio!" I said, horrified. "What the hell do we want with that? It's out of place on a prehistoric raft."

"Not at all—it's a safety precaution which won't have any effect on your theory so long as we don't send out any SOS for help. And we shall need the radio to send out weather observations and other reports. But it'll be no use for us to receive gale warnings because there are no reports for that part of the ocean, and, even if there were, what good would they be to us on a raft?"

His arguments gradually swamped all my protests, the main

ground for which was a lack of affection for push buttons and turning knobs.

"Curiously enough," I admitted, "I happen to have the best connections for getting into touch by radio over great distances with tiny sets. I was put into a radio section in the war. Every man in the right place, you know. But I shall certainly write a line to Knut Haugland and Torstein Raaby."

"Do you know them?"

"Yes. I met Knut for the first time in England in 1944. He'd been decorated by the British for having taken part in the parachute action that held up the German efforts to get the atomic bomb; he was the radio operator, you know, in the heavy water sabatoge at Rjukan. When I met him, he had just come back from another job in Norway; the Gestapo had caught him with a secret radio set inside a chimney in the Maternity Clinic in Oslo. The Nazis had located him by D/F, and the whole building was surrounded by German soldiers with machine-gun posts in front of every single door. Fehmer, the head of the Gestapo, was standing in the courtyard himself waiting for Knut to be carried down. But it was his own men who were carried down. Knut fought his way with his pistol from the attic down to the cellar, and from there out into the back yard, where he disappeared over the hospital wall with a hail of bullets after him. I met him at a secret station in an old English castle; he had come back to organize underground liaison among more than a hundred transmitting stations in occupied Norway.

"I myself had just finished my training as a parachutist, and our plan was to jump together in the Nordmark near Oslo. But just then the Russians marched into the Kirkenes region, and a small Norwegian detachment was sent from Scotland to Finnmark to take over the operations, so to speak, from the whole Russian army. I was sent up there instead. And there I met Torstein.

"It was real Arctic winter up in those parts, and the northern lights flashed in the starry sky which was arched over us, pitch black, all day and all night. When we came to the ash heaps of the burned area in Finnmark, frozen blue and wearing furs, a cheery fellow with blue eyes and bristly fair hair crept out of a little hut up in the mountains. This was Torstein Raaby. He had first escaped to England, where he went through special training, and then he'd been smuggled into Norway somewhere near Tromsö. He'd been in hiding with a little transmitting set close to the battleship 'Tirpitz' and for ten months he had sent daily reports to England about all that happened on board. He sent his reports at night by connecting his secret transmitter to a receiving aerial put up by a German officer. It was his regular reports that guided the British bombers who at last finished off the 'Tirpitz.'

"Torstein escaped to Sweden and from there over to England again, and then he made a parachute jump with a new radio set behind the German lines up in the wilds of Finnmark. When the Germans retreated, he found himself sitting behind our own lines and came out of his hiding place to help us with his little radio, as our main station had been destroyed by a mine. I'm ready to bet that both Knut and Torstein are fed up with hanging about at home now and would be glad to go for a little trip on a wooden raft."

"Write and ask them," Herman proposed.

So I wrote a short letter, without any disingenuous persuasions, to Erik, Knut, and Torstein:

"Am going to cross Pacific on a wooden raft to support a theory that the South Sea islands were peopled from Peru. Will you come? I guarantee nothing but a free trip to Peru and the South Sea islands and back, but you will find good use for your technical abilites on the voyage. Reply at once."

Next day the following telegram arrived from Torstein:
"Coming. Torstein."

The other two also accepted.

As sixth member of the party we had in view now one man and now another, but each time some obstacle arose. In the meantime Herman and I had to attack the supply problem. We did not mean to eat llama flesh or dried *kumara* potatoes on our trip, for we were not making it to prove that we had once been Indians ourselves. Our intention was to test the performance and quality of the Inca raft, its seaworthiness and loading capacity, and to ascertain whether the elements would really propel it across the sea to Polynesia with its crew still on board. Our native forerunners could certainly have managed to live on dried meat and fish and *kumara* potatoes on board, as that was their staple diet ashore. We were also going to try to find out, on the actual trip, whether they could have obtained additional supplies of fresh fish and rain water while crossing the sea. As our own diet I had thought of simple field service rations, as we knew them from the war.

Just at that time a new assistant to the Norwegian military ataché in Washington had arrived. I had acted as second in command of his company in Finnmark and knew that he was a "ball of fire," who loved to attack and solve with savage energy any problem set before him. Björn Rörholt was a man of that vital type which feels quite lost if it has fought its way out into the open without immediately sighting a new problem to tackle.

I wrote to him explaining the situation and asked him to use his tracking sense to smell out a contact man in the supply department of the American army. The chances were that the laboratory was experimenting with new field rations we could test, in the same way as we were testing equipment for the Air Force laboratory.

Two days later Björn telephoned us from Washington. He had been in contact with the foreign liaison section of the American War Department, and they would like to know what it was all about.

Herman and I took the first train to Washington.

We found Björn in his room in the military attaché's office. "I think it'll be all right," he said. "We'll be received at the foreign liaison section tomorrow provided we bring a proper letter from the colonel."

The "colonel" was Otto Munthe-Kaas, the Norwegian military attaché. He was well-disposed and more than willing to give us a proper letter of introduction when he heard what our business was.

When we came to fetch the document next morning, he suddenly rose and said he thought it would be best if he came with us himself. We drove out in the colonel's car to the Pentagon building to the offices of the War Department. The colonel and Björn sat in front in their smartest military turn-out, while Herman and I sat behind and peered through the windshield at the huge Pentagon building, which towered up on the plain before us. This gigantic building with thirty thousand clerks and sixteen miles of corridors was to form the frame of our impending raft conference with military "high-ups." Never, before or after, did the little raft seem to Herman and me so helplessly small.

After endless wanderings in ramps and corridors we reached the door of the foreign liaison section, and soon, surrounded by brand-new uniforms, we were sitting round a large mahogany table at which the head of the foreign liaison section himself presided.

The stern, broad-built West Point officer, who bulked big at the end of the table, had a certain difficulty at first in understanding what the connection between the American War Department and our wooden raft was, but the colonel's well-considered words, and the favorable result of a hurricane-like examination by the officers round the table, slowly brought him over to our side, and he read with interest the letter from the equipment laboratory of the Air Material Command. Then he rose and gave his staff a concise order to help us through the proper channels and, wishing us good luck for the present, marched out of the conference room. When the door had shut on him, a young staff captain whispered in my ear:

"I'll bet you'll get what you want. It sounds like a minor military operation and brings a little change into our daily office peacetime routine; besides, it'll be a good opportunity of methodically testing equipment."

The liaison office at once arranged a meeting with Colonel Lewis at the quartermaster general's experimental laboratory, and Herman and I were taken over there by car.

Colonel Lewis was an affable giant of an officer with a sportsman's bearing. He at once called in the men in charge of experiments in the different sections. All were amicably disposed and immediately suggested quantities of equipment they would like us to test thoroughly. They exceeded our wildest hopes as they rattled off the names of nearly everything we could want, from field rations to sunburn ointment and splashproof sleeping bags. Then they took us on an extensive tour to look at the things. We tasted special rations in smart packings; we tested matches which struck well even if they had been dipped in water, new primus stoves and water kegs, rubber bags and special boots, kitchen utensils and knives which would float, and all that an expedition could want.

I glanced at Herman. He looked like a good, expectant little boy walking through a chocolate shop with a rich aunt. The colonel walked in front demonstrating all these delights, and when the tour was completed staff clerks had made note of the kinds of goods and the quantities we required. I thought the battle was won and felt only an urge to rush home to the hotel in order to assume a horizontal position and think things over in peace and quiet. Then the tall, friendly colonel suddenly said:

"Well, now we must go in and have a talk with the boss; it's he who'll decide whether we can give you these things."

I felt my heart sink down into my boots. So we were to start our eloquence right from the beginning again, and heaven alone knew what kind of man the "boss" was!

We found that the boss was a little officer with an intensely earnest manner. He sat behind his writing table and examined us with keen blue eyes as we came into the office. He asked us to sit down.

"Well, what do these gentlemen want?" he asked Colonel Lewis sharply, without taking his eyes off mine.

"Oh, a few little things," Lewis hastened to reply. He explained the whole of our errand in outline, while the chief listened patiently without moving a finger.

"And what can they give us in return?" he asked, quite unimpressed.

"Well," said Lewis in a conciliatory tone, "we hoped that perhaps the expedition would be able to write reports on the new provisions and some of the equipment, based on the severe conditions in which they will be using it."

The intensely earnest officer behind the writing table leaned back in his chair with unaffected slowness, with his eyes still fixed on mine, and I felt myself sinking to the bottom of the deep leather chair as he said coolly:

"I don't see at all how they can give us anything in return."

There was dead silence in the room. Colonel Lewis fingered his collar, and neither of us said a word.

"But," the chief suddenly broke out, and now a gleam had come into the corner of his eye, "courage and enterprise count, too. Colonel Lewis, let them have the things!"

I was still sitting, half intoxicated with delight, in the cab which was taking us home to the hotel, when Herman began to laugh and giggle to himself at my side.

"Are you tight?" I asked anxiously.

"No," he laughed shamelessly, "but I've been calculating that the provisions we got include 684 boxes of pineapple, and that's my favorite dish."

There are a thousand things to be done, and mostly at the same time, when six men and a wooden raft and its cargo are to assemble at a place down on the coast of Peru. And we had three months and no Aladdin's lamp at our disposal.

We flew to New York with an introduction from the liaison office and met Professor Behre at Columbia University. He was head of the War Department's Geographical Research Committee, and it was he who pressed the buttons which at last brought Herman all his valuable instruments and apparatus for scientific measurements.

Then we flew to Washington to meet Admiral Glover at the Naval Hydrographic Institute. The good-natured old sea dog called in all his officers and pointed to the chart of the Pacific on the wall as he introduced Herman and me.

"These young gentlemen want to check up on our current maps. Help them!"

When the wheels had rolled a bit further, the English Colonel Lumsden called a conference at the British Military Mission in Washington to discuss our future problems and the chances of a favorable outcome. We received plenty of good advice and a selection of British equipment which was flown over from England to be tried out on the raft expedition. The British medical officer was an enthusiastic advocate of a mysterious shark powder. We were to sprinkle a few

pinches of the powder on the water if a shark became too
impudent, and the shark would vanish immediately.

"Sir," I said politely, "can we rely on this powder?"

"Well," said the Englishman, smiling, "that's just what we
want to find out ourselves!"

When time is short and plane replaces train, while taxi replaces legs, one's wallet crumples up like a withered herbar-
ium. When we had spent the cost of my return ticket to
Norway, we went and called on our friends and backers in
New York to get our finances straight. There we encountered
surprising and discouraging problems. The financial manager
was ill in bed with fever, and his two colleagues were power-
less till he was in action again. They stood firmly by our
economic agreement, but they could do nothing for the time
being. We were asked to postpone the business, a useless
request, for we could not stop the numerous wheels which
were now revolving vigorously. We could only hold on now;
it was too late to stop or brake. Our friends the backers
agreed to dissolve the whole syndicate in order to give us a
free hand to act quickly and independently without them.

So there we were in the street with our hands in our
trousers pockets.

"December, January, February," said Herman.

"And at a pinch March," said I, "but then we simply must
start!"

If all else seemed obscure, one thing was clear to us. Ours
was a journey with an objective, and we did not want to be
classed with acrobats who roll down Niagara in empty barrels
or sit on the knobs of flag staffs for seventeen days.

"No chewing-gum or pop backing," Herman said.

On this point we were in profound agreement.

We could get Norwegian currency. But that did not solve
the problems on our side of the Atlantic. We could apply
for a grant from some institution, but we could scarcely get
one for a disputed theory; after all, that was just why we
were going on the raft expedition. We soon found that neither
press nor private promoters dared to put money into what
they themselves and all the insurance companies regarded as

a suicide voyage; but, if we came back safe and sound, it would be another matter.

Things looked pretty gloomy, and for many days we could see no ray of hope. It was then that Colonel Munthe-Kaas came into the picture again.

"You're in a fix, boys," he said. "Here's a check to begin with. You can return it when you come back from the South Sea islands."

Several other people followed his example, and my private loan was soon big enough to tide us over without help from agents or others. We could fly to South America and start building the raft.

The old Peruvian rafts were built of balsa wood, which in a dry state is lighter than cork. The balsa tree grows in Peru, but only beyond the mountains in the Andes range, so the seafarers in Inca times went up along the coast to Ecuador, where they felled their huge balsa trees right down on the edge of the Pacific. We meant to do the same.

Today's travel problems are different from those of Inca times. We have cars and planes and travel bureaus but, so as not to make things altogether too easy, we have also impediments called frontiers, with brass-buttoned attendants who doubt one's alibi, maltreat one's luggage, and weigh one down with stamped forms—if one is lucky enough to get in at all. It was the fear of these men with brass buttons that decided us we could not land in South America with packing cases and trunks full of strange devices, raise our hats, and ask politely in broken Spanish to be allowed to come in and sail away on a raft. We should be clapped into jail.

"No," said Herman. "We must have an official introduction."

One of our friends in the dissolved triumvirate was a correspondent at the United Nations, and he offered to take us out there by car for aid. We were greatly impressed when we came into the great hall of the assembly, where men of all nations sat on benches side by side listening silently to the flow of speech from a black-haired Russian in front of the gigantic map of the world that decorated the back wall.

Our friend the correspondent managed in a quiet moment

to get hold of one of the delegates from Peru and, later, one of Ecuador's representatives. On a deep leather sofa in an antechamber they listened eagerly to our plan of crossing the sea to support a theory that men of an ancient civilization from their own country had been the first to reach the Pacific islands. Both promised to inform their governments and guaranteed us support when we came to their respective countries. Trygve Lie, passing through the anteroom, came over to us when he heard we were countrymen of his, and someone proposed that he should come with us on the raft. But there were billows enough for him on land. The assistant secretary of the United Nations, Dr. Benjamin Cohen from Chile, was himself a well-known amateur archaeologist, and he gave me a letter to the President of Peru, who was a personal friend of his. We also met in the hall the Norwegian ambassador, Wilhelm von Munthe of Morgenstierne, who from then on gave the expedition invaluable support.

So we bought two tickets and flew to South America. When the four heavy engines began to roar one after another, we sank into our seats exhausted. We had an unspeakable feeling of relief that the first stage of the program was over and that we were now going straight ahead to the adventure.

3 TO SOUTH AMERICA

Over the Equator—Balsa Problems—By Air to Quito—Head-Hunters and Bandidos—Over the Andes by Jeep—Into the Depths of the Jungle—At Quevedo—We fell Balsa Trees—Down the Palenque by Raft—The Beautiful Naval Harbor—At the Ministry of Marine in Lima—With the President of Peru—Danielsson Comes—Back to Washington—Twenty-Six Pounds of Paper—Herman's Baptism of Fire—We Build the Raft in the Naval Harbor—Warnings—Before the Start—Naming of the Kon-Tiki—Farewell to South America

As OUR PLANE CROSSED THE EQUATOR, IT BE-gan a slanting descent through the milk-white clouds which till then had lain beneath us like a blinding waste of snow in the burning sun. The fleecy vapor clung to the windows till it dissolved and remained hanging over us like clouds, and the bright green roof of a rolling, billowy jungle appeared. We flew in over the South American republic of Ecuador and landed at the tropical port of Guayaquil.

With yesterday's coats, vests, and overcoats over our arms we climbed out into the atmosphere of a hothouse to meet chattering southerners in tropical clothes and felt our shirts sticking to our backs like wet paper. We were embraced by customs and immigration officials and almost carried to a cab, which took us to the best hotel in the town, the only good one. Here we quickly found our way to our respective baths and lay down flat under the cold-water faucet. We had reached the country where the balsa tree grows and were to buy timber to build our raft.

The first day we spent in learning the monetary system and enough Spanish to find our way back to the hotel. On the second day we ventured away from our baths in steadily widening circles, and, when Herman had satisfied the longing of his childhood to touch a real palm tree and I was a walking bowl of fruit salad, we decided to go and negotiate for balsa.

Unfortunately this was easier said than done. We could certainly buy balsa in quantities but not in the form of whole logs, as we wanted it. The days when balsa trees were accessible down on the coast were past. The last war had put an end to them; they had been felled in thousands and shipped to the aircraft factories because the wood was so gaseous and light. We were told that the only place where large balsa trees now grew was in the jungle in the interior of the country.

"Then we must go inland and fell them ourselves," we said.

"Impossible," said the authorities. "The rains have just begun, and all the roads into the jungle are impassable because of flood water and deep mud. If you want balsa wood, you must come back to Ecuador in six months; the rains will be over then and the roads up country will have dried."

In our extremity we called on Don Gustavo von Buchwald, the balsa king of Ecuador, and Herman unrolled his sketch of the raft with the lengths of timber we required. The slight little balsa king seized the telephone eagerly and set his agents to work searching. They found planks and light boards and separate short blocks in every sawmill but they could not find one single serviceable log. There were two big logs, as dry as tinder, at Don Gustavo's own dump, but they would not take us far. It was clear that the search was useless.

"But a brother of mine has a big balsa plantation," said Don Gustavo encouragingly. "His name is Don Federico and he lives at Quevedo, a little jungle town up country. He can get you all you want as soon as we can get hold of him after the rains. It's no use now because of the jungle rain up country."

If Don Gustavo said a thing was no use, all the balsa experts in Ecuador would say it was no use. So here we were in Guayaquil with no timber for the raft and with no possibility of going in and felling the trees ourselves until several months later, when it would be too late.

"Time's short," said Herman.

"And balsa we must have," said I. "The raft must be an exact copy, or we shall have no guarantee of coming through alive."

A little school map we found in the hotel, with green jungle, brown mountains, and inhabited places ringed round in red, told us that the jungle stretched unbroken from the Pacific right to the foot of the towering Andes. I had an idea. It was clearly impracticable now to get from the coastal area through the jungle to the balsa trees at Quevedo, but suppose we could get to the trees from the inland side, by coming straight down into the jungle from the bare snow mountains of the Andes range? Here was a possibility, the only one we saw.

Out on the airfield we found a little cargo plane which was willing to take us up to Quito, the capital of this strange country, high up on the Andes plateau, 9,300 feet above sea level. Between packing cases and furniture we caught occasional glimpses of green jungle and shining rivers before we disappeared into the clouds. When we came out again, the lowlands were hidden under an endless sea of rolling vapor, but ahead of us dry mountainsides and bare cliffs rose from the sea of mist right up to a brilliant blue sky.

The plane climbed straight up the mountainside as in an invisible funicular railway, and, although the Equator itself was in sight, at last we had shining snow fields alongside us. Then we glided between the mountains and over a rich alpine plateau clad in spring green, on which we landed close to the world's most unusual capital.

Most of Quito's 175,000 inhabitants are pure or half-breed mountain Indians, for it was their forefathers' own capital long before Columbus and our own race knew America. The city is filled with ancient monasteries, containing art treasures of immeasurable value, and other magnificent buildings dating from Spanish times, towering over the roofs of low Indian houses built of bricks of sun-dried clay. A labyrinth of narrow alleys winds between the clay walls, and these we found swarming with mountain Indians in red-speckled cloaks and big homemade hats. Some were going to market with pack donkeys, while others sat hunched up along the adobe walls dozing in the hot sun. A few automobiles containing aristocrats of Spanish origin, going at half-speed and hooting ceaselessly, succeeded in finding a path along the one-way alleys among children and donkeys and barelegged Indians. The air up here on the high plateau was of such brilliant crystalline clearness that the mountains round us seemed to come into the street picture and contribute to its other-world atmosphere.

Our friend from the cargo plane, Jorge, nicknamed "the crazy flier," belonged to one of the old Spanish families in Quito. He installed us in an antiquated, amusing hotel and then went round, sometimes with and sometimes without us, trying to get us transport over the mountains and down into the jungle to Quevedo. We met in the evening in an old Spanish café, and Jorge was full of bad news; we must absolutely put out of our heads the idea of going to Quevedo. Neither men nor vehicle were to be obtained to take us over the mountains, and certainly not down into the jungle where the rains had begun and where there was danger of attack if one stuck fast in the mud. Only last year a party of ten American oil engineers had been found killed by poisoned arrows in the eastern part of Ecuador, where many Indians still went about in the jungle stark naked and hunted with poisoned arrows.

"Some of them are head-hunters," Jorge said in a hollow voice, seeing that Herman, quite unperturbed, was helping himself to more beef and red wine.

"You think I exaggerate," he continued in a low voice. "But, although it is strictly forbidden, there are still people in this country who make a living by selling shrunken human heads. It's impossible to control it, and to this very day the jungle Indians cut off the heads of their enemies among other nomad tribes. They smash up and remove the skull itself and fill the empty skin of the head with hot sand, so that the whole head shrinks till it's hardly bigger than a cat's head, without losing its shape or its features. These shrunken heads of enemies were once valuable trophies; now they're rare black-market goods. Half-breed middlemen see that they get down to the buyers on the coast, who sell them to tourists for fabulous prices."

Jorge looked at us triumphantly. He little knew that Herman and I that same day had been dragged into a porter's lodge and offered two of these heads at 1,000 sucres apiece. These heads nowadays are often fakes, made up from monkeys' heads, but these two were genuine enough, pure Indians and so true to life that every tiny feature was preserved. They were the heads of a man and a woman, both the size of oranges; the woman was actually pretty, though only the eyelashes and long black hair had preserved their natural size. I shuddered at Jorge's warning but expressed my doubts whether there were head-hunters west of the mountains.

"One can never know," said Jorge gloomily. "And what would you say if your friend disappeared and his head came into the market in miniature? That happened to a friend of mine once," he added, staring at me stubbornly.

"Tell us about it," said Herman, chewing his beef slowly and with only moderate enjoyment.

I laid my fork carefully aside, and Jorge told his story. He was once living with his wife on an outpost in the jungle, washing gold and buying up the take of the other gold-washers. The family had at that time a native friend who brought his gold regularly and sold it for goods. One day this friend was killed in the jungle. Jorge tracked down the murderer and threatened to shoot him. Now the murderer was one of those who were suspected of selling shrunken human heads, and Jorge promised to spare his life if he handed over the head at once. The murderer at once produced the head of Jorge's friend, now as small as a man's fist. Jorge was quite upset when he saw his friend again, for he was quite unchanged except that he had become so very small. Much moved, he took the little head home to his wife. She fainted when she saw it, and Jorge had to hide his friend in a trunk.

But it was so damp in the jungle that clusters of green mold formed on the head, so that Jorge had to take it out now and then and dry it in the sun. It hung very nicely by the hair on a clothesline, and Jorge's wife fainted every time she caught sight of it. But one day a mouse gnawed its way into the trunk and made a horrid mess of his friend. Jorge was much distressed and buried his friend with full ceremonies in a tiny little hole up on the airfield. For after all he was a human being, Jorge concluded.

"Nice dinner," I said to change the subject.

As we went home in the dark, I had a disagreeable feeling that Herman's hat had sunk far down over his ears. But he had only pulled it down to protect himself from the cold night wind from the mountains.

Next day we were sitting with our own Consul General Bryhn and his wife under the eucalyptus trees at their big country place outside the town. Bryhn hardly thought our planned jungle trip to Quevedo would lead to any drastic change in our hat sizes, but—there were robbers about in those very regions we had thought of visiting. He produced clippings from local papers announcing that soldiers were to be sent out, when the dry season came, to extirpate the *bandidos* who infested the regions around Quevedo. To go there now was the sheerest madness, and we would never get guides or transport. While we were talking to him, we saw a jeep from the American military attaché's office tear past along the road, and this gave us an idea. We went up to the American Embassy, accompanied by the consul general, and were able to see the military attaché himself. He was a trim, lighthearted young man in khaki and riding boots and asked laughingly why we had strayed to the top of the Andes when the local papers said we were to go to sea on a wooden raft.

We explained that the wood was still standing upright in the Quevedo jungle and we were up here on the roof of the continent and could not get to it. We asked the military attaché either (*a*) to lend us a plane and two parachutes or (*b*) to lend us a jeep with a driver who knew the country.

The military attaché at first sat speechless at our assurance;

then he shook his head despairingly and said with a smile, all right—since we gave him no third choice, he preferred the second!

At a quarter past five the next morning a jeep rolled up to our hotel entrance, and an Ecuadorian captain of engineers jumped out and reported himself at our service. His orders were to drive us to Quevedo, mud or no mud. The jeep was packed full of gasoline cans, for there were no gasoline pumps or even wheel tracks along the route we were to take. Our new friend, Captain Agurto Alexis Alvarez, was armed to the teeth with knives and firearms on account of the reports of *bandidos*. We had come to the country peacefully in business suits to buy timber for ready money down on the coast, and the whole of our equipment on board the jeep consisted of a bag of tinned food, except that we had hurriedly acquired a secondhand camera and a pair of tear-proof khaki breeches for each of us. In addition, the consul general had pressed upon us his big revolver with an ample supply of ammunition to exterminate everything that crossed our path. The jeep whizzed away through empty alleys where the moon shone ghostly pale on whitewashed adobe walls, till we came out into the country and raced at a giddy speed along a good sand road southward through the mountain region.

It was good going all along the range as far as the mountain village of Latacunga, where windowless Indian houses clustered blindly round a whitewashed country church with palms in a square. Here we turned off along a mule track which undulated and twisted westward over hill and valley into the Andes. We came into a world we had never dreamed of. It was the mountain Indians' own world—east of the sun and west of the moon—outside time and beyond space. On the whole drive we saw not a carriage or a wheel. The traffic consisted of barelegged goatherds in gaily colored ponchos, driving forward disorderly herds of stiff-legged, dignified llamas, and now and then whole families of Indians coming along the road. The husband usually rode ahead on a mule, while his little wife trotted behind with her entire collection of hats on her head and the youngest child in a bag on her back. All the time she ambled along, she spun wool with her

fingers. Donkeys and mules jogged behind at leisure, loaded
with boughs and rushes and pottery.

The farther we went, the fewer the Indians who spoke
Spanish, and soon Agurto's linguistic capacities were as useless as our own. A cluster of huts lay here and there up in
the mountains; fewer and fewer were built of clay, while
more and more were made of twigs and dry grass. Both the
huts and the sun-browned, wrinkle-faced people seemed to
have grown up out of the earth itself, from the baking effect
of the mountain sun on the rock walls of the Andes. They
belonged to cliff and scree and upland pasture as naturally
as the mountain grass itself. Poor in possessions and small in
stature, the mountain Indians had the wiry hardiness of wild
animals and the childlike alertness of a primitive people, and
the less they could talk, the more they could laugh. Radiant
faces with snow-white teeth shone upon us from all we saw.
There was nothing to indicate that the white man had lost
or earned a dime in these regions. There were no billboards
or road signs, and if a tin box or a scrap of paper was flung
down by the roadside, it was picked up at once as a useful
household article.

We went on up over sun-smitten slopes without a bush or
tree and down into valleys of desert sand and cactus, till
finally we climbed up and reached the topmost crest with
snow fields round the peak and a wind so bitingly cold that
we had to slacken speed in order not to freeze to bits as we sat
in our shirts longing for jungle heat. For long stretches we
had to drive across country between the mountains, over scree
and grassy ridges, searching for the next bit of road. But
when we reached the west wall, where the Andes range falls
precipitously to the lowlands, the mule track was cut along
shelves in the loose rock, and sheer cliffs and gorges were
all about us. We put all our trust in friend Agurto as he sat
crouched over the steering wheel, always swinging out when
we came to a precipice. Suddenly a violent gust of wind met
us; we had reached the outermost crest of the Andes chain,
where the mountain fell away sharply in a series of precipices
to the jungle far down in a bottomless abyss 12,000 feet beneath us. But we were cheated of the dizzy view over the sea

of jungle, for, as soon as we reached the edge, thick cloud banks rolled about us like steam from a witches' cauldron. But now our road ran down unhindered into the depths. Always down, in steep loops along gorges and bluffs and ridges, while the air grew damper and warmer and ever fuller of the heavy, deadening hothouse air which rose from the jungle world below.

And then the rain began. First gently, then it began to pour and beat upon the jeep like drumsticks, and soon the chocolate-colored water was flowing down the rocks on every side of us. We almost flowed down, too, away from the dry mountain plateaus behind us and into another world, where stick and stone and clay slope were soft and lush with moss and turf. Leaves shot up; soon they became giant leaves hanging like green umbrellas and dripping over the hillside. Then came the first feeble advanced posts of the jungle trees, with heavy fringes and beards of moss and climbing plants hanging from them. There was a gurgling and splashing everywhere. As the slopes grew gentler, the jungle rolled up swiftly like an army of green giant growths that swallowed up the little jeep as it splashed along the waterlogged clay road. We were in the jungle. The air was moist and warm and heavy with the smell of vegetation.

Darkness had fallen when we reached a cluster of palmroofed huts on a ridge. Dripping with warm water, we left the jeep for a night under a dry roof. The horde of fleas that attacked us in the hut were drowned in the next day's rain. With the jeep full of bananas and other tropical fruit we went on downhill through the jungle, down and down, though we thought we had reached bottom long ago. The mud grew worse but it did not stop us, and the robbers kept at an unknown distance.

Not till the road was barred by a broad river of muddy water rolling down through the jungle did the jeep give up. We stood stuck fast, unable to move either up or down along the riverbank. In an open clearing stood a hut where a few half-breed Indians were stretching out a jaguar skin on a sunny wall, while dogs and fowl were splashing about enjoying themselves on top of some cocoa beans spread out to dry in the sun. When the jeep came bumping along, the place came to life and some natives who spoke Spanish informed us that this was the Rio Palenque and that Quevedo was just on the other side. There was no bridge there, and the river was swift and deep, but they were willing to float us and the jeep over by raft. The queer contraption lay down by the bank. Twisted logs as thick as our arms were fastened together with vegetable fibers and bamboos to form a flimsy raft, twice the length and breadth of the jeep. With a plank under each wheel and our hearts in our mouths we drove the jeep out onto the logs, and though most of them were submerged under the muddy water, they did bear the jeep and us and four half-naked chocolate-colored men who pushed us off with long poles.

"Balsa?" Herman and I asked in the same breath.

"Balsa," one of the fellows nodded, with a disrespectful kick at the logs.

The current seized us and we whirled down the river, while the men pushed in their poles at the right places and kept the raft on an even diagonal course across the current and into quieter water on the other side. This was our first meeting with the balsa tree and our first trip on a balsa raft. We brought the raft safely to land at the farther bank and motored triumphantly into Quevedo. Two rows of tarred wooden houses with motionless vultures on the palm roofs formed a kind of street, and this was the whole place. The inhabitants dropped whatever they might be carrying, and black and brown, young and old, appeared swarming out of both doors and windows. They rushed to meet the jeep—a menacing, chattering tide of humanity. They scrambled on to it and under it and round it. We kept a tight hold on our worldly possessions while Agurto attempted desperate maneuvers at the steering wheel. Then the jeep had a puncture and went down on one knee. We had arrived at Quevedo and had to endure the embrace of welcome.

Don Federico's plantation lay a bit farther down the river. When the jeep came bumping into the yard along a path between the mango trees with Agurto, Herman, and me, the lean old jungle-dweller came to meet us at a trot with his nephew Angelo, a small boy who lived with him out in the wilds. We gave messages from Don Gustavo, and soon the jeep was standing alone in the yard while a fresh tropical shower streamed down over the jungle. There was a festive meal in Don Federico's bungalow; suckling pigs and chickens crackled over an open fire, while we sat round a dish loaded with tropical fruit and explained what we had come for. The jungle rain pouring down on the ground outside sent a warm sweet gust of scented blossoms and clay in through the window netting.

Don Federico had become as brisk as a boy. Why, yes, he had known balsa rafts since he was a child. Fifty years ago, when he lived down by the sea, the Indians from Peru still used to come sailing up along the coast on big balsa rafts to sell fish in Guayaquil. They could bring a couple of tons of dried fish in a bamboo cabin in the middle of the raft, or they might have wives and children and dogs and fowl on board. Such big balsa trees as they had used for their rafts would be hard to find now in the rains, for floodwater and mud had already made it impossible to get to the balsa plantation up in the forest, even on horseback. But Don Federico would do his best; there might still be some single trees growing wild in the forest nearer the bungalow, and we did not need many.

Late in the evening the rain stopped for a time, and we went for a turn under the mango trees round the bungalow. Here Don Federico had every kind of wild orchid in the world hanging down from the branches, with half-coconuts as flowerpots. Unlike cultivated orchids, these rare plants gave out a wonderful scent, and Herman was bending down to stick his nose into one of them when something like a long, thin, glittering eel emerged from the leaves above him. A lightning blow from Angelo's whip, and a wriggling snake fell to the ground. A second later it was held fast to the earth with a forked stick over its neck, and then its head was crushed.

"*Mortal*," said Angelo and exposed two curved poison fangs to show what he meant.

After that we thought we saw poisonous snakes lurking in the foliage everywhere and slipped into the house with

Angelo's trophy hanging lifeless across a stick. Herman sat down to skin the monster, and Don Federico was telling fantastic stories about poisonous snakes and boa constrictors as thick as dinner plates when we suddenly noticed the shadows of two enormous scorpions on the wall, the size of lobsters. They rushed at each other and engaged in a life-and-death battle with their pincers, with their hinder parts turned up and their curved poisonous sting at the tail ready for the deathblow. It was a horrible sight, and not till we moved the oil lamp did we see that it had cast a supernaturally gigantic shadow of two quite ordinary scorpions of the size of one's finger, which were fighting on the edge of the bureau.

"Let them be," Don Federico laughed. "One'll kill the other, and we want the survivor in the house to keep the cockroaches away. Just keep your mosquito net tight round the bed and shake your clothes before you put them on, and you'll be all right. I've often been bitten by scorpions and I'm not dead yet," added the old man, laughing.

I slept well, except that I woke up thinking of poisonous creatures every time a lizard or bat squeaked and scrabbled too noisily near my pillow.

Next morning we got up early to go and search for balsa trees.

"Better shake our clothes," said Agurto, and as he spoke a scorpion fell out of his shirt sleeve and shot down into a crack in the floor.

Soon after sunrise Don Federico sent his men out on horseback in all directions to look for accessible balsa trees along the paths. Our own party consisted of Don Federico, Herman, and myself, and we soon found our way to an open place where there was a gigantic old tree of which Don Federico knew. It towered high above the trees round about, and the trunk was three feet thick. In Polynesian style we christened the tree before we touched it; we gave it the name Ku, after a Polynesian deity of American origin. Then we swung the ax and drove it into the balsa trunk till the forest echoed our blows. But cutting a sappy balsa was like cutting cork with a blunt ax; the ax simple rebounded, and I had not delivered many strokes before Herman had to relieve me. The ax changed hands time after time, while the splinters flew and the sweat trickled in the heat of the jungle.

Late in the day Ku was standing like a cock on one leg, quivering under our blows; soon he tottered and crashed down heavily over the surrounding forest, big branches and small trees being pulled down by the giant's fall. We had torn the branches from the trunk and were beginning to rip off the bark in zigzags in Indian style when Herman suddenly dropped the ax and leaped into the air as if doing a Polynesian war dance, with his hand pressed to his leg. Out of his trouser leg fell a shining ant as big as a scorpion and with a long sting at its tail. It must have had a skull like a lobster's claw, for it was almost impossible to stamp it under one's heel on the ground.

"A kongo," Don Federico explained with regret. "The little brute's worse than a scorpion, but it isn't dangerous to a healthy man."

Herman was tender and sore for several days, but this did not prevent his galloping with us on horseback along the jungle paths, looking for more giant balsas in the forest. From time to time we heard creaking and crashing and a heavy thud somewhere in the virgin forest. Don Federico nodded with a satisfied air. It meant that his half-breed Indians had felled a new giant balsa for the raft. In a week Ku had been followed by Kane, Kama, Ilo, Mauri, Ra, Rangi, Papa, Taranga, Kura, Kukara, and Hiti—twelve mighty balsas, all christened in honor of Polynesian legendary figures whose names had once been borne with Tiki over the sea from Peru. The logs, glistening with sap, were dragged down through the jungle first by horses and at the last by Don Federico's tractor, which brought them to the riverbank in front of the bungalow.

The sap-filled logs were far from being as light as corks. They must have weighed a ton apiece, and we waited with great anxiety to see how they would float in the water. We rolled them out to the edge of the bank one by one; there we made fast a rope of tough, climbing plants to the ends of the logs that they might not vanish downstream when we let

them enter the water. Then we rolled them in turn down the
bank and into the river. There was a mighty splash. They
swung round and floated, about as much above as below the
surface of the water, and when we went out along them they
remained steady. We bound the timbers together with tough
lianas that hung down from the tops of the jungle trees, so
as to make two temporary rafts, one towing the other. Then
we loaded the rafts with all the bamboos and lianas we should
need later, and Herman and I went on board with two men
of a mysterious mixed race, with whom we had no common
language.

When we cut our moorings, we were caught by the whirling masses of water and went off downstream at a good pace.
The last glimpse we had in the drizzle, as we rounded the
first headland, was of our excellent friends standing on the
end of the point in front of the bungalow, waving. Then we
crept under a little shelter of green banana leaves and left
steering problems to the two brown experts who had stationed
themselves one in the bow and one astern, each holding a
huge oar. They kept the raft in the swiftest current with non-
chalant ease, and we danced downstream on a winding course
between sunken trees and sandbanks.

The jungle stood like a solid wall along the banks on both
sides, and parrots and other bright-colored birds fluttered out
of the dense foliage as we passed. Once or twice an alligator
hurled itself into the river and became invisible in the muddy
water. But we soon caught sight of a much more remarkable
monster. This was an iguana, or giant lizard, as big as a
crocodile but with a large throat and fringed back. It lay
dozing on the clay bank as if it had overslept from prehistoric
times and did not move as we glided past. The oarsmen made
signs to us not to shoot. Soon afterward we saw a smaller
specimen about three feet long. It was running away along a
thick branch which hung out over the raft. It ran only till it
was in safety, and then it sat, all shining blue and green, and
stared at us with cold snake's eyes as we passed. Later we
passed a fern-clad hillock, and on the top of it lay the biggest
iguana of all. It was like the silhouette of a fringed Chinese
dragon carved in stone as it stood out motionless against the

sky with chest and head raised. It did not as much as turn its head as we curved round it under the hillocks and vanished into the jungle.

Farther down we smelled smoke and passed several huts with straw roofs which lay in clearings along the bank. We on the raft were the objects of close attention from sinister-looking individuals on land, an unfavorable mixture of Indian, Negro, and Spaniard. Their boats, great dugout canoes, lay drawn up on to the bank.

When mealtimes came, we relieved our friends at the steering oars while they fried fish and breadfruit over a little fire regulated with wet clay. Roast chicken, eggs, and tropical fruits were also part of the menu on board, while the logs transported themselves and us at a fine speed down through the jungle toward the sea. What did it matter now if the water swept and splashed round us? The more it rained, the swifter the current ran.

When darkness fell over the river, an ear-splitting orchestra struck up on the bank. Toads and frogs, crickets and mosquitoes, croaked or chirped or hummed in a prolonged chorus of many voices. Now and again the shrill scream of a wild cat rang through the darkness, and soon another, and yet another, from birds scared into flight by the night prowlers of the jungle. Once or twice we saw the gleam of a fire in a native hut and heard bawling voices and the barking of dogs as we slid past in the night. But for the most part we sat alone with the jungle orchestra under the stars, till drowsiness and rain drove us into the cabin of leaves, where we went to sleep with our pistols loose in their holsters.

The farther downstream we drifted, the thicker became the huts and native plantations, and soon there were regular villages on the banks. The traffic here consisted of dugout canoes punted along with long poles, and now and then we saw a little balsa raft loaded with heaps of green bananas bound for market.

Where the Palenque joined the Rio Guayas, the water had risen so high that the paddle steamer was plying busily between Vinces and Guayaquil down on the coast. To save valuable time Herman and I each got a hammock on board

the paddle steamer and steamed off across the thickly popu-
lated flat country to the coast. Our brown friends were to
follow, drifting down alone with the timber.

At Guayaquil Herman and I parted. He was to remain at
the mouth of the Guayas to stop the balsa logs as they came
drifting down. Thence he was to take them, as cargo on a
coasting steamer, to Peru, where he was to direct the building
of the raft and make a faithful copy of the Indians' old-time
vessels. I myself took the regular plane southward to Lima,
the capital of Peru, to find a suitable place for building the
raft.

The plane ascended to a great height along the shore of
the Pacific, with the desert mountains in Peru on one side
and a glittering ocean far below us on the other. It was here
we were to put to sea on board the raft. The sea seemed
endless when seen from a plane high up. Sky and sea melted
into each other along an indefinable horizon far, far away to
the westward, and I could not rid myself of the thought that
even beyond that horizon many hundred similar sea plains
curved onward round a fifth of the earth before there was
any more land—in Polynesia. I tried to project my thoughts
a few weeks ahead, when we should be drifting on a speck
of a raft on that blue expanse below, but quickly dismissed
the thought again, for it gave me the same unpleasant feeling
inside as sitting in readiness to jump with a parachute.

On my arrival in Lima I took the street car down to the port
of Callao to find a place where we could build the raft. I
saw at once that the whole harbor was chock-full of ships and
cranes and warehouses, with customs sheds and harbor offices
and all the rest. And, if there was any open beach farther out,
it swarmed with bathers to such a degree that inquisitive
people would pull the raft and fittings to pieces as soon as our
backs were turned. Callao was now the most important port
in a country of seven million people, white and brown. Times
had changed for raft-builders in Peru even more than in
Ecuador, and I saw only one possibility—to get inside the high
concrete walls round the naval harbor, where armed men
stood on guard behind the iron gate and cast menacing and
suspicious looks on me and other unauthorized persons who

loafed past the walls. If one could only get in there, one would be safe.

I had met the Peruvian naval attaché in Washington and had a letter from him to support me. I went to the Ministry of Marine next day with the letter and sought an audience of the minister of marine, Manuel Nieto. He received in the morning in the elegant Empire drawing room of the Ministry, gleaming with mirrors and gilding. After a time he himself came in in full uniform, a short broadly built officer, as stern as Napoleon, straightforward and concise in his manner of speech. He asked why and I said why. I asked to be allowed to build a wooden raft in the naval dockyard.

"Young man," said the minister, drumming uneasily with his fingers. "You've come in by the window instead of the door. I'll be glad to help you, but the order must come from the foreign minister to me; I can't let foreigners into the naval area and give them the use of the dockyard as a matter of course. Apply to the Foreign Ministry in writing, and good luck."

I thought apprehensively of papers circulating and disappearing into the blue. Happy were the rude days of Kon-Tiki, when applications were an unknown hindrance!

To see the foreign minister in person was considerably harder. Norway had no local legation in Peru, and our helpful Consul General Bahr could, therefore, take me no farther than the counselors of the Foreign Ministry. I was afraid things would get no further. Dr. Cohen's letter to the President of the republic might come in useful now. So I sought through his adjutant an audience of His Excellency Don José Bustamante y Rivero, president of Peru. A day or two later I was told to be at the palace at twelve o'clock.

Lima is a modern city, with half a million inhabitants, and lies spread over a green plain at the foot of the desert mountains. Architecturally, and thanks not least to its gardens and plantations, it is surely one of the most beautiful capitals in the world—a bit of modern California or Riviera variegated with old Spanish architecture. The president's palace lies in the middle of the city and is strongly guarded by armed sentries in gaily colored costumes. An audience in Peru is a serious business, and few people have seen the president except on the screen. Soldiers in shining bandoleers escorted me upstairs and to the end of a long corridor; here my name was taken and registered by three civilians, and I was shown through a colossal oak door into a room with a long table and rows of chairs. A man dressed in white received me, asked me to sit down, and disappeared. A moment later a large door opened, and I was shown into a much handsomer room, where an imposing person in a spotless uniform advanced toward me.

"The President," I thought, drawing myself up. But no. The man in the gold-edged uniform offered me an antique straight-backed chair and disappeared. I had sat on the edge of my chair for barely a minute when yet another door opened and a servant bowed me into a large gilded room with gilded furniture and splendidly decorated. The fellow vanished as quickly as he had appeared, and I sat quite alone on an antique sofa with a view of a string of empty rooms whose doors stood open. It was so silent that I could hear someone coughing cautiously several rooms away. Then steady steps approached, and I jumped up and hesitatingly greeted an imposing gentleman in uniform. But, no, this too was not he. But I understood enough of what he said to gather that the President sent me his greetings and would be free very soon when a meeting of ministers was over.

Ten minutes later steady steps once more broke the silence, and this time a man with gold lace and epaulets came in. I sprang briskly from the sofa and bowed deeply. The man bowed still more deeply and led me through several rooms and up a staircase with thick carpets. Then he left me in a tiny little room with one leather-covered chair and one sofa. In came a little man in a white suit, and I waited resignedly to see where he intended to take me. But he took me nowhere, only greeted me amiably and remained standing. This was President Bustamante y Rivero.

The President had twice as much English as I had Spanish, so when we had greeted one another and he had begged me with a gesture to sit down, our common vocabulary was exhausted. Signs and gesticulations will do a lot, but they will not get one permission to build a raft in a naval harbor in Peru. The only thing I perceived was that the President did not understand what I was saying, and he grasped that still more clearly himself, for in a little while he disappeared and came back with the air minister. The air minister, General Reveredo, was a vigorous athletic man in an Air Force uniform. He spoke English splendidly with an American accent.

I apologized for the misunderstanding and said it was not to the airfield that I had been trying to ask for admission but to the naval harbor. The general laughed and explained that he had only been called in as interpreter. Bit by bit the theory was translated to the President, who listened closely and put sharp questions through General Reveredo. At last he said:

"If it is possible that the Pacific islands were first discovered from Peru, Peru has an interest in this expedition. If we can do anything for you, tell us."

I asked for a place where we could build the raft within the walls of the naval area, access to the naval workshops, a place for the storage of equipment and facilities for bringing it into the country, the use of the dry dock and of naval personnel to help us in the work, and a vessel to tow us out from the coast when we started.

"What is he asking for?" the President asked eagerly, so that I too understood.

"Nothing much," Reveredo answered, looking at me with a twinkle in his eye. And the President, satisfied, nodded as a sign of approval.

Before the meeting broke up, Reveredo promised that the foreign minister should receive orders from the President personally, and that Minister of Marine Nieto should be given a free hand to give us all the help we had asked for.

"God preserve you all!" said the General, laughing and shaking his head. The adjutant came in and escorted me out to a waiting messenger.

That day the Lima papers published a paragraph about the Norwegian raft expedition which was to start from Peru; at the same time they announced that a Swedish-Finnish scientific expedition had finished its studies among the jungle Indians in the Amazon regions. Two of the Swedish members of the Amazon expedition had come on up the river by canoe to Peru and had just arrived in Lima. One was Bengt Danielsson, from Uppsala University, who was now going to study the mountain Indians in Peru.

I cut out the paragraph, and was sitting in my hotel writing to Herman about the site for building the raft, when I was interrupted by a knock on the door. In came a tall sunburned fellow in tropical clothes, and, when he took off his white helmet, it looked as if his flaming red beard had burned his face and scorched his hair thin. That fellow came from the wilds, but his place was clearly a lecture room.

"Bengt Danielsson," I thought.

"Bengt Danielsson," said the man, introducing himself.

"He's heard about the raft," I thought and asked him to sit down.

"I've just heard of the raft plans," said the Swede.

"And now he's come to knock down the theory, because he's an ethnologist," I thought.

"And now I've come to ask if I may come with you on the raft," the Swede said peaceably. "I'm interested in the migration theory."

I knew nothing about the man except that he was a scientist and that he had come straight out of the depths of the jungle. But if a solitary Swede had the pluck to go out on a raft with five Norwegians, he could not be squeamish. And not even that imposing beard could hide his placid nature and gay humor.

Bengt became the sixth member of the crew, for the place was still vacant. And he was the only one who spoke Spanish.

When the passenger plane droned northward along the coast a few days later with me on board, I again looked down with respect on to the endless blue sea beneath us. It seemed to hang and float loose under the firmament itself. Soon we six were to be packed together like microbes on a mere speck, down there where there was so much water that it looked as if it overflowed all along the western horizon. We were to be part of a desolate world without being able to get more than a few steps away from one another. For the time being, at any rate, there was elbowroom enough between us. Herman was in Ecuador waiting for the timber. Knut Haugland and Torstein Raaby had just arrived in New York by air. Erik Hesselberg was on board ship from Oslo, bound for Panama. I myself was en route for Washington by air, and Bengt was in the hotel at Lima ready to start, waiting to meet the others.

No two of these men had met before, and they were all of entirely different types. That being so, we should have been on the raft for some weeks before we got tired of one another's stories. No storm clouds with low pressure and gusty weather held greater menace for us than the danger of psychological cloudburst among six men shut up together for months on a drifting raft. In such circumstances a good joke was often as valuable as a life belt.

Up in Washington there was still bitter winter weather when I came back—cold and snowy February. Björn had tackled the radio problem and had interested the Radio Amateur League of America in listening in for reports from the raft. Knut and Torstein were busy preparing the transmission, which was to be done partly with short-wave transmitters specially constructed for our purpose and partly with secret sabotage sets used during the war. There were a thousand things to prepare, big and small, if we were to do all that we planned on the voyage.

And the piles of paper in the files grew. Military and civilian documents—white, yellow, and blue—in English, Spanish, French, and Norwegian. Even a raft trip had to cost the paper industry half a fir tree in our practical age! Laws and regulations tied our hands everywhere, and knot after knot had to be loosened in turn.

"I'll swear this correspondence weighs twenty pounds," said Knut one day despairingly as he bent over his typewriter.

"Twenty-six," said Torstein drily. "I've weighed it."

My mother must have had a clear idea of the conditions in these days of dramatic preparation when she wrote: "And I only wish I knew you were all six safe on board the raft!"

Then one day an express telegram came from Lima. Herman had been caught in the backwash of a breaker and flung ashore, badly injured, with his neck dislocated. He was under treatment in Lima Hospital.

Torstein Raaby was sent down by air at once with Gerd
Vold, the popular London secretary of the Norwegian parachute saboteurs in the war, who was now helping us in Washington. They found Herman better; he had been hung up by
a strap round his head for half an hour while the doctors
twisted the atlas vertebra in his neck back into position. The
X-ray picture showed that the highest bone in his neck was
cracked and had been turned right around. Herman's splendid condition had saved his life, and he was soon back, blue
and green and stiff and rheumatic, in the naval dockyard,
where he had assembled the balsa wood and started the work.
He had to remain in the doctor's hands for several weeks, and
it was doubtful whether he would be able to make the voyage
with us. He himself never doubted it for a moment, despite
his initial rough handling in the embrace of the Pacific.

Then Erik arrived by air from Panama and Knut and I
from Washington, and so we were all assembled at the starting point in Lima.

Down in the naval dockyard lay the big balsa logs from
the Quevedo forest. It was really a pathetic sight. Fresh-cut
round logs, yellow bamboos, reeds, and green banana leaves
lay in a heap, our building materials, in between rows of
threatening gray submarines and destroyers. Six fair-skinned
northerners and twenty brown Peruvian seamen with Inca
blood in their veins swung axes and long machete knives and
tugged at ropes and knots. Trim naval officers in blue and
gold walked over and stared in bewilderment at these pale
strangers and their crude vegetable materials which had suddenly appeared in the midst of their proud naval yard.

For the first time for hundreds of years a balsa raft was
being built in Callao Bay. In these coastal waters, where Inca
legends affirm that their ancestors first learned to sail such
rafts from Kon-Tiki's vanished clan, modern Indians were
forbidden to build such rafts by men of our own race. Sailing
on an open raft can cost human lives. The descendants of the
Incas have moved with the times; like us, they have creases
in their trousers and are safely protected by the guns of their
naval craft. Bamboo and balsa belong to the primitive past;
here, too, life is marching on—to armor and steel.

The ultramodern dockyard gave us wonderful support. With Bengt as interpreter and Herman as chief constructor we had the run of the carpenter's and sailmaker's shops, as well as half the storage space as a dump for our equipment and a small floating pier where the timber was put into the water when the building began.

Nine of the thickest logs were chosen as sufficient to form the actual raft. Deep grooves were cut in the wood to prevent the ropes which were to fasten them and the whole raft together from slipping. Not a single spike, nail, or wire rope was used in the whole construction. The nine great logs were first laid loose side by side in the water so that they might all fall freely into their natural floating position before they were lashed securely together. The longest log, 45 feet long, was laid in the middle and projected a long way at both ends. Shorter and shorter logs were laid symmetrically on both sides of this, so that the sides of the raft were 30 feet long and the bow stuck out like a blunt plow. Astern the raft was cut off straight across, except that the three middle logs projected and supported a short thick block of balsa wood which lay athwart ship and held tholepins for the long steering oar. When the nine balsa logs were lashed securely together with separate lengths of inch-and-a-quarter hemp rope, the lighter balsa logs were made fast crossways over them at intervals of about 3 feet.

The raft itself was now complete, laboriously fastened together with about three hundred different lengths of rope, each firmly knotted. A deck of split bamboos was laid upon it, fastened to it in the form of separate strips and covered with loose mats of plaited bamboo reeds. In the middle of the raft, but nearer the stern, we erected a small open cabin of bamboo canes, with walls of plaited bamboo reeds and a roof of bamboo slats with leathery banana leaves overlapping one another like tiles. Forward of the cabin we set up two masts side by side. They were cut from mangrove wood, as hard as iron, and leaned toward each other, so that they were lashed together crosswise at the top. The big rectangular square sail was hauled up on a yard made of two bamboo stems bound together to secure double strength.

The nine big logs of timber which were to carry us over
the sea were pointed at their forward ends in native fashion
that they might glide more easily through the water, and
quite low splashboards were fastened to the bow above the
surface of the water.

At various places, where there were large chinks between
the logs, we pushed down in all five solid fir planks which
stood on their edges in the water under the raft. They were
scattered about without system and went down 5 feet into
the water, being 1 inch thick and 2 feet wide. They were
kept in place with wedges and ropes and served as tiny parallel keels or centerboards. Centerboards of this kind were used
on all the balsa rafts of Inca times, long before the time of
the discoveries, and were meant to prevent the flat wooden
rafts from drifting sideways with wind and sea. We did not
make any rail or protection round the raft, but we had a long
slim balsa log which afforded foothold along each side.

The whole construction was a faithful copy of the old
vessels in Peru and Ecuador except for the low splashboards
in the bow, which later proved to be entirely unnecessary.
After finishing the raft itself, of course, we could arrange
the details on board as we liked, so long as they had no effect
on the movement and quality of the vessel. We knew that
this raft was to be our whole world in the time that lay
before us and that, consequently, the smallest detail on board
would increase in dimensions and importance as the weeks
passed.

Therefore we gave the little deck as much variation as possible. The bamboo strips did not deck in the whole raft but
formed a floor forward of the bamboo cabin and along the
starboard side of it where the wall was open. The port side
of the cabin was a kind of back yard full of boxes and gear
made fast, with a narrow edge left to walk along. Forward
in the bow, and in the stern as far as the after wall of the
cabin, the nine gigantic logs were not decked in at all. So,
when we moved round the bamboo cabin, we stepped from
yellow bamboos and wickerwork down on to the round gray
logs astern and up again on to piles of cargo on the other
side. It was not many steps, but the psychological effect of

the irregularity gave us variation and compensated us for our limited freedom of movement. Up at the masthead we placed a wooden platform, not so much in order to have a lookout post, when at last we came to land, as to be able to clamber up while en route and look at the sea from another angle.

When the raft began to take shape and lay there among the warships, golden and fresh with ripe bamboos and green leaves, the minister of marine himself came to inspect us. We were immensely proud of our vessel as she lay there, a brave little reminder of Inca times among the threatening big warships. But the minister of marine was utterly horrified by what he saw. I was summoned to the naval office to sign a paper freeing the Navy from all responsibility for what we had built in its harbor, and to the harbor master to sign a paper saying that, if I left the harbor with men and cargo on board, it was entirely on my own responsibility and at my own risk.

Later a number of foreign naval experts and diplomats were admitted to the dockyard to see the raft. They were no more encouraging, and a few days afterward I was sent for by the ambassador of one of the Great Powers.

"Are your parents living?" he asked me. And, when I replied in the affirmative, he looked me straight in the eyes and said in a hollow voice, full of foreboding:

"Your mother and father will be very grieved when they hear of your death."

As a private individual he begged me to give up the voyage while there was yet time. An admiral who had inspected the raft had told him that we should never get across alive. In the first place, the raft's dimensions were wrong. It was so small that it would founder in a big sea; at the same time it was just long enough to be lifted up by two lines of waves at the same time, and with the raft filled with men and cargo the fragile balsa logs would break under the strain. And, what was worse, the biggest balsa exporter in the country had told him that the porous balsa logs would float only a quarter of the distance across the sea before they became so completely waterlogged that they would sink under us.

This sounded bad but, as we stuck to our guns, we were

given a Bible as a present to take with us on our voyage. All
in all, there was little encouragement to be had from the
experts who looked at the raft. Gales and perhaps hurricanes
would wash us overboard and destroy the low, open craft,
which would simply lie helpless and drift in circles about
the ocean before wind and sea. Even in an ordinary choppy
sea we should be continually drenched with salt water which
would take the skin off our legs and ruin everything on board.
If we added up all that the different experts, each in turn,
had pointed out as the vital flaw in the construction itself,
there was not a length of rope, not a knot, not a measure-
ment, not a piece of wood in the whole raft which would
not cause us to founder at sea. High wagers were made as to
how many days the raft would last, and a flippant naval
attaché bet all the whisky the members of the expedition
could drink for the rest of their lives if they reached the
South Sea islands alive.

Worst of all was when a Norwegian ship came into port
and we took the skipper and one or two of his most experienced sea dogs into the dockyard. We were eager to hear
their practical reactions. And our disappointment was great
when they all agreed that the blunt-bowed, clumsy craft
would never get any help from the sail, while the skipper
maintained that, if we kept afloat, the raft would take a year
or two to drift across with the Humboldt Current. The boat-
swain looked at our lashings and shook his head. We need
not worry. The raft would not hold together for a fortnight
before every single rope was worn through, for when at sea
the big logs would be continually moving up and down and
rubbing against one another. Unless we used wire ropes or
chains, we might as well pack up.

These were difficult arguments to stifle. If only one of them
proved to be right, we had not a chance. I am afraid I asked
myself many times if we knew what we were doing. I could
not counter the warnings one by one myself because I was
not a seaman. But I had in reserve one single trump in my
hand, on which the whole voyage was founded. I knew all
the time in my heart that a prehistoric civilization had been
spread from Peru and across to the islands at a time when

rafts like ours were the only vessels on that coast. And I drew the general conclusion that, if balsa wood had floated and lashings held for Kon-Tiki in 500 A.D., they would do the same for us now if we blindly made our raft an exact copy of his. Bengt and Herman had gone into the theory most thoroughly, and, while the experts lamented, all the boys took the thing quite calmly and had a royal time in Lima. There was just one evening when Torstein asked anxiously if I was sure the ocean currents went the right way. We had been to the movies and seen Dorothy Lamour dancing about in a straw skirt among palms and hula girls on a lovely South Sea island.

"That's where we must go," said Torstein. "And I'm sorry for you if the currents don't go as you say they do!"

When the day of our departure was approaching, we went to the regular passport control office to get permission to leave the country. Bengt stood first in the line as interpreter.

"What is your name?" asked a ceremonious little clerk, looking suspiciously over his spectacles at Bengt's huge beard.

"Bengt Emmerik Danielsson," Bengt answered respectfully.

The man put a long form into his typewriter.

"By what boat did you come to Peru?"

"Well, you see," Bengt explained, bending over the mild little man, "I didn't come by boat. I came to Peru by canoe."

The man looked at Bengt dumb with astonishment and tapped out "canoe" in an open space on the form.

"And by what boat are you leaving Peru?"

"Well, you see, again," said Bengt politely, "I'm not leaving Peru by boat. I'm leaving by raft."

"A likely story!" the clerk cried angrily and tore the paper out of the machine. "Will you please answer my questions properly?"

A few days before we sailed, provisions and water and all our equipment were stowed on board the raft. We took provisions for six men for four months, in the form of solid little cardboard cartons containing military rations. Herman had the idea of boiling asphalt and pouring it so as to make a level layer round each separate carton. Then we strewed sand on the cartons, to prevent them from sticking together, and stowed them, packed close, under the bamboo deck where they filled the space between the nine low crossbeams which supported the deck.

At a crystal-clear spring high up in the mountains we filled fifty-six small water cans with 275 gallons of drinking water. These, too, we made fast in between the crossbeams so that the sea might always splash round them. On the bamboo deck we lashed fast the rest of the equipment including large wicker baskets full of fruit, roots, and coconuts.

Knut and Torstein took one corner of the bamboo cabin for the radio, and inside the hut, down between the crossbeams, we made fast eight boxes. Two were reserved for scientific instruments and films; the other six were allotted one to each of us, with an intimation that each man could take with him as much private property as he could find room for in his own box. As Erik had brought several rolls of drawing paper and a guitar, his box was so full that he had to put his stockings in Torstein's. It took four seamen to carry Bengt's box on board. He brought nothing but books but he had managed to cram in seventy-three sociological and ethnological works. We laid plaited reed mats and our straw mattresses on top of the boxes and then we were ready to start.

First, the raft was towed out of the naval area and paddled round in the harbor for a while to see if the cargo was stowed evenly. Then she was towed across to the Callao Yacht Club, where invited guests and other persons interested were to be present at the naming of the raft the day before we sailed.

On April 27, 1947, the Norwegian flag was hoisted. Along a yard at the masthead waved the flags of the foreign countries which had given the expedition practical support. The quay was packed with people who wanted to see the strange craft christened. Both color and lineaments betrayed that many of them had remote ancestors who had sailed along the coast on balsa rafts. But there were also descendants of the old Spaniards, headed by representatives of the Peruvian Navy and the government, besides the ambassadors of the United States, Great Britain, France, China, Argentina, and Cuba; the former governor of the British colonies in the Pacific; the Swedish and Belgian ministers; and our friends from the little Norwegian colony with Consul General Bahr at their head. There were swarms of journalists and a clicking of movie cameras; indeed, the only things that were lacking were a brass band and a big drum. One thing was quite clear to us all—if the raft went to pieces outside the bay, we would paddle to Polynesia, each of us on a log, rather than dare come back here again.

Gerd Vold, the expedition's secretary and contact on the mainland, was to christen the raft with milk from a coconut, partly to be in harmony with the Stone Age and partly because, owing to a misunderstanding, the champagne had been put at the bottom of Torstein's private box. When our friends had been told in English and Spanish that the raft was named after the Incas' great forerunner—the sun-king who had vanished westward over the sea from Peru and appeared in Polynesia 1,500 years ago—Gerd Vold christened the raft *Kon-Tiki*. She smashed the coconut (previously cracked) so hard against the bow that milk and bits of coconut filled the hair of all those who stood reverently around.

Then the bamboo yard was hauled up and the sail shaken out, with Kon-Tiki's bearded head, painted in red by our artist Erik, in its center. It was a faithful copy of the sun-king's head cut in red stone on a statue in the ruined city of Tiahuanaco.

"Ah! Señor Danielsson," the foreman of our dockyard workers cried in delight when he saw the bearded face on the sail.

He had called Bengt Señor Kon-Tiki for two months, ever since we had shown him the bearded face of Kon-Tiki on a piece of paper. But now he had at last realized that Danielsson was Bengt's right name.

Before we sailed, we all had a farewell audience with the President, and then we went for a trip far up into the black mountains to look our fill on rock and scree before we drifted out into the endless ocean. While we were working on the raft down on the coast, we had stayed in a boardinghouse in a palm grove outside Lima and driven to and from Callao in an Air Ministry car with a private chauffeur whom Gerd had contrived to borrow for the expedition. Now we asked the chauffeur to drive us straight to the mountains, as far in as he could get in one day. We drove up over desert roads, along old irrigation canals from Inca times, till we came to the dizzy height of 12,000 feet above the raft's mast. Here we simply devoured rocks and mountain peaks and green grass with our eyes and tried to surfeit ourselves with the tranquil mountain mass of the Andes range that lay before us. We tried to convince ourselves that we were thoroughly tired of stone and solid earth and wanted to sail out and get to know the sea.

4 ACROSS THE PACIFIC

*A Dramatic Start—We Are Towed Out to Sea—A Wind
Springs Up—Fighting the Waves—Life in the Humboldt
Current—Plane Fails to Find Us—Logs absorb Water—
Wood against Ropes—Flying Fish for Meals—An Unusual
Bedfellow—Snakefish Makes a Blunder—Eyes in the Sea—
A Marine Ghost Story—We Meet the World's Biggest Fish—
A Sea-Turtle Hunt*

THERE WAS A BUSTLE IN CALLAO HARBOR THE
day the *Kon-Tiki* was to be towed out to sea. The minister
of marine had ordered the naval tug *Guardian Rios* to tow us
out of the bay and cast us off clear of the coastal traffic, out
where in times gone by the Indians used to lie fishing from
their rafts. The papers had published the news under both
red and black headlines, and there was a crowd of people
down on the quays from early in the morning of April 28.

We six who were to assemble on board all had little things
to do at the eleventh hour, and, when I came down to the
quay, only Herman was there keeping guard over the raft. I
intentionally stopped the car a long way off and walked the
whole length of the mole to stretch my legs thoroughly for
the last time for no one knew how long. I jumped on board
the raft, which looked an utter chaos of banana clusters, fruit
baskets, and sacks which had been hurled on board at the
very last moment and were to be stowed and made fast. In the
middle of the heap Herman sat resignedly holding on to a

cage with a green parrot in it, a farewell present from a
friendly soul in Lima.

"Look after the parrot a minute," said Herman. "I must go
ashore and have a last glass of beer. The tug won't be here
for hours."

He had hardly disappeared among the swarm on the quay
when people began to point and wave. And round the point
at full speed came the tug *Guardian Rios*. She dropped anchor
on the farther side of a waving forest of masts which blocked
the way in to the *Kon-Tiki* and sent in a large motorboat to
tow us out between the sailing craft. She was packed full of
seamen, officers, and movie photographers, and, while orders
rang out and cameras clicked, a stout towrope was made fast
to the raft's bow.

"*Un momento*," I shouted in despair from where I sat with
the parrot. "It's too early; we must wait for the others—*los
expedicionarios*," I explained and pointed toward the city.

But nobody understood. The officers only smiled politely,
and the knot at our bow was made fast in more than exem-
plary manner. I cast off the rope and flung it overboard with
all manner of signs and gesticulations. The parrot utilized
the opportunity afforded by all the confusion to stick its
beak out of the cage and turn the knob of the door, and
when I turned round it was strutting cheerfully about the
bamboo deck. I tried to catch it, but it shrieked rudely in
Spanish and fluttered away over the banana clusters. With
one eye on the sailors who were trying to cast a rope over the
bow I started a wild chase after the parrot. It fled shrieking
into the bamboo cabin, where I got it into a corner and
caught it by one leg as it tried to flutter over me. When I
came out again and stuffed my flapping trophy into its cage,
the sailors on land had cast off the raft's moorings, and we
were dancing helplessly in and out with the backwash of the
long swell that came rolling in over the mole. In despair I
seized a paddle and vainly tried to parry a violent bump as
the raft was flung against the wooden piles of the quay.
Then the motorboat started, and with a jerk the *Kon-Tiki*
began her long voyage.

My only companion was a Spanish-speaking parrot which

sat glaring sulkily in a cage. People on shore cheered and waved, and the swarthy movie photographers in the motor-boat almost jumped into the sea in their eagerness to catch every detail of the expedition's dramatic start from Peru. Despairing and alone I stood on the raft looking out for my lost companions, but none appeared. So we came out to the *Guardian Rios*, which was lying with steam up ready to lift anchor and start. I was up the rope ladder in a twinkling and made so much row on board that the start was postponed and a boat sent back to the quay. It was away a good while, and then it came back full of pretty *señoritas* but without a single one of the *Kon-Tiki's* missing men. This was all very well but it did not solve my problems, and, while the raft swarmed with charming *señoritas*, the boat went back on a fresh search for *los expedicionarios noruegos*.

Meanwhile Erik and Bengt came sauntering down to the quay with their arms full of reading matter and odds and ends. They met the whole stream of people on its way home and were finally stopped at a police barrier by a kindly official who told them there was nothing more to see. Bengt told the officer, with an airy gesture of his cigar, that they had not come to see anything; they themselves were going with the raft.

"It's no use," the officer said indulgently. "The *Kon-Tiki* sailed an hour ago."

"Impossible," said Erik, producing a parcel. "Here's the lantern!"

"And there's the navigator," said Bengt, "and I'm the steward."

They forced their way past, but the raft had gone. They trotted desperately to and fro along the mole where they met the rest of the party, who also were searching eagerly for the vanished raft. Then they caught sight of the boat coming in, and so we were all six finally united and the water was foaming round the raft as the *Guardian Rios* towed us out to sea.

It had been late in the afternoon when at last we started, and the *Guardian Rios* would not cast us off till we were clear of the coastal traffic next morning. Directly we were clear of

the mole we met a bit of a head sea, and all the small boats
which were accompanying us turned back one by one. Only
a few big yachts came with us out to the entrance to the bay
to see how things would go out there.

The *Kon-Tiki* followed the tug like an angry billy goat
on a rope, and she butted her bow into the head sea so that
the water rushed on board. This did not look very promising,
for this was a calm sea compared with what we had to expect.
In the middle of the bay the towrope broke, and our end of it
sank peacefully to the bottom while the tug steamed ahead.
We flung ourselves down along the side of the raft to fish
for the end of the rope, while the yachts went on and tried to
stop the tug. Stinging jellyfish as thick as washtubs splashed
up and down with the seas alongside the raft and covered
all the ropes with a slippery, stinging coating of jelly. When
the raft rolled one way, we hung flat over the side waving
our arms down toward the surface of the water, until our
fingers just touched the slimy towrope. Then the raft rolled
back again, and we all stuck our heads deep down into the
sea, while salt water and giant jellyfish poured over our backs.
We spat and cursed and pulled jellyfish fibers out of our hair,
but when the tug came back the rope end was up and ready
for splicing.

When we were about to throw it on board the tug, we suddenly drifted in under the vessel's overhanging stern and
were in danger of being crushed against her by the pressure
of the water. We dropped everything we had and tried to
push ourselves clear with bamboo sticks and paddles before it
was too late. But we never got a proper position, for when
we were in the trough of the sea we could not reach the iron
roof above us, and when the water rose again the *Guardian
Rios* dropped her whole stern down into the water and would
have crushed us flat if the suction had carried us underneath.
Up on the tug's deck people were running about and shouting; at last the propeller began to turn alongside us, and it
helped us clear of the backwash under the *Guardian Rios* in
the last second. The bow of the raft had had a few hard
knocks and had become a little crooked in the lashings, but
this fault rectified itself by degrees.

"When a thing starts so damnably, it's bound to end well," said Herman. "If only this towing could stop; it'll shake the raft to bits."

The towing went on all night at a slow speed and with only one or two small hitches. The yachts had bidden us farewell long ago, and the last coast light had disappeared astern. Only a few ships' lights passed us in the darkness. We divided the night into watches to keep an eye on the towrope, and we all had a good snatch of sleep. When it grew light next morning, a thick mist lay over the coast of Peru, while we had a brilliant blue sky ahead of us to westward. The sea was running in a long quiet swell covered with little white crests, and clothes and logs and everything we took hold of were soaking wet with dew. It was chilly, and the green water round us was astonishingly cold for 12° south.

We were in the Humboldt Current, which carries its cold masses of water up from the Antarctic and sweeps them north all along the coast of Peru till they swing west and out across the sea just below the Equator. It was out here that Pizarro, Zárate, and the other early Spaniards saw for the first time the Inca Indians' big sailing rafts, which used to go out for 50 to 60 sea miles to catch tunnies and dolphins in the same Humboldt Current. All day long there was an offshore wind out here, but in the evening the onshore wind reached as far out as this and helped the rafts home if they needed it.

In the early light we saw our tug lying close by, and we took care that the raft lay far enough away from her bow while we launched our little inflated rubber dinghy. It floated on the waves like a football and danced away with Erik, Bengt, and myself till we caught hold of the *Guardian Rios'* rope ladder and clambered on board. With Bengt as interpreter we had our exact position shown us on our chart. We were 50 sea miles from land in a northwesterly direction from Callao, and we were to carry lights the first few nights so as not to be sunk by coasting ships. Farther out we would not meet a single ship, for no shipping route ran through that part of the Pacific.

We took a ceremonious farewell of all on board, and many strange looks followed us as we climbed down into the dinghy and went tumbling back over the waves to the *Kon-Tiki*. Then the towrope was cast off and the raft was alone again. Thirty-five men on board the *Guardian Rios* stood at the rail waving for as long as we could distinguish outlines. And six men sat on the boxes on board the *Kon-Tiki* and followed the tug with their eyes as long as they could see her. Not till the black column of smoke had dissolved and vanished over the horizon did we shake our heads and look at one another.

"Good-by, good-by," said Torstein. "Now we'll have to start the engine, boys!"

We laughed and felt the wind. There was a rather light breeze, which had veered from south to southeast. We hoisted the bamboo yard with the big square sail. It only hung down slack, giving Kon-Tiki's face a wrinkled, discontented appearance.

"The old man doesn't like it," said Erik. "There were fresher breezes when he was young."

"It looks as if we were losing ground," said Herman, and he threw a piece of balsa wood overboard at the bow.

"One-two-three . . . thirty-nine, forty, forty-one."

The piece of balsa wood still lay quietly in the water alongside the raft; it had not yet moved halfway along our side.

"We'll have to go over with it," said Torstein optimistically.

"Hope we don't drift astern with the evening breeze," said Bengt. "It was great fun saying good-by at Callao, but I'd just as soon miss our welcome back again!"

Now the piece of wood had reached the end of the raft. We shouted hurrah and began to stow and make fast all the things that had been flung on board at the last moment. Bengt set up a primus stove at the bottom of an empty box, and soon after we were regaling ourselves on hot cocoa and biscuits and making a hole in a fresh coconut. The bananas were not quite ripe yet.

"We're well off now in one way," Erik chuckled. He was rolling about in wide sheepskin trousers under a huge Indian hat, with the parrot on his shoulder. "There's only one thing I don't like," he added, "and that's all the little-known cross-currents which can fling us right upon the rocks along the coast if we go on lying here like this."

We considered the possibility of paddling but agreed to wait for a wind.

And the wind came. It blew up from the southeast quietly and steadily. Soon the sail filled and bent forward like a swelling breast, with Kon-Tiki's head bursting with pugnacity. And the *Kon-Tiki* began to move. We shouted westward ho! and hauled on sheets and ropes. The steering oar was put into the water, and the watch roster began to operate. We threw balls of paper and chips of wood overboard at the bow and stood aft with our watches.

"One, two, three. . . . eighteen, nineteen—now!"

Paper and chips passed the steering oar and soon lay like pearls on a thread, dipping up and down in the trough of the waves astern. We went forward yard by yard. The *Kon-Tiki* did not plow through the sea like a sharp-prowed racing craft. Blunt and broad, heavy and solid, she splashed sedately forward over the waves. She did not hurry, but when she had once got going she pushed ahead with unshakable energy.

At the moment the steering arrangements were our greatest problem. The raft was built exactly as the Spaniards described it, but there was no one living in our time who could give us a practical advance course in sailing an Indian raft. The problem had been thoroughly discussed among the experts on shore but with meager results. They knew just as little about it as we did. As the southeasterly wind increased in strength, it was necessary to keep the raft on such a course that the sail was filled from astern. If the raft turned her side too much to the wind, the sail suddenly swung round and banged against cargo and men and bamboo cabin, while the whole raft turned round and continued on the same course stern first. It was a hard struggle, three men fighting with the sail and three others rowing with the long steering oar to get the nose of the wooden raft round and away from the wind. And, as soon as we got her round, the steersman had to take good care that the same thing did not happen again the next minute.

The steering oar, nineteen feet long, rested loose between two tholepins on a large block astern. It was the same steering oar our native friends had used when we floated the timber down the Palenque in Ecuador. The long mangrove-wood pole was as tough as steel but so heavy that it would sink if it fell overboard. At the end of the pole was a large oar blade of fir wood lashed on with ropes. It took all our strength to hold this long steering oar steady when the seas drove against it, and our fingers were tired out by the convulsive grip which was necessary to turn the pole so that the oar blade stood straight up in the water. This last problem was finally solved by our lashing a crosspiece to the handle of the steering oar so that we had a sort of lever to turn. And meanwhile the wind increased.

By the late afternoon the trade wind was already blowing at full strength. It quickly stirred up the ocean into roaring seas which swept against us from astern. For the first time we fully realized that here was the sea itself come to meet us; it was bitter earnest now—our communications were cut. Whether things went well now would depend entirely on the balsa raft's good qualities in the open sea. We knew that, from now onward, we should never get another onshore wind or chance of turning back. We were in the path of the real trade wind, and every day would carry us farther and farther out to sea. The only thing to do was to go ahead under full sail; if we tried to turn homeward, we should only drift farther out to sea stern first. There was only one possible course, to sail before the wind with our bow toward the sunset. And, after all, that was the object of our voyage—to follow the sun in its path as we thought Kon-Tiki and the old sun-worshipers must have done when they were driven out to sea from Peru.

We noted with triumph and relief how the wooden raft rose up over the first threatening wave crests that came foaming toward us. But it was impossible for the steersman to hold the oar steady when the roaring seas rolled toward him and lifted the oar out of the tholepins, or swept it to one side so that the steersman was swung round like a helpless acrobat. Not even two men at once could hold the oar steady when the seas rose against us and poured down over the steersmen aft. We hit on the idea of running ropes from the oar blade to each side of the raft; and with other ropes holding the oar in place in the tholepins it obtained a limited freedom of movement and could defy the worst seas if only we ourselves could hold on.

As the troughs of the sea gradually grew deeper, it became clear that we had moved into the swiftest part of the Humboldt Current. This sea was obviously caused by a current and not simply raised by the wind. The water was green and cold and everywhere about us; the jagged mountains of Peru had vanished into the dense cloud banks astern. When darkness crept over the waters, our first duel with the elements began. We were still not sure of the sea; we were still uncertain whether it would show itself a friend or an enemy in the intimate proximity we ourselves had sought. When, swallowed up by the darkness, we heard the general noise from the sea around us suddenly deafened by the hiss of a roller close by and saw a white crest come groping toward us on a level with the cabin roof, we held on tight and waited uneasily to feel the masses of water smash down over us and the raft.

But every time there was the same surprise and relief. The *Kon-Tiki* calmly swung up her stern and rose skyward unperturbed, while the masses of water rolled along her sides. Then we sank down again into the trough of the waves and waited for the next big sea. The biggest seas often came two or three in succession, with a long series of smaller seas in between. It was when two big seas followed each other too closely that the second broke on board aft, because the first was still holding our bow in the air. It became, therefore, an unbreakable law that the steering watch must have ropes round their waists, the other ends of which were made fast to the raft, for there were no bulwarks. Their task was to keep the sail filled by holding stern to sea and wind.

We had made an old boat's compass fast to a box aft so that Erik could check our course and calculate our position and speed. For the time being it was uncertain where we were, for the sky was overclouded and the horizon one

single chaos of rollers. Two men at a time took turns as steering watch and, side by side, they had to put all their strength
into the fight with the leaping oar, while the rest of us tried
to snatch a little sleep inside the open bamboo cabin.

When a really big sea came, the men at the helm left the
steering to the ropes and, jumping up, hung on to a bamboo
pole from the cabin roof, while the masses of water thundered in over them from astern and disappeared between the
logs or over the side of the raft. Then they had to fling themselves at the oar again before the raft could turn round and
the sail thrash about. For, if the raft took the seas at an angle,
the waves could easily pour right into the bamboo cabin.
When they came from astern, they disappeared between the
projecting logs at once and seldom came so far forward as
the cabin wall. The round logs astern let the water pass as
if through the prongs of a fork. The advantage of a raft was
obviously this: the more leaks the better. Through the gaps
in our floor the water ran out but never in.

About midnight a ship's light passed in a northerly direction. At three another passed on the same course. We waved
our little paraffin lamp and hailed them with flashes from an
electric torch, but they did not see us and the lights passed
slowly northward into the darkness and disappeared. Little
did those on board realize that a real Inca raft lay close to
them, tumbling among the waves. And just as little did we
on board the raft realize that this was our last ship and the
last trace of men we should see till we had reached the other
side of the ocean.

We clung like flies, two and two, to the steering oar in the
darkness and felt the fresh sea water pouring off our hair
while the oar hit us till we were tender both behind and
before and our hands grew stiff with the exertion of hanging
on. We had a good schooling those first days and nights; it
turned landlubbers into seamen. For the first twenty-four
hours every man, in unbroken succession, had two hours at
the helm and three hours' rest. We arranged that every hour
a fresh man should relieve one of the two steersmen who
had been at the helm for two hours.

Every single muscle in the body was strained to the uttermost throughout the watch to cope with the steering. When we were tired out with pushing the oar, we went over to the other side and pulled, and when arms and chest were sore with pressing, we turned our backs while the oar kneaded us green and blue in front and behind. When at last the relief came, we crept half-dazed into the bamboo cabin, tied a rope round our legs, and fell asleep with our salty clothes on before we could get into our sleeping bags. Almost at the same moment there came a brutal tug at the rope; three hours had passed, and one had to go out again and relieve one of the two men at the steering oar.

The next night was still worse; the seas grew higher instead of going down. Two hours on end of struggling with the steering oar was too long; a man was not much use in the second half of his watch, and the seas got the better of us and hurled us round and sideways, while the water poured on board. Then we changed over to one hour at the helm and an hour and a half's rest. So the first sixty hours passed, in one continuous struggle against a chaos of waves that rushed upon us, one after another, without cessation. High waves and low waves, pointed waves and round waves, slanting waves and waves on top of other waves.

The one of us who suffered worst was Knut. He was let off steering watch, but to compensate for this he had to sacrifice to Neptune and suffered silent agonies in a corner of the cabin. The parrot sat sulkily in its cage, hanging on with its beak and flapping its wings every time the raft gave an unexpected pitch and the sea splashed against the wall from astern. The *Kon-Tiki* did not roll excessively. She took the seas more steadily than any boat of the same dimensions, but it was impossible to predict which way the deck would lean each time, and we never learned the art of moving about the raft easily, for she pitched as much as she rolled.

On the third night the sea went down a bit, although it was still blowing hard. About four o'clock an unexpected deluge came foaming through the darkness and knocked the raft right round before the steersmen realized what was happening. The sail thrashed against the bamboo cabin and threatened to tear both the cabin and itself to pieces. All

hands had to go on deck to secure the cargo and haul on
sheets and stays in the hope of getting the raft on her right
course again, so that the sail might fill and curve forward
peacefully. But the raft would not right herself. She would
go stern foremost, and that was all. The only result of all our
hauling and pushing and rowing was that two men nearly
went overboard in a sea when the sail caught them in the
dark.

The sea had clearly become calmer. Stiff and sore, with
skinned palms and sleepy eyes, we were not worth a row of
beans. Better to save our strength in case the weather should
call us out to a worse passage of arms. One could never know.
So we furled the sail and rolled it round the bamboo yard.
The *Kon-Tiki* lay sideways on to the seas and took them like
a cork. Everything on board was lashed fast, and all six of us
crawled into the little bamboo cabin, huddled together, and
slept like mummies in a sardine tin.

We little guessed that we had struggled through the hardest steering of the voyage. Not till we were far out on the
ocean did we discover the Incas' simple and ingenious way
of steering a raft.

We did not wake till well on in the day, when the parrot
began to whistle and halloo and dance to and fro on its perch.
Outside the sea was still running high but in long, even
ridges and not so wild and confused as the day before. The
first thing we saw was that the sun was beating down on
the yellow bamboo deck and giving the sea all round us a
bright and friendly aspect. What did it matter if the seas
foamed and rose high so long as they only left us in peace
on the raft? What did it matter if they rose straight up in
front of our noses when we knew that in a second the raft
would go over the top and flatten out the foaming ridge like
a steam roller, while the heavy threatening mountain of
water only lifted us up in the air and rolled groaning and
gurgling under the floor? The old masters from Peru knew
what they were doing when they avoided a hollow hull
which could fill with water, or a vessel so long that it would
not take the waves one by one. A cork steam roller—that was
what the balsa raft amounted to.

Erik took our position at noon and found that, in addition to our run under sail, we had made a big deviation northward along the coast. We still lay in the Humboldt Current just 100 sea miles from land. The great question was whether we would get into the treacherous eddies south of the Galapagos Islands. This could have fatal consequences, for up there we might be swept in all directions by strong ocean currents making toward the coast of Central America. But, if things went as we calculated, we should swing west across the sea with the main current before we got as far north as the Galapagos. The wind was still blowing straight from southeast. We hoisted the sail, turned the raft stern to sea, and continued our steering watches.

Knut had now recovered from the torments of seasickness, and he and Torstein clambered up to the swaying masthead, where they experimented with mysterious radio aerials which they sent up both by balloon and by kite. Suddenly one of them shouted from the radio corner of the cabin that he could hear the naval station at Lima calling us. They were telling us that the American ambassador's plane was on its way out from the coast to bid us a last good-by and see what we looked like at sea. Soon after we obtained direct contact with the operator in the plane and then a completely unexpected chat with the secretary to the expedition, Gerd Vold, who was on board. We gave our position as exactly as we could and sent direction-finding signals for hours. The voice in the ether grew stronger and weaker as ARMY-119 circled round near and far and searched. But we did not hear the drone of the engines and never saw the plane. It was not easy to find the low raft down in the trough of the seas, and our own view was strictly limited. At last the plane had to give it up and returned to the coast. It was the last time anyone tried to search for us.

The sea ran high in the days that followed, but the waves came hissing along from the southeast with even spaces between them and the steering went more easily. We took the sea and wind on the port quarter, so that the steersman got fewer seas over him and the raft went more steadily and did not swing round. We noted anxiously that the southeast trade

wind and the Humboldt Current were, day after day, sending us straight across on a course leading to the countercur-
rents round the Galapagos Islands. And we were going due
northwest so quickly that our daily average in those days was
55 to 60 sea miles, with a record of 71 sea miles in one day.

"Are the Galapagos a nice place to go to?" Knut asked cautiously one day, looking at our chart where a string of pearls
indicating our positions was marked and resembled a finger
pointing balefully toward the accursed Galapagos Islands.

"Hardly," I said. "The Inca Tupak Yupanqui is said to
have sailed from Ecuador to the Galapagos just before the
time of Columbus, but neither he nor any other native settled
there because there was no water."

"O.K.," said Knut. "Then we damned well won't go there.
I hope we don't anyhow."

We were now so accustomed to having the sea dancing
round us that we took no account of it. What did it matter if
we danced round a bit with a thousand fathoms of water under us, so long as we and the raft were always on top? It was
only that here the next question arose—how long could we
count on keeping on top? It was easy to see that the balsa logs
absorbed water. The aft crossbeam was worse than the others;
on it we could press our whole finger tip into the soaked
wood till the water squelched. Without saying anything I
broke off a piece of the sodden wood and threw it overboard.
It sank quietly beneath the surface and slowly vanished down
into the depths. Later I saw two or three of the other fellows
do exactly the same when they thought no one was looking.
They stood looking reverently at the waterlogged piece of
wood sinking quietly into the green water.

We had noted the water line on the raft when we started,
but in the rough sea it was impossible to see how deep we
lay, for one moment the logs were lifted out of the water and
the next they went deep down into it. But, if we drove a
knife into the timber, we saw to our joy that the wood was
dry an inch or so below the surface. We calculated that, if
the water continued to force its way in at the same pace, the
raft would be lying and floating just under the surface of
the water by the time we could expect to be approaching

land. But we hoped that the sap further in would act as an impregnation and check the absorption.

Then there was another menace which troubled our minds a little during the first weeks. The ropes. In the daytime we were so busy that we thought little about it, but, when darkness had fallen and we had crept into bed on the cabin floor, we had more time to think, feel, and listen. As we lay there, each man on his straw mattress, we could feel the reed matting under us heaving in time with the wooden logs. In addition to the movements of the raft itself all nine logs moved reciprocally. When one came up, another went down with a gentle heaving movement. They did not move much, but it was enough to make one feel as if one were lying on the back of a large breathing animal, and we preferred to lie on a log lengthways. The first two nights were the worst, but then we were too tired to bother about it. Later the ropes swelled a little in the water and kept the nine logs quieter.

But all the same there was never a flat surface on board which kept quite still in relation to its surroundings. As the foundation moved up and down and round at every joint, everything else moved with it. The bamboo deck, the double mast, the four plaited walls of the cabin, and the roof of slats with the leaves on it—all were made fast just with ropes and twisted about and lifted themselves in opposite directions. It was almost unnoticeable but it was evident enough. If one corner went up, the other corner came down, and if one half of the roof dragged all its laths forward, the other half dragged its laths astern. And, if we looked out through the open wall, there was still more life and movement, for there the sky moved quietly round in a circle while the sea leaped high toward it.

The ropes took the whole pressure. All night we could hear them creaking and groaning, chafing and squeaking. It was like one single complaining chorus round us in the dark, each rope having its own note according to its thickness and tautness.

Every morning we made a thorough inspection of the ropes. We were even let down with our heads in the water over the edge of the raft, while two men held us tight by

the ankles, to see if the ropes on the bottom of the raft were
all right. But the ropes held. A fortnight the seamen had
said. Then all the ropes would be worn out. But, in spite of
this consensus of opinion, we had not so far found the smallest sign of wear. Not till we were far out to sea did we find
the solution. The balsa wood was so soft that the ropes wore
their way slowly into the wood and were protected, instead
of the logs wearing the ropes.

After a week or so the sea grew calmer, and we noticed
that it became blue instead of green. We began to go west-
northwest instead of due northwest and took this as the first
faint sign that we had got out of the coastal current and had
some hope of being carried out to sea.

The very first day we were left alone on the sea we had
noticed fish round the raft, but we were too much occupied
with the steering to think of fishing. The second day we
went right into a thick shoal of sardines, and soon afterward
an eight-foot blue shark came along and rolled over with its
white belly uppermost as it rubbed against the raft's stern,
where Herman and Bengt stood barelegged in the seas, steering. It played round us for a while but disappeared when we
got the hand harpoon ready for action.

Next day we were visited by tunnies, bonitos, and dolphins, and when a big flying fish thudded on board we used
it as bait and at once pulled in two large dolphins (dorados)
weighing from twenty to thirty-five pounds each. This was
food for several days. On steering watch we could see many
fish we did not even know, and one day we came into a
school of porpoises which seemed quite endless. The black
backs tumbled about, packed close together, right in to the
side of the raft, and sprang up here and there all over the sea
as far as we could see from the masthead. And the nearer
we came to the Equator, and the farther from the coast, the
commoner flying fish became. When at last we came out into
the blue water where the sea rolled by majestically, sunlit and
serene, ruffled by gusts of wind, we could see them glittering
like a rain of projectiles which shot from the water and flew
in a straight line till their power of flight was exhausted and
they vanished beneath the surface.

If we set the little paraffin lamp out at night, flying fish were attracted by the light and, large and small, shot over the raft. They often struck the bamboo cabin or the sail and tumbled helpless on the deck. Unable to get a take-off by swimming through the water, they just remained lying and kicking help-lessly, like large-eyed herrings with long breast fins. It some-times happened that we heard an outburst of strong language from a man on deck when a cold flying fish came unexpect-edly, at a good speed, slap into his face. They always came at a good pace and snout first, and if they caught one full in the face they made it burn and tingle. But the unprovoked attack was quickly forgiven by the injured party, for, with all its drawbacks, we were in a maritime land of enchantment where delicious fish dishes came hurling through the air. We used to fry them for breakfast, and whether it was the fish, the cook, or our appetites, they reminded us of fried trout-lings once we had scraped the scales off.

The cook's first duty, when he got up in the morning, was to go out on deck and collect all the flying fish that had landed on board in the course of the night. There were usually half a dozen or more, and once we found twenty-six fat flying fish on the raft. Knut was much upset one morning because, when he was standing operating with the frying pan, a flying fish struck him on the hand instead of landing right in the cooking fat.

Our neighborly intimacy with the sea was not fully realized by Torstein till he woke one morning and found a sardine on his pillow. There was so little room in the cabin that Torstein had to lie with his head in the doorway and, if anyone inadvertently trod on his face when going out at night, he bit him in the leg. He grasped the sardine by the tail and confided to it understandingly that all sardines had his entire sympathy. We conscientiously drew in our legs so that Torstein should have more room the next night, but then something happened which caused Torstein to find himself a sleeping place on top of all the kitchen utensils in the radio corner.

It was a few nights later. It was overcast and pitch dark, and Torstein had placed the paraffin lamp close by his head, so that the night watches could see where they were treading when they crept in and out over his head. About four o'clock Torstein was awakened by the lamp tumbling over and something cold and wet flapping about his ears. "Flying fish," he thought and felt for it in the darkness to throw it away. He caught hold of something long and wet, which wriggled like a snake, and let go as if he had burned himself. The unseen visitor twisted itself away and over to Herman, while Torstein tried to get the lamp lighted again. Herman started up, too, and this made me wake, thinking of the octopus which came up at night in these waters.

When we got the lamp lighted, Herman was sitting in triumph with his hand gripping the neck of a long thin fish which wriggled in his hands like an eel. The fish was over three feet long, as slender as a snake, with dull black eyes and a long snout with a greedy jaw full of long sharp teeth. The teeth were as sharp as knives and could be folded back into the roof of the mouth to make way for what was swallowed. Under Herman's grip a large-eyed white fish, about eight inches long, was suddenly thrown up from the stomach and out of the mouth of the predatory fish, and soon after up came another like it. These were clearly two deep-water fish, much torn by the snakefish's teeth. The snakefish's thin skin was bluish violet on the back and steel blue underneath, and it came loose in flakes when we took hold of it.

Bengt too was awakened at last by all the noise, and we held the lamp and the long fish under his nose. He sat up drowsily in his sleeping bag and said solemnly:

"No, fish like that don't exist."

With which he turned over quietly and fell asleep again.

Bengt was not far wrong. It appeared later that we six sitting round the lamp in the bamboo cabin were the first men to have seen this fish alive. Only the skeleton of a fish like this one had been found a few times on the coast of South America and the Galapagos Islands; ichthyologists called it *Gempylus*, or snake mackerel, and thought it lived at the bottom of the sea at a great depth because no one had ever seen it alive. But, if it lived at a great depth, it must have done so by day when the sun blinded its big eyes. For on dark nights *Gempylus* was abroad high over the surface of the sea; we on the raft had experience of that.

A week after the rare fish had landed on Torstein's sleeping bag, we had another visit. Again it was four in the morning, and the new moon had set so that it was dark but the stars were shining. The raft was steering easily, and when my watch was over I took a turn along the edge of the raft to see if everything was shipshape for the new watch. I had a rope round my waist, as the watch always had, and, with the paraffin lamp in my hand, I was walking carefully along the outermost log to get round the mast. The log was wet and slippery, and I was furious when someone quite unexpectedly caught hold of the rope behind me and jerked till I nearly lost my balance. I turned round wrathfully with the lantern, but not a soul was to be seen. There came a new tug at the rope, and I saw something shiny lying writhing on the deck. It was a fresh *Gempylus*, and this time it had got its teeth so deep into the rope that several of them broke before I got the rope loose. Presumably the light of the lantern had flashed along the curving white rope, and our visitor from the depths of the sea had caught hold in the hope of jumping up and snatching an extra long and tasty tidbit. It ended its days in a jar of Formalin.

The sea contains many surprises for him who has his floor on a level with the surface and drifts along slowly and noiselessly. A sportsman who breaks his way through the woods may come back and say that no wild life is to be seen. Another may sit down on a stump and wait, and often rustlings and cracklings will begin and curious eyes peer out. So it is on the sea, too. We usually plow across it with roaring engines and piston strokes, with the water foaming round our bow. Then we come back and say that there is nothing to see far out on the ocean.

Not a day passed but we, as we sat floating on the surface of the sea, were visited by inquisitive guests which wriggled and waggled about us, and a few of them, such as dolphins and pilot fish, grew so familiar that they accompanied the raft across the sea and kept round us day and night.

When night had fallen and the stars were twinkling in the

dark tropical sky, a phosphorescence flashed around us in ri-
valry with the stars, and single glowing plankton resembled
round live coals so vividly that we involuntarily drew in our
bare legs when the glowing pellets were washed up round
our feet at the raft's stern. When we caught them, we saw
that they were little brightly shining species of shrimp. On
such nights we were sometimes scared when two round shining eyes suddenly rose out of the sea right alongside the raft
and glared at us with an unblinking hypnotic stare. The visitors were often big squids which came up and floated on the
surface with their devilish green eyes shining in the dark like
phosphorus. But sometimes the shining eyes were those of
deep-water fish which came up only at night and lay staring,
fascinated by the glimmer of light before them. Several times,
when the sea was calm, the black water round the raft was
suddenly full of round heads two or three feet in diameter,
lying motionless and staring at us with great glowing eyes. On
other nights balls of light three feet and more in diameter
would be visible down in the water, flashing at irregular intervals like electric lights turned on for a moment.

We gradually grew accustomed to having these subterra-
nean or submarine creatures under the floor, but nevertheless
we were just as surprised every time a new species appeared.
About two o'clock on a cloudy night, when the man at the
helm had difficulty in distinguishing black water from black
sky, he caught sight of a faint illumination down in the water
which slowly took the shape of a large animal. It was impossible to say whether it was plankton shining on its body,
or whether the animal itself had a phosphorescent surface,
but the glimmer down in the black water gave the ghostly
creature obscure, wavering outlines. Sometimes it was round-
ish, sometimes oval, or triangular, and suddenly it split into
two parts which swam to and fro under the raft independently of each other. Finally there were three of these large
shining phantoms wandering round in slow circles under us.

They were real monsters, for the visible parts alone were
some five fathoms long, and we all quickly collected on deck
and followed the ghost dance. It went on for hour after hour,
following the course of the raft. Mysterious and noiseless, our

shining companions kept a good way beneath the surface, mostly on the starboard side where the light was, but often they were right under the raft or appeared on the port side. The glimmer of light on their backs revealed that the beasts were bigger than elephants but they were not whales, for they never came up to breathe. Were they giant ray fish which changed shape when they turned over on their sides? They took no notice at all if we held the light right down on the surface to lure them up, so that we might see what kind of creatures they were. And, like all proper goblins and ghosts, they had sunk into the depths when the dawn began to break.

We never got a proper explanation of this nocturnal visit from the three shining monsters, unless the solution was afforded by another visit we received a day and a half later in the full midday sunshine. It was May 24, and we were lying drifting on a leisurely swell in exactly 95° west by 7° south. It was about noon, and we had thrown overboard the guts of two big dolphins we had caught earlier in the morning. I was having a refreshing plunge overboard at the bow, lying in the water but keeping a good lookout and hanging on to a rope end, when I caught sight of a thick brown fish, six feet long, which came swimming inquisitively toward me through the crystal-clear sea water. I hopped quickly up on to the edge of the raft and sat in the hot sun looking at the fish as it passed quietly, when I heard a wild war whoop from Knut, who was sitting aft behind the bamboo cabin. He bellowed "Shark!" till his voice cracked in a falsetto, and, as we had sharks swimming alongside the raft almost daily without creating such excitement, we all realized that this must be something extra-special and flocked astern to Knut's assistance.

Knut had been squatting there, washing his pants in the swell, and when he looked up for a moment he was staring straight into the biggest and ugliest face any of us had ever seen in the whole of our lives. It was the head of a veritable sea monster, so huge and so hideous that, if the Old Man of the Sea himself had come up, he could not have made such an impression on us. The head was broad and flat like a frog's, with two small eyes right at the sides, and a toadlike jaw

which was four or five feet wide and had long fringes droop-
ing from the corners of the mouth. Behind the head was an
enormous body ending in a long thin tail with a pointed tail
fin which stood straight up and showed that this sea monster
was not any kind of whale. The body looked brownish under the water, but both head and body were thickly covered
with small white spots.

The monster came quietly, lazily swimming after us from
astern. It grinned like a bulldog and lashed gently with its
tail. The large round dorsal fin projected clear of the water
and sometimes the tail fin as well, and, when the creature
was in the trough of the swell, the water flowed about the
broad back as though washing round a submerged reef. In
front of the broad jaws swam a whole crowd of zebra-striped
pilot fish in fan formation, and large remora fish and other
parasites sat firmly attached to the huge body and traveled
with it through the water, so that the whole thing looked like
a curious zoological collection crowded round something that
resembled a floating deep-water reef.

A twenty-five-pound dolphin, attached to six of our largest
fishhooks, was hanging behind the raft as bait for sharks, and
a swarm of the pilot fish shot straight off, nosed the dolphin
without touching it, and then hurried back to their lord and
master, the sea king. Like a mechanical monster it set its machinery going and came gliding at leisure toward the dolphin which lay, a beggarly trifle, before its jaws. We tried to
pull the dolphin in, and the sea monster followed slowly,
right up to the side of the raft. It did not open its mouth but
just let the dolphin bump against it, as if to throw open the
whole door for such an insignificant scrap was not worth
while. When the giant came close up to the raft, it rubbed
its back against the heavy steering oar, which was just lifted
up out of the water, and now we had ample opportunity of
studying the monster at the closest quarters—at such close
quarters that I thought we had all gone mad, for we roared
stupidly with laughter and shouted overexcitedly at the completely fantastic sight we saw. Walt Disney himself, with all
his powers of imagination, could not have created a more

hair-raising sea monster than that which thus suddenly lay with its terrific jaws along the raft's side.

The monster was a whale shark, the largest shark and the largest fish known in the world today. It is exceedingly rare, but scattered specimens are observed here and there in the tropical oceans. The whale shark has an average length of fifty feet, and according to zoologists it weighs fifteen tons. It is said that large specimens can attain a length of sixty feet; one harpooned baby had a liver weighing six hundred pounds and a collection of three thousand teeth in each of its broad jaws.

Our monster was so large that, when it began to swim in circles round us and under the raft, its head was visible on one side while the whole of its tail stuck out on the other. And so incredibly grotesque, inert, and stupid did it appear when seen fullface that we could not help shouting with laughter, although we realized that it had strength enough in its tail to smash both balsa logs and ropes to pieces if it attacked us. Again and again it described narrower and narrower circles just under the raft, while all we could do was to wait and see what might happen. When it appeared on the other side, it glided amiably under the steering oar and lifted it up in the air, while the oar blade slid along the creature's back.

We stood round the raft with hand harpoons ready for action, but they seemed to us like toothpicks in relation to the mammoth beast we had to deal with. There was no indication that the whale shark ever thought of leaving us again; it circled round us and followed like a faithful dog, close up to the raft. None of us had ever experienced or thought we should experience anything like it; the whole adventure, with the sea monster swimming behind and under the raft, seemed to us so completely unnatural that we could not really take it seriously.

In reality the whale shark went on encircling us for barely an hour, but to us the visit seemed to last a whole day. At last it became too exciting for Erik, who was standing at a corner of the raft with an eight-foot hand harpoon, and, encouraged by ill-considered shouts, he raised the harpoon above his head. As the whale shark came gliding slowly toward him and its broad head moved right under the corner of the raft, Erik thrust the harpoon with all his giant strength down between his legs and deep into the whale shark's gristly head. It was a second or two before the giant understood properly what was happening. Then in a flash the placid half-wit was transformed into a mountain of steel muscles.

We heard a swishing noise as the harpoon line rushed over the edge of the raft and saw a cascade of water as the giant stood on its head and plunged down into the depths. The three men who were standing nearest were flung about the place, head over heels, and two of them were flayed and burned by the line as it rushed through the air. The thick line, strong enough to hold a boat, was caught up on the side of the raft but snapped at once like a piece of twine, and a few seconds later a broken-off harpoon shaft came up to the surface two hundred yards away. A shoal of frightened pilot fish shot off through the water in a desperate attempt to keep up with their old lord and master. We waited a long time for the monster to come racing back like an infuriated submarine, but we never saw anything more of him.

We were now in the South Equatorial Current and moving in a westerly direction just 400 sea miles south of the Galapagos. There was no longer any danger of drifting into the Galapagos currents, and the only contacts we had with this group of islands were greetings from big sea turtles which no doubt had strayed far out to sea from the islands. One day we saw a thumping turtle lying struggling with its head and one great fin above the surface of the water. As the swell rose, we saw a shimmer of green and blue and gold in the water under the turtle, and we discovered that it was engaged in a life-and-death struggle with dolphins. The fight was apparently quite one-sided; it consisted in twelve to fifteen big-headed, brilliantly colored dolphins attacking the turtle's neck and fins and apparently trying to tire it out, for the turtle could not lie for days on end with its head and paddles drawn inside its shell.

When the turtle caught sight of the raft, it dived and made straight for us, pursued by the glittering fish. It came close up to the side of the raft and was showing signs of wanting to climb up on to the timber when it caught sight of us already standing there. If we had been more practiced, we could have captured it with ropes without difficulty as the huge carapace paddled quietly along the side of the raft. But we spent the time that mattered in staring, and when we had the lasso ready the giant turtle had already passed our bow. We flung the little rubber dinghy into the water, and Herman, Bengt, and Torstein went in pursuit of the turtle in the round nutshell, which was not a great deal bigger than what swam ahead of them. Bengt, as steward, saw in his mind's eye endless meat dishes and a most delicious turtle soup.

But the faster they rowed, the faster the turtle slipped through the water just below the surface, and they were not more than a hundred yards from the raft when the turtle suddenly disappeared without a trace. But they had done one good deed at any rate. For when the little yellow rubber dinghy came dancing back over the water, it had the whole glittering school of dolphins after it. They circled round the new turtle, and the boldest snapped at the oar blades which dipped into the water like fins; meanwhile, the peaceful turtle escaped successfully from all its ignoble persecutors.

5 HALFWAY

THE WEEKS PASSED. WE SAW NO SIGN EITHER
of a ship or of drifting remains to show that there were other
people in the world. The whole sea was ours, and, with all
the gates of the horizon open, real peace and freedom were
wafted down from the firmament itself.

It was as though the fresh salt tang in the air, and all the
blue purity that surrounded us, had washed and cleansed
both body and soul. To us on the raft the great problems of
civilized man appeared false and illusory—like perverted pro-
ducts of the human mind. Only the elements mattered. And
the elements seemed to ignore the little raft. Or perhaps they
accepted it as a natural object, which did not break the harmony of the sea but adapted itself to current and sea like
bird and fish. Instead of being a fearsome enemy, flinging
itself at us, the elements had become a reliable friend which
steadily and surely helped us onward. While wind and waves

pushed and propelled, the ocean current lay under us and pulled, straight toward our goal.

If a boat had cruised our way on any average day out at sea, it would have found us bobbing quietly up and down over a long rolling swell covered with little white-crested waves, while the trade wind held the orange sail bent steadily toward Polynesia.

Those on board would have seen, at the stern of the raft, a brown bearded man with no clothes on, either struggling desperately with a long steering oar while he hauled on a tangled rope, or, in calm weather, just sitting on a box dozing in the hot sun and keeping a leisurely hold on the steering oar with his toes.

If this man happened not to be Bengt, the latter would have been found lying on his stomach in the cabin door with one of his seventy-three sociological books. Bengt had further been appointed steward and was responsible for fixing the daily rations. Herman might have been found anywhere at any time of the day—at the masthead with meteorological instruments, underneath the raft with diving goggles on checking a centerboard, or in tow in the rubber dinghy, busy with balloons and curious measuring apparatus. He was our technical chief and responsible for meteorological and hydrographical observations.

Knut and Torstein were always doing something with their wet dry batteries, soldering irons, and circuits. All their wartime training was required to keep the little radio station going in spray and dew a foot above the surface of the water. Every night they took turns sending our reports and weather observations out into the ether, where they were picked up by chance radio amateurs who passed the reports on to the Meteorological Institute in Washington and other destinations. Erik was usually sitting patching sails and splicing ropes, or carving in wood and drawing sketches of bearded men and odd fish. And at noon every day he took the sextant and mounted a box to look at the sun and find out how far we had moved since the day before. I myself had enough to do with the logbook and reports and the collecting of plankton, fishing, and filming. Every man had his sphere of responsibility, and no one interfered with the others' work. All difficult jobs, like steering watch and cooking, were divided equally. Every man had two hours each day and two hours each night at the steering oar. And duty as cook was in accordance with a daily roster. There were few laws and regulations on board, except that the night watch must have a rope round his waist, that the lifesaving rope had its regular place, that all meals were consumed outside the cabin wall, and that the "right place" was only at the farthest end of the logs astern. If an important decision was to be taken on board, we called a powwow in Indian style and discussed the matter together before anything was settled.

An ordinary day on board the Kon-Tiki began with the last night watch shaking some life into the cook, who crawled out sleepily on to the dewy deck in the morning sun and began to gather flying fish. Instead of eating the fish raw, according to both Polynesian and Peruvian recipes, we fried them over a small primus stove at the bottom of a box which stood lashed fast to the deck outside the cabin door. This box was our kitchen. Here there was usually shelter from the southeast trade wind which regularly blew on to our other quarter. Only when the wind and sea juggled too much with the primus flame did it set fire to the wooden box, and once, when the cook had fallen asleep, the whole box became a mass of flames which spread to the very wall of the bamboo cabin. But the fire on the wall was quickly put out when the smoke poured into the hut, for, after all, we had never far to go for water on board the Kon-Tiki.

The smell of fried fish seldom managed to wake the snorers inside the bamboo cabin, so the cook usually had to stick a fork into them or sing "Breakfast's ready!" so out of tune that no one could bear to listen to him any longer. If there were no sharks' fins alongside the raft, the day began with a quick plunge in the Pacific, followed by breakfast in the open air on the edge of the raft.

The food on board was above reproach. The cuisine was divided into two experimental menus, one dedicated to the quartermaster and the twentieth century, one to Kon-Tiki and the fifth century. Torstein and Bengt were the subjects of the first experiment and restricted their diet to the slim little packages of special provisions which we had squeezed down into the hole between the logs and the bamboo deck. Fish and marine food, however, had never been their strong suit. Every few weeks we untied the lashings which held down the bamboo deck and took out fresh supplies, which we lashed fast forward of the bamboo cabin. The tough layer of asphalt outside the cardboard proved resistant, while the hermetically sealed tins lying loose beside it were penetrated and ruined by the sea water which continually washed round our provisions.

Kon-Tiki, on his original voyage across the sea, had no asphalt or hermetically sealed tins; nevertheless he had no serious food problems. In those days, too, supplies consisted of what the men took with them from land and what they obtained for themselves on the voyage. We may assume that, when Kon-Tiki sailed from the coast of Peru after his defeat by Lake Titicaca, he had one of two objectives in mind. As the spiritual representative of the sun among a solely sun-worshiping people, it is very probable that he ventured straight out to sea to follow the sun itself on its journey in the hope of finding a new and more peaceful country. An alternative possibility for him was to sail his rafts up the coast of South America in order to found a new kingdom out of reach of his persecutors. Clear of the dangerous rocky coast and hostile tribes along the shore, he would, like ourselves, fall an easy prey to the southeast trade wind and the Humboldt Current and, in the power of the elements, he would drift in exactly the same large semicircle right toward the sunset.

Whatever these sun-worshipers' plans were when they fled from their homeland, they certainly provided themselves with supplies for the voyage. Dried meat and fish and sweet potatoes were the most important part of their primitive diet. When the raftsmen of that time put to sea along the desert coast of Peru, they had ample supplies of water on board. Instead of clay vessels they generally used the skin of giant bottle gourds, which was resistant to bumps and blows, while even more adapted to raft use were the thick canes of giant

bamboos. They perforated through all the knots in the center
and poured water in through a little hole at the end, which
they stopped with a plug or with pitch or resin. Thirty or
forty of these thick bamboo canes could be lashed fast along
the raft under the bamboo deck, where they lay shaded and
cool with fresh sea water—about 79° Fahrenheit in the Equatorial Current—washing about them. A store of this kind
would contain twice as much water as we ourselves used on
our whole voyage, and still more could be taken by simply
lashing on more bamboo canes in the water underneath the
raft, where they weighed nothing and occupied no space.

We found that after two months fresh water began to
grow stale and have a bad taste. But by then one is well
through the first ocean area, in which there is little rain, and
has arrived in regions where heavy rain showers can main-
tain the water supply. We served out a good quart of water
per man daily, and it was by no means always that the ration
was consumed.

Even if our predecessors had started from land with inade-
quate supplies, they would have managed well enough as
long as they drifted across the sea with the current, in which
fish abounded. There was not a day on our whole voyage on
which fish were not swimming round the raft and could
not easily be caught. Scarcely a day passed without flying
fish, at any rate, coming on board of their own accord. It
even happened that large bonitos, delicious eating, swam on
board with the masses of water that came from astern and lay
kicking on the raft when the water had vanished down between the logs as a sieve. To starve to death was impossible.

The old natives knew well the device which many shipwrecked men hit upon during the war—chewing thirst-
quenching moisture out of raw fish. One can also press the
juices out by twisting pieces of fish in a cloth, or, if the
fish is large, it is a fairly simple matter to cut holes in its
side, which soon become filled with ooze from the fish's
lymphatic glands. It does not taste good if one has anything
better to drink, but the percentage of salt is so low that
one's thirst is quenched.

The necessity for drinking water was greatly reduced if we

bathed regularly and lay down wet in the shady cabin. If a shark was patrolling majestically round about us and preventing a real plunge from the side of the raft, one had only to lie down on the logs aft and get a good grip of the ropes with one's fingers and toes. Then we got several bathfuls of crystal-clear Pacific pouring over us every few seconds.

When tormented by thirst in a hot climate, one generally assumes that the body needs water, and this may often lead to immoderate inroads on the water ration without any benefit whatever. On really hot days in the tropics you can pour tepid water down your throat till you taste it at the back of your mouth, and you are just as thirsty. It is not liquid the body needs then, but, curiously enough, salt. The special rations we had on board included salt tablets to be taken regularly on particularly hot days, because perspiration drains the body of salt. We experienced days like this when the wind had died away and the sun blazed down on the raft without mercy. Our water ration could be ladled into us till it squelched in our stomachs, but our throats malignantly demanded much more. On such days we added from 20 to 40 per cent of bitter, salt sea water to our fresh-water ration and found, to our surprise, that this brackish water quenched our thirst. We had the taste of sea water in our mouths for a long time afterward but never felt unwell, and moreover we had our water ration considerably increased.

One morning, as we sat at breakfast, an unexpected sea splashed into our gruel and taught us quite gratuitously that the taste of oats removed the greater part of the sickening taste of sea water!

The old Polynesians had preserved some curious traditions, according to which their earliest forefathers, when they came sailing across the sea, had with them leaves of a certain plant which they chewed, with the result that their thirst disappeared. Another effect of the plant was that in an emergency they could drink sea water without being sick. No such plants grew in the South Sea islands; they must, therefore, have originated in their ancestors' homeland. The Polynesian historians repeated these statements so often that modern scientists investigated the matter and came to the conclusion that the only known plant with such an effect was the coca plant, which grew only in Peru. And in prehistoric Peru this very coca plant, which contains cocaine, was regularly used both by the Incas and by their vanished forerunners, as is shown by discoveries in pre-Inca graves. On exhausting mountain journeys and sea voyages they took with them piles of these leaves and chewed them for days on end to remove the feelings of thirst and weariness. And over a fairly short period the chewing of coca leaves will even allow one to drink sea water with a certain immunity.

We did not test coca leaves on board the *Kon-Tiki*, but we had on the foredeck large wicker baskets full of other plants, some of which had left a deeper imprint on the South Sea islands. The baskets stood lashed fast in the lee of the cabin wall, and as time passed yellow shoots and green leaves of potatoes and coconuts shot up higher and higher from the wickerwork. It was like a little tropical garden on board the wooden raft.

When the first Europeans came to the Pacific islands, they found large plantings of sweet potatoes on Easter Island and in Hawaii and New Zealand, and the same plant was also cultivated on the other islands, but only within the Polynesian area. It was quite unknown in the part of the world which lay farther west. The sweet potato was one of the most important cultivated plants in these remote islands where the people otherwise lived mainly on fish, and many of the Polynesians' legends centered round this plant. According to tradition it had been brought by no less a personage than Tiki himself, when he came with his wife Pani from their ancestors' original homeland, where the sweet potato had been an important article of food. New Zealand legends affirm that the sweet potato was brought over the sea in vessels which were not canoes but consisted of "wood bound together with ropes."

Now, as is known, America is the only place in the rest of the world where the potato grew before the time of the Europeans. And the sweet potato Tiki brought with him to the islands, *Ipomoea batatas*, is exactly the same as that which the Indians have cultivated in Peru from the oldest times.

Dried sweet potatoes were the most important travel provisions both for the seafarers of Polynesia and for the natives in old Peru. In the South Sea islands the sweet potato will grow only if carefully tended by man, and, as it cannot withstand sea water, it is idle to explain its wide distribution over these scattered islands by declaring that it could have drifted over 4,000 sea miles with ocean currents from Peru. This attempt to explain away so important a clue to the Polynesians' origin is particularly futile seeing that philologists have pointed out that on all the widely scattered South Sea islands the name of the sweet potato is *kumara,* and *kumara* is just what the sweet potato was called among the old Indians in Peru. The name followed the plant across the sea.

Another very important Polynesian cultivated plant we had with us on board the *Kon-Tiki* was the bottle gourd, *Lagenaria vulgaris.* As important as the fruit itself was the skin, which the Polynesians dried over a fire and used to hold water. This typical garden plant also, which again cannot propagate itself in a wild state by drifting across the sea alone, the old Polynesians had in common with the original population of Peru. Bottle gourds, converted into water containers, are found in prehistoric desert graves on the coast of Peru and were used by the fishing population there centuries before the first men came to the islands in the Pacific. The Polynesian name for the bottle gourd, *kimi,* is found again among the Indians in Central America, where Peruvian civilization has its deepest roots.

In addition to a few chance tropical fruits, most of which we ate up in a few weeks' time before they spoiled, we had on board a third plant which, along with the sweet potato, has played the greatest part in the history of the Pacific. We had two hundred coconuts, and they gave us exercise for our teeth and refreshing drinks. Several of the nuts soon began to sprout, and, when we had been just ten weeks at sea, we had half a dozen baby palms a foot high, which had already opened their shoots and formed thick green leaves. The coconut grew before Columbus' time both on the Isthmus of Panama and in South America. The chronicler Oviedo writes that the coconut palm was found in great numbers along the coast of Peru when the Spaniards arrived. At that time it had long existed on all the islands in the Pacific.

Botanists have still no certain proof in which direction it spread over the Pacific. But one thing has now been discovered. Not even the coconut, with its famous shell, can spread over the ocean without men's help. The nuts we had in baskets on deck remained eatable and capable of germinating the whole way to Polynesia. But we had laid about half among the special provisions below deck, with the waves washing around them. Every single one of these was ruined by the sea water. And no coconut can float over the sea faster than a balsa raft moves with the wind behind it. It was the eyes of the coconut which sucked in the sea water so that the nut spoiled. Refuse collectors, too, all over the ocean took care that no edible thing that floated should get across from one world to the other.

Solitary petrels and other sea birds which can sleep on the sea we met thousands of sea miles from the nearest land. Sometimes, on quiet days far out on the blue sea, we sailed close to a white, floating bird's feather. If, on approaching the little feather, we looked at it closely, we saw that there were two or three passengers on board it, sailing along at their ease before the wind. When the Kon-Tiki was about to pass, the passengers noticed that a vessel was coming which was faster and had more space, and so all came scuttling sideways at top speed over the surface and up on to the raft, leaving the feather to sail on alone. And so the Kon-Tiki soon began to swarm with stowaways. They were small pelagic crabs. As big as a fingernail, and now and then a good deal larger, they were tidbits for the Goliaths on board the raft, if we managed to catch them.

The small crabs were the policemen of the sea's surface, and they were not slow to look after themselves when they saw anything eatable. If one day the cook failed to notice a flying fish in between the logs, next day it was covered with from eight to ten small crabs, sitting on the fish and helping themselves with their claws. Most often they were frightened and scurried away to hide when we came in view, but aft, in a little hole by the steering block, lived a crab which was quite tame and which we named Johannes.

Like the parrot, who was everyone's amusing pet, the crab Johannes became one of our community on deck. If the man at the helm, sitting steering on a sunshiny day with his back to the cabin, had not Johannes for company, he felt utterly lonely out on the wide blue sea. While the other small crabs scurried furtively about and pilfered like cockroaches on an ordinary boat, Johannes sat broad and round in his doorway with his eyes wide open, waiting for the change of watch. Every man who came on watch had a scrap of biscuit or a bit of fish for him, and we needed only to stoop down over the hole for him to come right out on his doorstep and stretch out his hands. He took the scraps out of our fingers with his claws and ran back into the hole, where he sat down in the doorway and munched like a schoolboy, cramming his food into his mouth.

The crabs clung like flies to the soaked coconuts, which burst when they fermented, or caught plankton washed on board by the waves. And these, the tiniest organisms in the sea, were good eating too even for us Goliaths on the raft, when we learned how to catch a number of them at once so that we got a decent mouthful.

It is certain that there must be very nourishing food in these almost invisible plankton which drift about with the current on the oceans in infinite numbers. Fish and sea birds which do not eat plankton themselves live on other fish or sea animals which do, no matter how large they themselves may be. Plankton is a general name for thousands of species of visible and invisible small organisms which drift about near the surface of the sea. Some are plants (*phyto*-plankton), while others are loose fish ova and tiny living creatures (*zoo*-plankton). Animal plankton live on vegetable plankton, and vegetable plankton live on ammoniac, nitrates, and nitrites which are formed from dead animal plankton. And while they reciprocally live on one another, they all form food for everything which moves in and over the sea. What they cannot offer in size they can offer in numbers.

In good plankton waters there are thousands in a glassful.

More than once persons have starved to death at sea because they did not find fish large enough to be spitted, netted, or hooked. In such cases it has often happened that they have literally been sailing about in strongly diluted, raw fish soup. If, in addition to hooks and nets, they had had a utensil for straining the soup they were sitting in, they would have found a nourishing meal—plankton. Some day in the future, perhaps, men will think of harvesting plankton from the sea to the same extent as now they harvest grain on land. A single grain is of no use, either, but in large quantities it becomes food.

The marine biologist Dr. A. D. Bajkov told us of plankton and sent us a fishing net which was suited to the creatures we were to catch. The "net" was a silk net with almost three thousand meshes per square inch. It was sewn in the shape of a funnel with a circular mouth behind an iron ring, eighteen inches across, and was towed behind the raft. Just as in other kinds of fishing, the catch varied with time and place. Catches diminished as the sea grew warmer farther west, and we got the best results at night, because many species seemed to go deeper down into the water when the sun was shining.

If we had no other way of whiling away time on board the raft, there would have been entertainment enough in lying with our noses in the plankton net. Not for the sake of the smell, for that was bad. Nor because the sight was appetizing, for it looked a horrible mess. But because, if we spread the plankton out on a board and examined each of the little creatures separately with the naked eye, we had before us fantastic shapes and colors in unending variety.

Most of them were tiny shrimplike crustaceans (*copepods*) or fish ova floating loose, but there were also larvae of fish and shellfish, curious miniature crabs in all colors, jellyfish, and an endless variety of small creatures which might have been taken from Walt Disney's *Fantasia*. Some looked like fringed, fluttering spooks cut out of cellophane paper, while others resembled tiny red-beaked birds with hard shells instead of feathers. There was no end to Nature's extravagant inventions in the plankton world; a surrealistic artist might well own himself bested here.

Where the cold Humboldt Current turned west south of the Equator, we could pour several pounds of plankton porridge out of the bag every few hours. The plankton lay packed together like cake in colored layers—brown, red, gray, and green according to the different fields of plankton through which we had passed. At night, when there was phosphorescence about, it was like hauling in a bag of sparkling jewels. But, when we got hold of it, the pirates' treasure turned into millions of tiny glittering shrimps and phosphorescent fish larvae that glowed in the dark like a heap of live coals. When we poured them into a bucket, the squashy mess ran out like a magic gruel composed of glowworms. Our night's catch looked as nasty at close quarters as it had been pretty at long range. And, bad as it smelled, it tasted correspondingly good if one just plucked up courage and put a spoonful of it into one's mouth. If this consisted of many dwarf shrimps, it tasted like shrimp paste, lobster, or crab. If it was mostly deep-sea fish ova, it tasted like caviar and now and then like oysters.

The inedible vegetable plankton were either so small that they washed away with the water through the meshes of the net, or they were so large that we could pick them up with our fingers. "Snags" in the dish were single jellylike coelenterates like glass balloons and jellyfish about half an inch long. These were bitter and had to be thrown away. Otherwise everything could be eaten, either as it was or cooked in fresh water as gruel or soup. Tastes differ. Two men on board thought plankton tasted delicious, two thought they were quite good, and for two the sight of them was more than enough. From a nutrition standpoint they stand on a level with a larger shellfish, and, spiced and properly prepared, they can certainly be a first-class dish for all who like marine food.

That these small organisms contain calories enough has been proved by the blue whale, which is the largest animal in the world and yet lives on plankton. Our own method of capture, with the little net which was often chewed up by hungry fish, seemed to us sadly primitive when we sat on the raft and saw a passing whale send up cascades of water as it

simply filtered plankton through its celluloid beard. And one
day we lost the whole net in the sea.

"Why don't you plankton-eaters do like him?" Torstein and
Bengt said contemptuously to the rest of us, pointing to a
blowing whale. "Just fill your mouths and blow the water out
through your mustaches!"

I have seen whales in the distance from boats, and I have
seen them stuffed in museums, but I have never felt toward
the gigantic carcass as one usually feels toward proper warm-
blooded animals, for example a horse or an elephant. Biologi-
cally, indeed, I had accepted the whale as a genuine mammal,
but in its essence it was to all intents and purposes a large
cold fish. We had a different impression when the great
whales came rushing toward us, close to the side of the raft.

One day, when we were sitting as usual on the edge of the
raft having a meal, so close to the water that we had only to
lean back to wash out our mugs, we started when suddenly
something behind us blew hard like a swimming horse and
a big whale came up and stared at us, so close that we saw a
shine like a polished shoe down through its blowhole. It was
so unusual to hear real breathing out at sea, where all living
creatures wriggle silently about without lungs and quiver
their gills, that we really had a warm family feeling for our
old distant cousin the whale, who like us had strayed so far
out to sea. Instead of the cold, toadlike whale shark, which
had not even the sense to stick up its nose for a breath of
fresh air, here we had a visit from something which recalled
a well-fed jovial hippopotamus in a zoological gardens and
which actually breathed—that made a most pleasant impression on me—before it sank into the sea again and disappeared.

We were visited by whales many times. Most often they
were small porpoises and toothed whales which gamboled
about us in large schools on the surface of the water, but
now and then there were big cachalots, too, and other giant
whales which appeared singly or in small schools. Sometimes
they passed like ships on the horizon, now and again sending
a cascade of water into the air, but sometimes they steered
straight for us. We were prepared for a dangerous collision
the first time a big whale altered course and came straight

toward the raft in a purposeful manner. As it gradually grew
nearer, we could hear its blowing and puffing, heavy and
long drawn, each time it rolled its head out of the water. It
was an enormous, thick-skinned, ungainly land animal that
came toiling through the water, as unlike a fish as a bat is unlike a bird. It came straight toward our port side, where we
stood gathered on the edge of the raft, while one man sat
at the masthead and shouted that he could see seven or eight
more making their way toward us.

The big, shining, black forehead of the first whale was not
more than two yards from us when it sank beneath the surface of the water, and then we saw the enormous blue-black
bulk glide quietly under the raft right beneath our feet. It lay
there for a time, dark and motionless, and we held our breath
as we looked down on the gigantic curved back of a mammal
a good deal longer than the whole raft. Then it sank slowly
through the bluish water and disappeared from sight. Meanwhile the whole school were close upon us, but they paid no
attention to us. Whales which have abused their giant
strength and sunk whaling boats with their tails have presumably been attacked first. The whole morning we had them
puffing and blowing round us in the most unexpected places
without their even pushing against the raft or the steering
oar. They quite enjoyed themselves gamboling freely among
the waves in the sunshine. But about noon the whole school
dived as if on a given signal and disappeared for good.

It was not only whales we could see under the raft. If we
lifted up the reed matting we slept on, through the chinks between the logs we saw right down into the crystal-blue
water. If we lay thus for a while, we saw a breast fin or tail
fin waggle past and now and again we saw a whole fish. If the
chinks had been a few inches wider, we could have lain comfortably in bed with a line and fished under our mattresses.

The fish which most of all attached themselves to the raft
were dolphins and pilot fish. From the moment the first dolphins joined us in the current off Callao, there was not a day
on the whole voyage on which we had not large dolphins
wriggling round us. What drew them to the raft we do not
know, but, either there was a magical attraction in being

able to swim in the shade with a moving roof above them, or there was food to be found in our kitchen garden of seaweed and barnacles that hung like garlands from all the logs and from the steering oar. It began with a thin coating of smooth green, but then the clusters of seaweed grew with astonishing speed, so that the *Kon-Tiki* looked like a bearded sea-god as she tumbled along among the waves. Inside the green seaweed was a favorite resort of tiny small fry and our stow-aways, the crabs.

There was a time when ants began to get the upper hand on board. There had been small black ants in some of the logs, and, when we had got to sea and the damp began to penetrate into the wood, the ants swarmed out and into the sleeping bags. They were all over the place, and bit and tormented us till we thought they would drive us off the raft. But gradually, as it became wetter out at sea, they realized that this was not their right element, and only a few isolated specimens held out till we reached the other side. What did best on the raft, along with the crabs, were barnacles from an inch to an inch and a half long. They grew in hundreds, especially on the lee side of the raft, and as fast as we put the old ones into the soup kettle new larvae took root and grew up. The barnacles tasted fresh and delicate; we picked the seaweed as salad and it was eatable, though not so good. We never actually saw the dolphins feeding in the vegetable garden, but they were constantly turning their gleaming bellies upward and swimming under the logs.

The dolphin (dorado), which is a brilliantly colored tropical fish, must not be confused with the creature, also called dolphin, which is a small, toothed whale. The dolphin was ordinarily from three feet three inches to four feet six inches long and had much flattened sides with an enormously high head and neck. We jerked on board one which was four feet eight inches long with a head thirteen and one-half inches high. The dolphin had a magnificent color. In the water it shone blue and green like a bluebottle with a glitter of golden-yellow fins. But if we hauled one on board, we sometimes saw a strange sight. As the fish died, it gradually changed color and became silver gray with black spots and, finally, a quite uniform silvery white. This lasted for four or five minutes, and then the old colors slowly reappeared. Even in the water the dolphin could occasionally change color like a chameleon, and often we saw a "new kind" of shining copper-colored fish, which on a closer acquaintance proved to be our old companion the dolphin.

The high forehead gave the dolphin the appearance of a bulldog flattened from the side, and it always cut through the surface of the water when the predatory fish shot off like a torpedo after a fleeing shoal of flying fish. When the dolphin was in a good humor, it turned over on its flat side, went ahead at a great speed, and then sprang high into the air and tumbled down like a flat pancake. It came down on the surface with a regular smack and a column of water rose up. It was no sooner down in the water than it came up in another leap, and yet another, away over the swell. But, when it was in a bad temper—for example, when we hauled it up on to the raft—then it bit. Torstein limped about for some time with a rag round his big toe because he had let it stray into the mouth of a dolphin, which had used the opportunity to close its jaws and chew a little harder than usual. After our return home we heard that dolphins attack and eat people when bathing. This was not very complimentary to us, seeing that we had bathed among them every day without their showing any particular interest. But they were formidable beasts of prey, for we found both squids and whole flying fish in their stomachs.

Flying fish were the dolphins' favorite food. If anything splashed on the surface of the water, they rushed at it blindly in the hope of its being a flying fish. In many a drowsy morning hour, when we crept blinking out of the cabin and, half asleep, dipped a toothbrush into the sea, we became wide-awake with a jump when a thirty-pound fish shot out like lightning from under the raft and nosed at the toothbrush in disappointment. And, when we were sitting quietly at breakfast on the edge of the raft, a dolphin might jump up and make one of its most vigorous sideway splashes, so that the sea water ran down our backs and into our food.

One day, when we were sitting at dinner, Torstein made a

reality of the tallest of fish stories. He suddenly laid down his fork and put his hand into the sea, and, before we knew what was happening, the water was boiling and a big dolphin came tumbling in among us. Torstein had caught hold of the tail end of a fishing line which came quietly gliding past, and on the other end hung a completely astonished dolphin which had broken Erik's line when he was fishing a few days before.

There was not a day on which we had not six or seven dolphins following us in circles round and under the raft. On bad days there might be only two or three, but, on the other hand, as many as thirty or forty might turn up the day after. As a rule it was enough to warn the cook twenty minutes in advance if we wanted fresh fish for dinner. Then he tied a line to a short bamboo stick and put half a flying fish on the hook. A dolphin was there in a flash, plowing the surface with its head as it chased the hook, with two or three more in its wake. It was a spendid fish to play and, when freshly caught, its flesh was firm and delicious to eat, like a mixture of cod and salmon. It kept for two days, and that was all we needed, for there were fish enough in the sea.

We became acquainted with pilot fish in another way. Sharks brought them and left them to be adopted by us after the sharks' death. We had not been long at sea before the first shark visited us. And sharks soon became an almost daily occurrence. Sometimes the shark just came swimming up to inspect the raft and went on in search of prey after circling round us once or twice. But most often the sharks took up a position in our wake just behind the steering oar, and there they lay without a sound, stealing from starboard to port and occasionally giving a leisurely wag of their tails to keep pace with the raft's placid advance. The blue-gray body of the shark always looked brownish in the sunlight just below the surface, and it moved up and down with the seas so that the dorsal fin always stuck up menacingly. If there was a high sea, the shark might be lifted up by the waves high above our own level, and we had a direct side view of the shark as in a glass case as it swam toward us in a dignified manner with its fussy retinue of small pilot fish ahead of its jaws. For a few seconds it looked as if both the shark and its striped companions would swim right on board, but then the raft would lean over gracefully to leeward, rise over the ridge of waves, and descend on the other side.

To begin with, we had a great respect for sharks on account of their reputation and their alarming appearance. There was an unbridled strength in the streamlined body, consisting of one great bundle of steel muscles, and a heartless greed in the broad flat head with the small, green cat's eyes and the enormous jaws which could swallow footballs. When the man at the helm shouted "Shark alongside to starboard" or "Shark alongside to port," we used to come out in search of hand harpoons and gaffs and station ourselves along the edge of the raft. The shark usually glided round us with the dorsal fin close up to the logs. And our respect for the shark increased when we saw that the gaffs bent like spaghetti when we struck them against the sandpaper armor on the shark's back, while the spearheads of the hand harpoons were broken in the heat of the battle. All we gained by getting through the shark's skin and into the gristle or muscle was a hectic struggle, in which the water boiled round us till the shark broke loose and was off, while a little oil floated up and spread itself out over the surface.

To save our last harpoon head we fastened together a bunch of our largest fishhooks and hid them inside the carcass of a whole dolphin. We slung the bait overboard with a precautionary multiplication of steel lines fastened to a piece of our own life line. Slowly and surely the shark came, and, as it lifted its snout above the water, it opened its great crescent-shaped jaws with a jerk and let the whole dolphin slip in and down. And there it stuck. There was a struggle in which the shark lashed the water into foam, but we had a good grip on the rope and hauled the big fellow, despite its resistance, as far as the logs aft, where it lay awaiting what might come and only gaped as though to intimidate us with its parallel rows of sawlike teeth. Here we profited by a sea to slide the shark up over the low end logs, slippery with seaweed and, after casting a rope round the tail fin, we ran well out of way till the war dance was over.

In the gristle of the first shark we caught this way we found our own harpoon head, and we thought at first that this was the reason for the shark's comparatively small fighting spirit. But later we caught shark after shark by the same method, and every time it went just as easily. Even if the shark could jerk and tug and certainly was fearfully heavy to play, it became quite spiritless and tame and never made full use of its giant strength if we only managed to hold the line tight without letting the shark gain an inch in the tug of war. The sharks we got on board were usually from six to ten feet long, and there were blue sharks as well as brown sharks. The last-named had a skin outside the mass of muscles through which we could not drive a sharp knife unless we struck with our whole strength, and often not even then. The skin of the belly was as impenetrable as that of the back; the five gill clefts behind the head on each side were the only vulnerable point.

When we hauled in a shark, black slippery remora fish were usually fixed tight to its body. By means of an oval sucking disc on the top of the flat head, they were fastened so tight that we could not get them loose by pulling their tails. But they themselves could break loose and skip away to take hold at another place in a second. If they grew tired of hanging tightly to the shark when their host gave no sign of returning to the sea, they leaped off and vanished down between the chinks in the raft to swim away and find themselves another shark. If the remora does not find a shark, it attaches itself to the skin of another fish for the time being. It is generally as long as the length of a finger up to a foot. We tried the natives' old trick which they sometimes use when they have been lucky enough to secure a live remora. They tie a line to its tail and let it swim away. It then tries to suck itself on to the first fish it sees and clings so tightly that a lucky fisherman may haul in both fishes by the remora's tail. We had no luck. Every single time we let a remora go with a line tied to its tail, it simply shot off and sucked itself fast to one of the logs of the raft, in the belief that it had found an extra-fine big shark. And here it hung, however hard we tugged on the line. We gradually acquired a number of these small remoras which hung on and dangled obstinately among the shells on the side of the raft, traveling with us right across the Pacific.

But the remora was stupid and ugly and never became such an agreeable pet as its lively companion the pilot fish. The pilot fish is a small cigar-shaped fish with zebra stripes, which swims rapidly in a shoal ahead of the shark's snout. It received its name because it was thought that it piloted its half-blind friend the shark about in the sea. In reality, it simply goes along with the shark, and, if it acts independently, it is only because it catches sight of food within its own range of vision. The pilot fish accompanied its lord and master to the last second. But, as it could not cling fast to the giant's skin, as the remora does, it was completely bewildered when its old master suddenly disappeared up into the air and did not come down again. Then the pilot fish scurried about in a distracted manner, searching wildly, but always came back and wriggled along astern of the raft, where the shark had vanished skyward. But as time passed and the shark did not come down again, they had to look round for a new lord and master. And none was nearer to hand than the *Kon-Tiki* herself.

If we let ourselves down over the side of the raft, with our heads down in the brilliantly clear water, we saw the raft as the belly of a sea monster, with the steering oar as its tail and the centerboards hanging down like blunt fins. In between them all the adopted pilot fish swam, side by side, and took no notice of the bubbling human head except that one or two of them darted swiftly aside and peered right up its nose, only to wriggle back again unperturbed and take their places in the ranks of eager swimmers.

Our pilot fish patrolled in two detachments; most of them swam between the centerboards, the others in a graceful fan formation ahead of the bow. Now and then they shot away from the raft to snap up some edible trifle we passed, and after meals, when we washed our crockery in the water alongside, it was as if we had emptied a whole cigar case of striped pilot fish among the scraps. There was not a single scrap they did not examine, and, so long as it was not vegetable food,

down it went. These queer little fish huddled under our protecting wings with such childlike confidence that we, like
the shark, had a fatherly protective feeling toward them.
They became the *Kon-Tiki's* marine pets, and it was taboo
on board to lay hands on a pilot fish.

We had in our retinue pilot fish which were certainly in
their childhood, for they were hardly an inch long, while most
were about six inches. When the whale shark rushed off at
lightning speed after Erik's harpoon had entered its skull,
some of its old pilot fish strayed over to the victor; they were
two feet long. After a succession of victories the *Kon-Tiki*
soon had a following of forty or fifty pilot fish, and many of
them liked our quiet forward movement, and our daily scraps,
so much that they followed us for thousands of miles over the
sea.

But occasionally some were faithless. One day, when I was
at the steering oar, I suddenly noticed that the sea was boiling to southward and saw an immense shoal of dolphins come
shooting across the sea like silver torpedoes. They did not
come as usual, splashing along comfortably on their flat sides,
but came rushing at frantic speed more through the air than
through the water. The blue swell was whipped into white
foam in one single turmoil of splashing fugitives, and behind
them came a black back dashing along on a zigzag course
like a speedboat. The desperate dolphins came shooting
through and over the surface right up to the raft; here they
dived, while about a hundred crowded together in a tightly
packed shoal and swung away to eastward, so that the whole
sea astern was a glittering mass of colors. The gleaming back
behind them half rose above the surface, dived in a graceful
curve under the raft, and shot astern after the shoal of dolphins. It was a devilish-big fellow of a blue shark that seemed
to be nearly twenty feet long. When it disappeared, a number
of our pilot fish had gone too. They had found a more exciting
sea hero to go campaigning with.

The marine creature against which the experts had begged
us to be most on our guard was the octopus, for it could get
on board the raft. The National Geographic Society in Washington had shown us reports and dramatic magnesium photo-

graphs from an area in the Humboldt Current where
monstrous octopuses had their favorite resort and came up on
to the surface at night. They were so voracious that, if one of
them fastened on to a piece of meat and remained on the
hook, another came and began to eat its captured kinsman.
They had arms which could make an end of a big shark and
set ugly marks on great whales, and a devilish beak like an
eagle's hidden among their tentacles. We were reminded that
they lay floating in the darkness with phosphorescent eyes
and that their arms were long enough to feel about in every
small corner of the raft, if they did not care to come right on
board. We did not at all like the prospect of feeling cold arms
round our necks, dragging us out of our sleeping bags at
night, and we provided ourselves with saber-like machete
knives, one for each of us, in case we should wake to the
embrace of fumbling tentacles. There was nothing which
seemed more disagreeable to us when we started, especially as
the marine experts in Peru got on to the same subject and
showed us on the chart where the worst area was—right in
the Humboldt Current itself.

For a long time we saw no sign of a squid, either on board
or in the sea. But then one morning we had the first warning
that they must be in those waters. When the sun rose, we
found a progeny of an octopus on board, in the form of a
little baby the size of a cat. It had come up on deck unaided
in the course of the night and now lay dead with its arms
twined round the bamboo outside the cabin door. A thick,
black, inky liquid was smeared over the bamboo deck and
lay in a pool round the squid. We wrote a page or two in the
logbook with cuttlefish ink, which was like India ink, and
then flung the baby overboard for the pleasure of the dolphins.

We saw in this minor incident the harbinger of larger
night visitors. If the baby could clamber on board, its hungry
progenitor could no doubt do the same. Our forefathers must
have felt the same as we did when they sat in their Viking
ships and thought of the Old Man of the Sea. But the next
incident completely bewildered us. One morning we found
a single smaller young squid on the top of the roof of palm

leaves. This puzzled us very much. It could not have climbed
up there, as the only ink marks were smeared in a ring round
it in the middle of the roof. Nor had it been dropped by a sea
bird, for it was completely intact with no beak marks. We
came to the conclusion that it had been flung up on to the
roof by a sea which had come on board, but none of those
on night watch could remember any such sea that night. As
the nights passed, we regularly found more young squids on
board, the smallest of them the size of one's middle finger.

It was soon usual to find a small squid or two among the
flying fish about the deck in the morning, even if the sea had
been calm in the night. And they were young ones of the real
devilish kind, with eight long arms covered with sucking
discs and two still longer with thornlike hooks at the end. But
large squids never gave a sign of coming on board. We saw
the shine of phosphorescent eyes drifting on the surface on
dark nights, and on one single occasion we saw the sea boil
and bubble while something like a big wheel came up and
rotated in the air, while some of our dolphins tried to escape
by hurling themselves desperately through space. But why
the big ones never came on board, when the small ones were
constant night visitors, was a riddle to which we found no
answer until two months later—two months rich in experience
—after we were out of the ill-famed octopus area.

Young squids continued to come aboard. One sunny morning we all saw a glittering shoal of something which shot up
out of the water and flew through the air like large raindrops,
while the sea boiled with pursuing dolphins. At first we
took it for a shoal of flying fish, for we had already had three
different kinds of these on board. But, when they came near
and some of them sailed over the raft at a height of four or
five feet, one ran straight into Bengt's chest and fell slap on
the deck. It was a small squid. Our astonishment was great.
When we put it into a sailcloth bucket it kept on taking off
and shooting up to the surface, but it did not develop speed
enough in the small bucket to get more than half out of the
water.

It is a known fact that the squid ordinarily swims on the
principle of the rocket-propelled airplane. It pumps sea water

Plans being discussed before the start in the Explorers Club in New York. From left to right: Chief of Clannfhearghuis, Herman Watzinger, **Thor Heyerdahl (1914–   )**, Greenland explorer Peter Freuchen.

BIOGRAPHICAL BACKGROUND

Thor Heyerdahl was born on October 6, 1914, the son of a prosperous and intellectual family in the city of Larvik, Norway. His father, also Thor Heyerdahl, the president of a brewery and mineral water plant, infected his family with his extraordinary enthusiasm for skiing, hiking, hunting, and fishing. His mother, Alison Lyng Heyerdahl, had pursued scientific studies in folk art, zoology, and the history of primitive races; her interest and accomplishments qualified her to serve as the chairman of the Larvik museum.

After receiving his bachelor's degree from the Larvik *Gymnasium* in 1933, young Thor Heyerdahl spent three and a half years at the University of Oslo. He was a candidate for a graduate degree in zoology; his studies, however, were much more varied than is usual for graduate students—mathematics, philosophy, genetics, geography, and Polynesian ethnology, together with zoology, his chosen field.

On Christmas Eve 1936, Heyerdahl took a wife. He and his bride, planning to combine a romantic honeymoon with field research for his thesis, at once set off for Fatu Hiva, one of the Marquesas Islands in French Polynesia. Like good scientists and true children of romance, Thor and Liv Heyerdahl lived intimately with the Polynesians in thorough-going Polynesian style for the year and a half of their stay.

The young scientist collected beetles and fish, which he dutifully preserved in glass jars. In the course of his field trips, however, he came upon ancient temples that had been overwhelmed by jungle growth. The red stone carvings he found there particularly fascinated him. Talking about his finds with his Polynesian friends gradually shifted his primary interest to anthropology, for which his university studies had partially prepared him.

In *Kon-Tiki* (pp. 11M–13M), Heyerdahl recounts the genesis of his theory of Polynesian origins. The theory is interesting enough to merit a brief summary in this Supplement.

Native traditions, combined with the striking lack of archeological evidence for earlier settlement, make it certain that the islands were peopled for the first time within the last fifteen hundred years. Where did the people come from? The Polynesians were a very high-level stone-age people, ignorant of metalcraft, weaving, pottery manufacture, and the principle of the wheel, but nonetheless truly civilized. Cultures like theirs existed to the east, in America, but were extinct throughout the rest of the world. Ocean currents and prevailing winds would have made east-to-west travel much easier than travel in the opposite direction over shorter distances; what is more, both Peruvian rafts and British Columbian war canoes were capable of long sea voyages. Why might not the Polynesians have come from America instead of Asia, the homeland supposed by almost all scholars?

Polynesian tradition confirms the Heyerdahl theory by speaking of the racial progenitors as coming from a mountainous land to the east. Artifacts from Peru and British Columbia closely resemble Polynesian artifacts, and Polynesian legend includes many elements of aboriginal American folklore. Many cultivated plants in Polynesia are demonstrably of American origin. Physical similarities exist between the Polynesians and various American peoples, including a mysterious white race attested both by tradi-

Note: The page references above and on the following pages direct your attention to passages in the text (T for Top of page, M for Middle, and B for Bottom).

tion and archeology as having laid the foundations of civilization in the Americas.

Heyerdahl returned to Norway and published a book about his South Sea island stay. After a year of library research in Oslo, he spent nearly three years doing library research in the United States and Canada and pursuing anthropological field studies in British Columbia. From 1942 until the end of World War II, he led a military life —first in the Free Norwegian Air Force, then in a special parachute unit, and finally as a lieutenant in an invasion unit operating in Arctic Norway.

When published, *Kon-Tiki,* in the highly praised translation by F. H. Lyon, was widely acclaimed as an adventure yarn, and even Heyerdahl himself had to admit that it did not prove his theories, only that a balsa raft could cross the Pacific and that Peru was not out of the question in considering east-to-west migration in ancient times.

In 1958, Heyerdahl published *Aku-Aku* in an attempt to prove that the migration from Peru to the South Pacific did occur, the feasibility of which *Kon-Tiki* had established. "Heyerdahl tells a story well, as every reader of *Kon-Tiki* knows," conceded *The New York Times,* but once again fellow scientists begged to differ with the Norwegian's theories.

Heyerdahl was undaunted and studied ancient Egyptian tomb paintings to design a papyrus boat that might prove a theory of cultural migration from Egypt to South America. The boat (named *Ra* in honor of the ancient sun god) was constructed on ancient lines at Gizah in 1969, dragged across the desert on primitive wooden tracks, taken to the harbor of Safi in Morocco by modern truck, and set sail on May 25, 1969, with Heyerdahl and a crew of six. After fifty-six days, the *Ra* foundered because of improper loading, and the mission had to be aborted after sailing some 2700 of the 4000 miles to the projected landing in Yucatán.

The ship was abandoned, but the theory was not.

With the determination that all readers of *Kon-Tiki* expected, Heyerdahl constructed *Ra II* and in 1970 again sailed from Safi. This time the boat stayed afloat. He and a crew of eight reached Bridgetown in the Barbadoes after fifty-seven days, proving (at least to their own satisfaction) that ancient Egyptians, perhaps blown off course by strong trade winds, had brought their highly developed culture to the Caribbean and Central America. Was this the way that such "Egyptian" knowledge as astronomy, surgery, mummification, pyramid building, and so on, and such customs as the marriage of royal brothers and sisters were brought to South and Central America? In the search for the secrets of the past, the indomitable courage of our modern adventures equals, and may some day explain, the exploits of their ancient predecessors.

HISTORICAL BACKGROUND

The two basic drives underlying the Kon-Tiki expedition (as well as the reader's favorable reaction to it), the *quest for adventure* and the *quest for knowledge,* have been present in some form or other among all races at almost every stage of their history. The particular forms relevant to the Kon-Tiki story, however, are peculiarly European and American. And they have developed only in the last five hundred years.

From the most ancient times, bold warriors delighted in the opportunity to win glory on the field of battle. They wanted adventures so that they could boast about them. And there was little worth boasting about apart from killing people. At the time of the Crusades, however, returning pilgrims found that the traveler to far-off lands was as thoroughly envied as the terrible warrior. Later, successful explorers found themselves as much esteemed as conquering generals. The emphasis gradually shifted from killing people to doing dangerous things and surviving them. Because most men like to think of themselves as being the sort of men that others esteem, they have gradually come to appreciate danger for its own sake. Skiing and mountaineering for fun would have seemed like insanity to Julius Caesar. To us, they seem a natural expression of a basic human hunger; this hunger, however, is in fact a sophisticated elaboration of the primitive desire to be regarded as the roughest fighter in the neighborhood.

Nowadays, men like Mallory and Herzog and Sir Edmund Hillary risk their lives to climb vast rock-piles in the Himalayas. There is nothing at the top of the mountain but air, and only a little of that; but they have to climb the mountain "because it is there" to be climbed. Even though they gain glory when they succeed, the thirst for glory has little effect on what they do. They would climb just as zealousy if they had no chance of getting their name in the papers. Their concept of adventure is radically different from that of a medieval knight.

A similar spirit animated Charles Lindbergh and now animates the astronauts. Such men, however, are also interested in finding out something. They are aware, as their remote ancestors were not, that reliable new knowledge is based in experiment and observation. The astronauts are in a real sense both engineers and scholars. Lindbergh's later career indicates that he was by temperament very similar to them. They have a zest for danger, but they are disciplined to risk their lives in the service of knowledge.

Some persons who have no love for danger will face it manfully when they think the stakes are high enough. In our time, this common-sense approach is more characteristic of war heroes than it is of such adventures as astronauts and arctic explorers. A man like Thor Heyerdahl must have a personal hunger for adventure if he is to carry out a dangerous test in person, rather than wait for a less careful man to do it in his place. With the possible exception of Bengt Danielsson, the sailors of the *Kon-Tiki* were glad that their assignment was a perilous one. Danger alone would not have attracted them—but danger sanctified by scientific purpose drew them as a light draws a moth.

The characteristic of man we are dealing with is relatively new. We search older history in vain for instances of it. Even at the beginning of our own era, it was displayed quite imperfectly by the greatest adventurers the world knew. We think of such explorers as Magellan and Hudson as the Lindberghs of their own time, willing to embrace the same kind of perilous assignment. We are not entirely wrong. But in view of the materialistic and religious motives of our bravest ancestors, the Magellans, although different from the Charlemagnes or the Alexanders, were not quite like Lindbergh.

Put to the severest tests, most of us are not, either. But there is a little of his kind of spirit of adventure in all of us, even the most timid—and there has been since the beginning of the nineteenth century, at the latest. We can understand the attraction of danger without referring to opportunities for glory. We can understand, too, the readiness of braver men to take risks for the sake of measuring the capability of their equipment or testing a theory or gathering scientific data.

The voyage of the *Kon-Tiki* manifests one special aspect of adventure that belongs peculiarly to our own century. Our ancestors rarely attempted difficult tasks without using the best equipment they could lay their hands on. The more daring among us, however, adventurously emulate their hardiness; we try to survive a year in the woods with no tools or even clothing, but what we are able to fashion for ourselves on the spot, or we sail a duplicate of the *Mayflower* across the Atlantic, or we go hunting armed with bow and arrow. Heyerdahl and his companions, crossing the Pacific exactly as men of the Stone Age may have done, thrill us and themselves with their practical demonstration that the primitive vigor of humanity survives undiminished in this age of machines.

PICTORIAL BACKGROUND

Above: Over the Andes for wood—our jeep on a mountain road 13,000 feet above sea level. Indians with pack donkeys, Indian women spinning wool as they walk, and flocks of llamas were the only living creatures we met.

Above: The six members of the *Kon-Tiki* expedition. From left to right: Knut Haugland, Bengt Danielsson, the author, Erik Hesselberg, Torstein Raaby, Herman Watzinger.

Above: In the Ecuadorian jungle we found our balsa logs. We felled the biggest trees we could find, peeled off the bark in Indian style, and built a makeshift raft on which we drifted down the Palenque and the Guayas to the Pacific.

Below: Building the raft in Peru. We lashed the nine big balsa logs together with ordinary hemp ropes, using neither nails nor metal in any form.

Kon-Tiki ready to start in Callao Harbor. Like the Indians' prehistoric vessels on the west coast of South America, our raft had an open bamboo cabin and two masts lashed together with a square sail between. The woman secretary of the expedition, Gerd Vold *(above left)*, named the raft by smashing a coconut against the bow. The raft received the name *Kon-Tiki* in memory of the Peruvian sun-god, who long ago vanished westward across the sea.

Above: Erik puts the finishing touch to the raft. A Peruvian sailor helps him to fix a tholepin of the hardest wood for the steering oar.

Below: Thank you and good-by! The tug *Guardian Rios* turns back and leaves us to our fate.

Under full sail out at sea. Nature was our only teacher, the last raftsmen having died several hundred years before, and we went through a hard school in our first weeks in the Humboldt Current off the coast of South America.

Above: The kitchen department. Before our fresh fruit ran out, we had entered waters where fish abounded. We cooked our food on a couple of primus stoves, which stood on the bottom of a wooden box, and generally had our meals on the starboard side of the raft in front of the entrance to the cabin. Like our prehistoric forerunners, we also had with us sweet potatoes and gourds from Peru.

Below: A fresh breeze. With a good wind we danced over the waves so that the raft groaned and creaked; 71 sea miles in a day was our record.

Top: Toward Polynesia in sunny weather. With the help of ocean currents and trade winds we moved westward without interruption. Our average speed was as much as 42½ sea miles a day.

Above: The cook's first duty in the morning was to collect all the flying fish which had landed on deck during the night.

15

Below: View astern from the mast. Many thousand tons of water poured in astern daily and vanished between the logs.

Above: Steering watch. We divided the day and night into watches of two hours. Although the waves often towered round us as high as our mast tops, the raft always rode over them in style. Author at the steering oar.

Below: An unusual bedfellow. We were the first to see a living snake mackerel (Latin name *Gempylus*). It jumped on board one night and got into Torstein's sleeping bag.

Above: Evening. Watzinger takes the last weather observation; we eat our supper outside the cabin entrance; the lantern is hung up; and the sun sinks into the Pacific with a brilliant display of colors.

Below: A bout with a tunny was an exciting sport. There were fish enough in the sea to feed a whole flotilla of rafts.

Above: Beneath Kon-Tiki's bearded face. The head on the sail was copied from a stone carving of Kon-Tiki, the prehistoric chieftain who led a fair-skinned civilized people across the Pacific 1,500 years ago.

Below: Windless weather and tropical heat troubled us very little. When the sea was calm, we made long trips in our little rubber boat.

Inside the bamboo cabin we were protected against both wind and tropical sun. The walls were of plaited bamboo and the roof of banana leaves, so that we almost felt we were in a virgin forest instead of at sea. *From left*: Watzinger, Haugland, Raaby, Danielsson, the author.

Watzinger with a bonito. This fish was certainly the best eating. It sometimes happened that bonitos swam on board with the waves.

Above: When we were halfway across, we were about 2,000 sea miles from land both ahead and astern. We felt we were living in a strange world — "east of the sun and west of the moon."

Below: Provisions were stored between the logs and the bamboo deck. Our Peruvian parrot always came fluttering along when we opened a box of food.

Hold on, Haugland! If the intervals between the waves were too short, water often came on board from astern, and the helmsman had a hard job to prevent himself from being washed overboard.

Top: The whale shark which paid us a visit. It is the world's biggest fish and can be as much as 60 feet long. Its body is covered with white spots, and its jaws are nearly 5 feet wide.

Above: The dorsal fin projected menacingly from the water when the monster approached the raft.

Below: Whales often visited us, and the raft seemed pretty small alongside them. Sometimes they followed us for hours before they disappeared.

Above: Heave ho! The ropes became slack in tropical sun and squalls, and we often had to make them taut.

Below: An idyllic scene: Hesselberg playing and singing in his "watch below."

Above: Catching sharks with our hands. Sharks followed us throughout the voyage and we got to know them thoroughly. Top left, a shark eating out of the author's hand. Its black head projects from the water and snaps a dolphin in half with the utmost ease. Just as it is about to dive, the author seizes its tail fin, as rough as sandpaper. The shark is slowly hauled on deck. As soon as the tail fin comes above water the shark is helpless, and when at last the stomach sinks down toward the head it is almost paralyzed.

Below: One strong jerk and the shark is on deck. Then we have to jump out of the way and keep at a distance till the shark has ceased to snap around.

Top: A blue shark with its conqueror. Shark flesh was edible only if soaked in salt water for twenty-four hours. But we often cleared the water of sharks to be on the safe side in case one of us should fall overboard.

Above: A day's catch. Nine sharks, two tunnies, and a lot of bonitos. The flying fish, squids, and remora fish in the foreground all came on board of their own accord.

Below: The raft would certainly have come off badly in a collision with a whale. But however deliberately the whales seemed to come rushing straight toward the raft, they always dived under it at the last moment.

Our daily bread. Dolphins followed us throughout the voyage and were the best eating imaginable. They bit at once if we used flying fish as bait.

Hesselberg making a diving basket. If we received unwelcome attentions when we dived under the raft, we just crouched inside the basket and were quickly hauled on board.

Top: Haugland goes down to inspect the lashings on the raft's bottom. The author holds him firmly by the legs.

Above: Where Haugland went down, a shark was hauled up — an easy matter, as the deck was only a foot or two above the surface of the water.

Below: Raaby in the radio corner. Haugland and Raaby had their radio station behind a cardboard partition decorated by Danielsson. They were in contact with amateurs in many different countries and sent regular reports to the U.S. Weather Bureau.

Above left: Studying the chart. Hesselberg took observations daily and marked our drift on the chart. Not till after three months, when we reached the Tuamotu group, did a serious navigation problem arise — how were we to land?

Above right: The first birds from Polynesia which welcomed us. We followed the same course as they when they flew home at evening.

Below: Land in sight! After 93 days we sighted land for the first time. It was the island Puka Puka. But the wind and current took us out to sea again.

On opposite page top: Kon-Tiki approaching land. The tricolor was hoisted as we steered toward the French island Angatau. We had reached Polynesia.

Center: The first natives coming out. Toward evening several canoes appeared with natives eager to help us ashore. But the raft drifted out to sea again, and finally Angatau disappeared astern.

Bottom: A reef with a witches' caldron of seething breakers barred the approach to the island Raroia. The raft was heavily pounded and finally flung up by the waves on to the coral reef surrounding the island.

Above: The wreck was washed higher up on to the reef every day. The Raroia reef—25 miles long—is (like all the other islands in the Tuamotu group) the work of industrious little coral polyps.

Below left: Salvage work. Danielsson — safe and sound, but his head still aching from a blow from the mast — dragging his mattress out of the wreckage. The most important cargo has already been salvaged.

Below right: Chaos. After the stranding the raft was hardly recognizable. The masts were broken, the cabin crushed, the bamboo deck twisted up to form a barricade, and our belongings strewn all over the place.

Top: An uninhabited South Sea island, protected by the coral reef, was our first home across the ocean. It was a curious experience to feel solid ground under our feet again after 101 days at sea.

Above: We were able to save most of our equipment and carried it to the island in our rubber boat, which we had found a long way in on the reef. We waded across to the island seen in the background, but that too was uninhabited.

Left: Big fresh green coconuts hung from the trees in clusters. With coconuts, hermit crabs, and fish we were not short of food.

Above: A coconut from Peru was planted on the island where we had been shipwrecked. The coconut palm grew on the coast of tropical America and in the South Sea islands before Columbus' time. As the nuts will not withstand sea water for any length of time, they must have been spread with man's assistance.

Below: "All well, all well" — Raaby and Haugland sent out this message hour after hour to prevent relief expeditions from coming to search for us. "If all's well, why worry?" asked an American radio "ham" who picked up the message. In the foreground Hesselberg is shown turning the hand generator.

Above left: Polynesians arrive. After a week on our desert island an outrigger canoe appeared. The natives on board lived in a village on the other side of the lagoon; they had found wreckage and seen a light from our island.

Above right: "*Ke-ke-te-huru-huru* (Heave ho)!" shouted the natives as they dragged the raft to land. After several days she had finally been washed over the reef.

Below: Kon-Tiki in the Raroia lagoon. It may be safely assumed that no other vessel will repeat our raft's exploit in clearing the breakers and then sailing as trimly over land as over water.

Above: The raft arrives at Tahiti in tow of the government schooner *Tamara.*

Below left: Tiki was the name of the first great chief on Tahiti. He was regarded by the inhabitants as their divine ancestor, and stone statues of South American type were erected in his honor on many of the islands.

Below right: Teriieroo a Teriierooiterai is the name of the last chief on Tahiti. He was on the quay to meet us when we arrived. Ten years before he had adopted the author as his son and had given him the name Terai Mateata (Blue Sky).

Above: The country which Tiki found. Low coral islands, like those of the Tuamotu group, and lofty mountainous islands like Tahiti and Moorea were found by Kon-Tiki, Son of the Sun, when he came from Peru with the first men on balsa rafts.

Left: Hula dance on Tahiti. Purea was related to the last queen of the island. After Tiki another Indian race came to these islands in big double canoes from British Columbia via Hawaii. The Polynesian race is a mixture of these two immigrant peoples.

A Tahitian belle. When we came to the native village on Raroia, the natives started festivities that lasted the fourteen days we spent on the island. Our stay on Tahiti was of the same nature, but lasted longer.

At the White House. After our return to Washington, President Truman received the members of the expedition. The American flag that had accompanied us across the Pacific was presented to him. From left: (half hidden) Knut Haugland, the author, Herman Watzinger, President Truman, My Lykke (counselor to the Embassy), Erik Hesselberg, and Torstein Raaby. Bengt Danielsson had remained on the West Coast.

LITERARY ALLUSIONS AND NOTES

Norwegian Independence Day (p. 9M):
In the Stone and Bronze Ages, along the coast of Finnmark in the north and north of Standlandet, "Nordic" peoples settled in what we now call Norway. Reaching a period of greatness 1217–1319, Norway eventually came under Danish rule, and from 1814 to 1905, was united with Sweden. In 1905, Prince Charles of Denmark (married to Maud, youngest daughter of Edward VII of Great Britain) was chosen King of Norway and took the title of Haakon VII. To a patriot like Heyerdahl, a true descendant of the brave Vikings of old, Independence Day would be very important.

Goethe (p. 10T):
Bengt is reading a work by Johann Wolfgang von Goethe (1749–1832), the great German poet, dramatist, and scientist, author of *Wilhelm Meister* and *Faust*.

Easter Island (p. 15T):
Throughout this book, Heyerdahl refers to this island named by the Dutch navigator Jakob Roggeven (p. 140M) and its mysterious monoliths and hieroglyphics, a subject he dealt with in his *Aku-Aku: The Secret of Easter Island* (1958). Heyerdahl argues that white men from the east carved the monoliths and were later wiped out (*c.* 1680) by the Polynesians, but Alfred Metraux in the work translated as *Easter Island, a Stone-Age Civilization of the Pacific* (1957) regards the huge statues as much more recent and the work of the Polynesians, uninfluenced by Egyptian or Hindu or similar cultures.

Trygve Lie (p. 40T):
This Norwegian statesman (b. 1896) became well known to Americans when he served as the first Secretary-General of the United Nations (1946–1953).

washing gold (p. 45B):
Gold is not only mined from the earth, but is also found in alluvial placer deposits and can be "washed," panned,

dredged, or hydraulically mined. F. H. Lyon, translating from Heyerdahl's Norwegian text, might have written "panned" here.

Herman's hat (p. 46T):
Heyerdahl is making a joke on the idea of the "swelled head" of the proud. Here, an abashed person is said to have a shrunken head. Throughout *Kon-Tiki*—see the "sacrifice to Neptune" on page 81M for another example —Heyerdahl's wit lightens the tone occasionally and spices the narrative with humor. A sense of humor was certainly necessary for every member of this trying expedition and, in fact, that quality enabled Heyerdahl to recognize at least one excellent recruit and sign him on after the briefest of interviews.

east of the sun and west of the moon (p. 47B):
This expression, meaning "outside time and beyond space," is known to English-speaking readers chiefly through a popular song of that title of the last generation.

Humboldt Current (p. 66M):
Kon-Tiki makes much of the current discovered by one of the greatest of scientists, Friedrich Heinrich Alexander, Freiherr (Count) von Humboldt (1769–1859), who explored the Orinoco and Amazon rivers, the Andes of Peru, and so on. In fact, the Humboldt Current made Heyerdahl's whole voyage possible, as the book explains.

Pizzaro, Zárate (p. 75M):
Francisco Pizarro (*c.* 1476–1541) was the Spanish *conquistador* of Peru. The whole incredible tale is told in Prescott's classic *History of the Conquest of Peru* (1855), which gives all details of Zárate and the other Spaniards.

Tupak Yupanqui (p. 84T):
Under the Incan rulers Pachacuti (*c.* 1438–1471) and his son Tupak Yupanqui (1471–1493), the Peruvian empire reached its greatest power, and such cities as Machu Pichu flourished.

Old Man of the Sea (p. 91B):
A bogeyman of folklore, the Old Man of the Sea was a Viking superstition, as mentioned on page 117B.

whale shark (p. 93T):

This is described as "the largest fish known in the world today," although the whale is a mammal, not a fish. See the mention of the "blue whale," page 107B. On the voyage over untracked ocean, the crew of *Kon-Tiki* were able to see many rare forms of sea life, and the expedition had important features for marine biologists, other scientists, and anthropologists. Dr. A. D. Bajkov, the marine biologist mentioned on page 106M, is but one of the many scientists who contributed to and benefited from this voyage.

Walt Disney (p. 106B):

The creator of Mickey Mouse and many other animated features, Disney produced *Fantasia,* the first attempt to interpret music through cartoon characters. The reference to the "seven little dwarfs" of the Snow White story (p. 221B) is as likely to be drawn from Disney's *Snow White and the Seven Dwarfs* (1938) as from the old fairy tale.

Haakon (p. 149B):

This is the man (1872–1957) mentioned above who ruled as King Haakon VII of Norway (1905–57). During the German Occupation of his country (1940–45), he headed a government in exile in London. Many Norwegians fought with British forces or in guerrilla bands against the Germans, as did Heyerdahl himself.

Great Bear . . . Pleiades (pp. 151M, 152B):

The ancients saw pictures in the constellations of the heavens and named them after animals (Dragon, Swan, Lion, Bear), mythological personages (Orion, Perseus, Hercules, the seven Pleiades—daughters of Atlas and the nymph Pleidone, changed into stars when pursued by the hunter Orion), or objects (Crown, Scales). Despite these fancies, ancient people were well versed in astronomy and could navigate by the stars, as could both Heyerdahl's crew and the ancients who may have traveled the same seas.

witches' dance (p. 173T):

The reference is to the deadly, roiling seas.

"Tom Brown's baby . . ." (p. 178B):

This parody on the familiar Civil War song "John Brown's Body" is a trifle more sedate in Heyerdahl's version—he uses the word "nose"—than the common form. The song helps set the tone of the occasion.

Robinson Crusoe (p. 200T):

The true adventures of the Scottish sailor Alexander Selkirk were immortalized in the novel (with two sequels) *Robinson Crusoe* (1719) in which Daniel Defoe (1660?–1731) wrote convincingly of man alone against the elements, cast away on a desert island with no companion but his faithful man Friday. Like the crew member here, Robinson Crusoe wore a large hat.

Christiania (p. 209T):

Teka's education is out of date: the capital of Norway is Oslo. Founded about 1050, Oslo suffered a great fire in 1624 and when rebuilt was renamed Christiania by Christian IV, but reverted to its original name in 1925. Teka's familiarity with the "crooner" Bing Crosby, however, shows him more up to date in some respects, though his question as to whether Heyerdahl knows Crosby is naive.

"Marseillaise" (p. 214T):

This song from the French Revolution, of course, is the national anthem of France, the country that controls the Society Islands and other parts of Oceania.

Captain Cook (p. 216B):

The English explorer and navigator James Cook (1728–79) circumnavigated the globe and discovered many territories before he was murdered by natives in the Hawaiian islands.

Quel bateau? (p. 225M):

This French phrase asks "What boat?" Fortunately, Heyerdahl is generally careful to translate for us expressions in less familiar Polynesian languages, just as he helpfully identifies many of the persons and places he mentions so that the reader needs no reference books or notes such as those for Pitcairn (p. 17M), the chronicler Oviedo (p. 103B), Tiahuanaco (p. 69M), and so on, which are sufficiently clear in the text.

CRITICAL EXCERPTS

1. *There has been much discussion in scientific groups about Heyerdahl's theories concerning the early settlement of Polynesia by prehistoric raft-borne Peruvians. Waldemar Kaempffert, writing in the New York* Times *(August 17, 1947), found similarities between Heyerdahl's theories and those of the late Professor G. N. Lewis of the University of California and of the late A. Posnansky, a German engineer who gathered and interpreted somewhat similar material he came upon in Bolivia about an extinct blond race which had ruled regions of South America. Although the majority of anthropologists confute Heyerdahl's hypotheses (they are of the opinion that the origins of the Polynesian people are Asiatic), in the words of Kaempffert, Heyerdahl "certainly proved by his epic voyage that it is possible to reach Polynesia from Peru on a balsa raft." This point, the Norwegian ethnologist reiterated later, was all he had set out to prove.*

Current Biography, 1947.

2. *If you love water, it is no jump from a duck pond to the Pacific. The most audacious story of seafaring since the war is told and well told in* Kon-Tiki . . . *by Thor Heyerdahl. Heyerdahl, a Norwegian zoologist, had been prospecting for the origins of the Polynesian race in the late 1930s, and at the first opportunity after the war, in 1947, he gathered together a ship's company of six Scandinavians: war veterans, explorers, and a meteorologist—men who had learned to operate radio in the Resistance, parachutists who were not afraid of the unknown. Thor's matter-of-fact invitation was this: "Am going to cross Pacific on a wooden raft to support a theory that the South Sea islands were peopled from Peru. Will you come? . . . You will find good use for your technical abilities. . . . Reply at once." They accepted to a man, and in December Heyerdahl, their young captain, flew down to Peru to launch the expedition.*

The raft covered 4300 miles in 101 days, and following the life aboard is an astonishing adventure for readers of any age. The voyage did not necessarily prove the captain's theory, but it did prove the character of the six men, and that's why the book is so good.

> Edward Weeks, "Stone Age Voyage," Atlantic Bookshelf, *The Atlantic*, CLXXXVI.

3. *No brief review can give any idea of the tremendous experience that this book allows the reader to share in. Technically, the writing is fine, part of the credit for which must go to F. H. Lyon, translator from the Norwegian. . . .*

> D. B. Theall, *Catholic World*, CLXXII.

4. *The whole story—from its beginnings in Heyerdahl's theory, through the long voyage and in the experiences after he was ashore—is as great an adventure as it is possible to imagine. That means it's as good as "Robinson Crusoe," plus the fact that "Kon-Tiki" is true.*

> Emmett Dedmon, *Chicago Sun*, September 5, 1950.

5. *This review can easily be written in four words: "Wow! What a book!" It has spine chilling, nerve tingling, spirit lifting adventure on every page and in every one of its 80 action photografs [sic]. It is the fiction of a Conrad or a Melville brought to reality. It might be added that the writing is of itself worthy of either pen.*

> W. M. Krogman, *Chicago Sunday Tribune*, September 9, 1950.

6. *Beware! Fair warning! If you pick up this book in the morning, your day will be ruined. If you open it in the evening, you'll get no sleep that night. Kon-Tiki will cling to you like a South sea jellyfish, pursue you like a school of dolphins,*

sweep you onward and away from your normal pursuits as irresistibly as the Humboldt current.

Christian Century, LXVII, September 27, 1950.

7. *While this is not the first time that a log has been turned into literature, it has seldom been done so superbly. The book is cast in terms of men-against-the-sea, which gives it a general rather than particular appeal. Specialists in archaeology, ethnology, icthyology, and other fields will be among its avid readers.*

Roland Sawyer, *Christian Science Monitor,* September 7, 1950.

8. *The Norwegian author had a theory that civilization had come to the South Sea Islands from South America with the prevailing winds and currents. And there was a Polynesian legend of a great Chief Tiki who had come from the east. So he built a balsa log raft lashed together with ropes, just as the old chief's men would have done it, and with five companions and a parrot set out to drift across the Pacific Ocean. The 4300-mile trip took almost 100 days, but the raft did land in Polynesia. The writing here is taut and vivid; there is no padding. The adventure story of the year!*

Margaret C. Scoggin, *Horn Book Magazine,* XXVI, November, 1950.

9. *A completely unorthodox viewpoint finds convincing claims in a story that ranks with the best of the classics of adventure.*

Kirkus Book Service, XVIII, August 15, 1950

10. *Regarded merely as an adventure, this voyage of six hardy Norsemen challenges both wonder and admiration: and the story is nowhere spoilt in the telling.*

"H. D. N.," *Manchester Guardian,* April 11, 1950.

11. *Mr. Heyerdahl's account of the voyage, admirably translated by Mr. F. H. Lyon, is the most fascinating description of intelligent courage that I have read.*

> R. C. Wright, *New Statesman and Nation,* XXXIX, April 1, 1950.

12. *It is the deep connection with nature and a tremendous simplicity that makes this book great as few books of our time are great. . . . Its pages reflect a minimum of philosophical overtones. But on every page there is a perceptiveness of the sea and the sky that has delicacy and sureness.*

> Alfred Stanford, *New York Herald Tribune Book Review,* September 13, 1950.

13. *Mr. Heyerdahl's fellow-scientists were not so readily satisfied: their argument was that it would have been impossible to get from Peru to any of the Polynesian islands on a raft. The only way Mr. Heyerdahl could think of refuting their objections was to construct such a raft and float from Peru to Polynesia himself. And so, with five companions and a rather charming Norwegian stubbornness, he proceeded to do just that. His book is a record of the voyage, one of the most remarkable feats in seafaring history. . . . No brief retelling of the story of the voyage can do it justice. Mr. Heyerdahl's theory and his development of it are just as exciting as the adventures on the raft. This is an enthralling book, and I don't think I can be very far off in calling it the most absorbing sea tale of our time.*

> Hamilton Basso, "Six Men on a Raft," *The New Yorker,* XXVI, September 1, 1950.

14. *Fridtjof Nansen would have greeted the author of this book as a brother. Like the long drift of the "Fram" in the Polar ice, the crossing of the Pacific on a raft expressed a Norwegian scientist's readiness to risk everything for a theory in which he believed. Thor Heyerdahl, a biologist working in the Marquesas, heard the Polynesian tradition that their*

islands had been peopled by a mythical hero, Kon-Tiki, who had come over the sea from the East. Later, in Peru, he found a Tiki identified with Virakocha in legends that told of his defeat on Lake Titicaca and of his disappearance overseas to the West. Convinced that both sets of legends referred to the same man and the same sea voyage, and with much other evidence to support him, he came to the conclusion that Polynesia had been reached by a people who migrated from Peru. He wrote a thesis on the subject, but could not persuade anybody to take it seriously. He was told that none of the peoples of South America could have crossed the Pacific for the simple reason that they had no boats. He remembered Pizarro's Ruiz meeting a big raft with a square sail somewhere south of Panama. "Yes," said the scientists, "but who would cross the Pacific on a raft?" "I will," said Thor Heyerdahl.

The voyage itself is a new honour for Norway, already rich in such exploits, and men of every nation will rejoice in Thor Heyerdahl's high-spirited, gallant and modest-minded book. At the end of it all its scientific author says quietly that the voyage does not in itself prove his theory, but it does prove that balsa rafts have qualities hitherto unknown to men of our time, and that "the Pacific islands are located well inside the range of prehistoric travel from Peru."

> Arthur Ransome, "Stone-Age Voyage," Reviews of the Week, *The Spectator*, CLXXXIV, March 31, 1950.

15. *Given the imaginative birth of this adventure, its brilliant audacity, its gambler's throw with death, its resource in peril and its success, any book about it would perhaps write itself. Mr. Heyerdahl has made it a superb adventure story which all the world may, and probably will, read. He has woven into many pages a particular enchantment which proves him a writer as well as a dreamer and man of action, and his translator a skilful interpreter.*

> *Times Literary Supplement*, London, April 7, 1950.

with great force through a closed tube alongside its body and can thus shoot backward in jerks at a high speed; with all its tentacles hanging behind it in a cluster over its head it becomes streamlined like a fish. It has on its sides two round, fleshy folds of skin which are ordinarily used for steering and quiet swimming in the water. But our experience showed that defenseless young squids, which are a favorite food of many large fish, can escape their pursuers by taking to the air in the same way as flying fish. They had made the principle of the rocket aircraft a reality long before human genius hit upon the idea. They pump sea water through themselves till they got up a terrific speed, and then they steer up at an angle from the surface by unfolding the pieces of skin like wings. Like the flying fish, they make a glider flight over the waves for as far as their speed can carry them. After that, when we had to begin to pay attention, we often saw them sailing along for fifty to sixty yards, singly and in two's and three's. The fact that cuttlefish can "glide" has been a novelty to all the zoologists we have met.

As the guest of natives in the Pacific I have often eaten squid; it tastes like a mixture of lobster and India rubber. But on board the *Kon-Tiki* squid came last on the menu. If we got them on deck gratis, we just exchanged them for something else. We made the exchange by throwing out a hook, with the squid on it, and pulling it in again with a big fish kicking at the end of it. Even tunny and bonito liked young squids, and they were food which came at the head of our menu.

But we did not run up against acquaintances only, as we lay drifting over the sea's surface. The diary contains many entries of this type:

—11/5. *Today a huge marine animal twice came up to the surface alongside us as we sat at supper on the edge of the raft. It made a fearful splashing and disappeared. We have no idea what it was.*

—6/6. *Herman saw a thick dark-colored fish with a broad white body, thin tail, and spikes. It jumped clear of the sea on the starboard side several times.*

—16/6. *Curious fish sighted on port bow. Six feet long,*

maximun breadth one foot; long, brown, thin snout, large dorsal fin near head and a smaller one in the middle of the back, heavy sickle-shaped tail fin. Kept near surface and swam at times by wriggling its body like an eel. It dived when Herman and I went out in the rubber dinghy with a hand harpoon. Came up later but dived again and disappeared.

—Next day: Erik was sitting at the masthead, 12 noon, when he saw thirty or forty long, thin, brown fish of the same kind as yesterday. Now they came at a high speed from the port side and disappeared astern like a big, brown, flat shadow in the sea.

—18/6. Knut observed a snakelike creature, two to three feet long and thin, which stood straight up and down in the water below the surface and dived by wriggling downward like a snake.

On several occasions we glided past a large dark mass, the size of the floor of a room, that lay motionless under the surface of the water like a hidden reef. It was presumably the giant ray of evil repute but it never moved, and we never went close enough to make out its shape clearly.

With such company in the water time never passed slowly. It was even more entertaining when we had to dive down into the sea ourselves and inspect the ropes on the underside of the raft. One day one of the centerboards broke loose and slipped down under the raft, where it was caught up in the ropes without our being able to get hold of it. Herman and Knut were the best divers. Twice Herman swam under the raft and lay there among dolphins and pilot fish, tugging and pulling at the board. He had just come up for the second time, and was sitting on the edge of the raft to recover his breath, when an eight-foot shark was detected not more than ten feet from his legs, moving steadily up from the depths toward the tips of his toes. Perhaps we did the shark an injustice, but we suspected it of evil intentions and rammed a harpoon into its skull. The shark felt aggrieved and a splashy struggle took place, as a consequence of which the shark disappeared leaving a sheet of oil on the surface, while the centerboard remained unsalved, lying caught up under the raft.

Then Erik had the idea of making a diving basket. We had

not many raw materials to which we could have recourse, but we had bamboos and ropes and an old chip basket which had contained coconuts. We lengthened the basket upward with bamboos and plaited ropework, and then let one another down in the basket alongside the raft. Our enticing legs were then concealed in the basket, and, even if the plaited ropework above had only a psychological effect on both us and the fish, in any case we could duck down into the basket in a flash if anything with hostile intentions made a dash at us, and have ourselves pulled up out of the water by the others on deck.

This diving basket was not merely useful but gradually became a perfect place of entertainment for us on board. It gave us a first-class opportunity to study the floating aquarium we had under the raft floor.

When the sea was content to run in a calm swell, we crawled into the basket one by one and were let down under water for as long as our breath lasted. There was a curiously transfigured, shadowless flow of light down in the water. As soon as we had our eyes under the surface, light no longer seemed to have a particular direction, as up in our own above-water world. Refraction of light came as much from below as from above; the sun no longer shone—it was present everywhere. If we looked up at the bottom of the raft, it was brightly illuminated all over, with the nine big logs and the whole network of rope lashings bathed in a magic light and with a flickering wreath of spring-green seaweed all round the sides and along the whole length of the steering oar. The pilot fish swam formally in their ranks like zebras in fishes' skins, while big dolphins circled round with restless, vigilant, jerky movements, eager for prey. Here and there the light fell on the sappy red wood of a centerboard which stuck downward out of a chink, and on them sat peaceful colonies of white barnacles rhythmically beckoning for oxygen and food with their fringed yellow gills. If anyone came too near them, they hastily closed their red- and yellow-edged shells and shut the door till they felt the danger was over.

The light down here was wonderfully clear and soothing for us who were accustomed to the tropical sun on deck. Even when we looked down into the bottomless depths of the sea,

where it is eternal black night, the night appeared to us a
brilliant light blue on account of the refracted rays of the sun.
To our astonishment, we saw fish far down in the depths of
the clear, clean blue when we ourselves were only just below
the surface. They might have been bonitos, and there were
other kinds which swam at such a depth that we could not
recognize them. Sometimes they were in immense shoals, and
we often wondered whether the whole ocean current was full
of fish, or whether those down in the depths had intentionally
assembled under the *Kon-Tiki* to keep us company for a few
days.

What we liked best was a dip under the surface when the
great gold-finned tunnies were paying us a visit. Occasionally
they came to the raft in big shoals, but most often just two or
three came together and swam round us in quiet circles for
several days on end, unless we were able to lure them on to
the hook. From the raft they looked simply like big, heavy,
brown fish without any distinctive adornment, but if we crept
down to them in their own element they spontaneously
changed both color and shape. The change was so bewildering
that several times we had to come up and take our bearings
afresh to see if it was the same fish we had been looking at
across the water. The big fellows paid no attention to us whatever—they continued their majestic maneuvers unperturbed
—but now they had acquired a marvelous elegance of form,
the equal of which we never saw in any other fish, and their
color had become metallic with a suffusion of pale violet.
Powerful torpedoes of shining silver and steel, with perfect
proportions and streamlined shape, they had only to move
one or two fins slightly to set their 150 to 200 pounds gliding
about in the water with the most consummate grace.

The closer we came into contact with the sea and what had
its home there, the less strange it became and the more at
home we ourselves felt. And we learned to respect the old
primitive peoples who lived in close converse with the Pacific
and therefore knew it from a quite different standpoint from
our own. True, we have now estimated its salt content and
given tunnies and dolphins Latin names. They had not done

that. But, nevertheless, I am afraid that the picture the primitive peoples had of the sea was a truer one than ours.

There were not many fixed marks out here at sea. Waves and fish, sun and stars, came and went. There was not supposed to be land of any sort in the 4,300 sea miles that separated the South Sea islands from Peru. We were therefore greatly surprised when we approached 100° west and discovered that a reef was marked on the Pacific chart right ahead of us on the course we were following. It was marked as a small circle, and, as the chart had been issued the same year, we looked up the reference in *Sailing Directions for South America*. We read that "breakers were reported in 1906 and again in 1926 to exist about 600 miles southwestward of Galapagos Islands, in latitude 6° 42′ S., longitude 99° 43′ W. In 1927 a steamer passed one mile westward of this position but saw no indication of breakers, and in 1934 another passed one mile southward and saw no evidence of breakers. The motor vessel 'Cowrie,' in 1935, obtained no bottom at 160 fathoms in this position."

According to the chart the place was clearly still regarded as a doubtful one for shipping, but, as a deep-draught vessel runs a greater risk by going too near a shoal than we should with a raft, we decided to steer straight for the point marked on the chart and see what we found. The reef was marked a little farther north than the point we seemed to be making for, so we laid the steering oar over to starboard and trimmed the square sail so that the bow pointed roughly north and we took sea and wind from the starboard side. Now it came about that a little more Pacific splashed into our sleeping bags than we were accustomed to, especially as at the same time the weather began to freshen considerably. But we saw to our satisfaction that the *Kon-Tiki* could be maneuvered surely and steadily at a surprisingly wide angle into the wind, so long as the wind was still on our quarter. Otherwise the sail swung round, and we had the same mad circus business to get the raft under control again.

For two days and nights we drove the raft north-northwest. The seas ran high and became incalculable as the trade wind began to fluctuate between southeast and east, but we were lifted up and down over all the waves that rushed against us. We had a constant lookout at the masthead, and when we rode over the ridges the horizon widened considerably. The crests of the seas reached six feet above the level of the roof of the bamboo cabin, and, if two vigorous seas rushed together, they rose still higher in combat and flung up a hissing watery tower which might burst down in unexpected directions. When night came, we barricaded the doorway with provision boxes, but it was a wet night's rest. We had hardly fallen asleep when the first crash on the bamboo wall came, and, while a thousand jets of water sprayed in like a fountain through the bamboo wickerwork, a foaming torrent rushed in over the provisions and on to us.

"Ring up the plumber," I heard a sleepy voice remark, as we hunched ourselves up to give the water room to run out through the floor. The plumber did not come, and we had a lot of bathwater in our beds that night. A big dolphin actually came on board unintentionally in Herman's watch.

Next day the seas were less confused, as the trade wind had decided that it would now blow for a time from due east. We relieved one another at the masthead, for now we might expect to reach the point we were making for late in the afternoon. We noticed more life than usual in the sea that day. Perhaps it was only because we kept a better lookout than usual.

During the forenoon we saw a big swordfish approaching the raft close to the surface. The two sharp pointed fins which stuck up out of the water were six feet apart, and the sword looked almost as long as the body. The swordfish swept in a curve close by the man at the helm and disappeared behind the wave crests. When we were having a rather wet and salty midday meal, the carapace, head, and sprawling fins of a large sea turtle were lifted up by a hissing sea right in front of our noses. When that wave gave place to two others, the turtle was gone as suddenly as it had appeared. This time too we saw the gleaming whitish-green of dolphins' bellies tumbling about in the water below the armored reptile. The area was unusually rich in tiny flying fish an inch long, which sailed along in big shoals and often came on board. We also noted single skuas and were regularly visited by frigate birds, with forked tails like giant swallows, which cruised over the raft. Frigate birds are usually regarded as a sign that land is near, and the optimism on board increased.

"Perhaps there is a reef or a sandbank there all the same," some of us thought. And the most optimistic said: "Suppose we find a little green grassy island—one can never know since so few people have been here before. Then we'll have discovered a new land—Kon-Tiki Island!"

From noon onward Erik was more and more diligent in climbing up on the kitchen box and standing blinking through the sextant. At 6:20 P.M. he reported our position as latitude 6° 42′ south by longitude 99° 42′ west. We were 1 sea mile due east of the reef on the chart. The bamboo yard was lowered and the sail rolled up on deck. The wind was due east and would take us slowly right to the place. When the sun went down swiftly into the sea, the full moon in turn shone out in all its brilliance and lit up the surface of the sea, which undulated in black and silver from horizon to horizon. Visibility from the masthead was good. We saw breaking seas everywhere in long rows, but no regular surf which would indicate a reef or shoal. No one would turn in; all stood looking out eagerly, and two or three men were aloft at once.

As we drifted in over the center of the marked area, we sounded all the time. All the lead sinkers we had on board were fastened to the end of a fifty-four-thread silk rope more than 500 fathoms long, and, even if the rope hung rather aslant on account of the raft's leeway, at any rate the lead hung at a depth of some 400 fathoms. There was no bottom east of the place, or in the middle of it, or west of it. We took one last look over the surface of the sea, and, when we had assured ourselves that we could safely call the area surveyed and free from shallows of any kind, we set sail and laid the oar over in its usual place, so that wind and sea were again on our port quarter.

And so we went on with the raft on her natural free course. The waves came and went as before between the open logs aft. We could now sleep and eat dry, even if the heaving seas round us took charge in earnest and raged for several days while the trade wind vacillated from east to southeast.

On this little sailing trip up to the spurious reef we had learned quite a lot about the effectiveness of the centerboards as a keel, and when, later in the voyage, Herman and Knut dived under the raft together and salved the fifth centerboard, we learned still more about these curious pieces of board, something which no one has understood since the Indians themselves gave up this forgotten sport. That the board did the work of a keel and allowed the raft to move at an angle to the wind—that was plain sailing. But when the old Spaniards declared that the Indians to a large extent "steered" their balsa rafts on the sea with "certain centerboards which they pushed down into the chinks between the timbers," this sounded incomprehensible both to us and to all who had concerned themselves with the problem. As the centerboard was simply held tight in the narrow chink, it could not be turned sideways and serve as a helm.

We discovered the secret in the following manner: The wind was steady and the sea had gone down again, so that the Kon-Tiki had kept a steady course for a couple of days without our touching the lashed steering oars. We pushed the recovered centerboard down into a chink aft, and in a moment the Kon-Tiki altered course several degrees from west toward northwest and proceeded steadily and quietly on her new course. If we pulled this centerboard up again, the raft swung back on to her previous course. But if we pulled it only halfway up, the raft swung only halfway back on her old course. By simply raising and lowering the centerboards we could effect changes of course and keep to them without touching the steering oar.

This was the Incas' ingenious system. They had worked out a simple system of balances by which pressure of the wind on the sail made the mast the fixed point. The two arms were respectively the raft forward of and the raft aft of the mast. If the aggregate centerboard surface aft was heavier, the bow swung freely round with the wind; but if the centerboard surface forward was heavier, the stern swung round with the wind. The centerboards which are nearest the mast have, of

course, the least effect on account of the relation between arm
and power. If the wind was due astern, the centerboards
ceased to be effective, and then it was impossible to keep the
raft steady without continually working the steering oar. If
the raft lay thus at full length, she was a little too long to ride
the seas freely. As the cabin door and the place where we
had meals were on the starboard side, we always took the seas
on board on our port quarter.

We could certainly have continued our voyage by making
the steersman stand and pull a centerboard up and down in
a chink instead of hauling sidewise on the ropes of the steering oar, but we had now grown so accustomed to the steering
oar that we just set a general course with the centerboards
and preferred to steer with the oar.

The next great stage on our voyage was as invisible to the
eye as the shoal which existed only on the map. It was the
forty-fifth day at sea; we had advanced from the 78th degree
of longitude to the 108th and were exactly halfway to the
first islands ahead. There were over 2,000 sea miles between
us and South America to the east, and it was the same distance
on to Polynesia in the west. The nearest land in any direction
was the Galapagos Islands to east-northeast and Easter Island
due south, both more than 500 sea miles away on the boundless ocean. We had not seen a ship, and we never did see
one, because we were off the routes of all ordinary shipping
traffic in the Pacific.

But we did not really feel these enormous distances, for the
horizon glided along with us unnoticed as we moved and
our own floating world remained always the same—a circle
flung up to the vault of the sky with the raft itself as center,
while the same stars rolled on over us night after night.

6 ACROSS THE PACIFIC

A Queer Craft—Out in the Dinghy—Unhindered Progress—
Absence of Sea Signs—At Sea in a Bamboo Hut—On the
Longitude of Easter Island—The Mystery of Easter Island—
The Stone Giants—Red-Stone Wigs—The "Long-Ears"—
Tiki Builds a Bridge—Suggestive Place Names—Catching
Sharks with Our Hands—The Parrot—LI 2 B Calling—
Sailing by the Stars—Three Seas—A Storm—Blood Bath
in the Sea, Blood Bath on Board—Man Overboard—
Another Storm—The Kon-Tiki Becomes Rickety—Messengers
from Polynesia

WHEN THE SEA WAS NOT TOO ROUGH, WE WERE
often out in the little rubber dinghy taking photographs. I
shall not forget the first time the sea was so calm that two
men felt like putting the balloon-like little thing into the
water and going for a row. They had hardly got clear of the
raft when they dropped the little oars and sat roaring with
laughter. And, as the swell lifted them away and they disappeared and reappeared among the seas, they laughed so
loud every time they caught a glimpse of us that their voices
rang out over the desolate Pacific. We looked around us with
mixed feelings and saw nothing comic but our own hirsute
faces; but as the two in the dinghy should be accustomed to
those by now, we began to have a lurking suspicion that they
had suddenly gone mad. Sunstroke, perhaps. The two fellows
could hardly scramble back on board the *Kon-Tiki* for sheer

laughter and, gasping, with tears in their eyes they begged us just to go and see for ourselves.

Two of us jumped down into the dancing rubber dinghy and were caught by a sea which lifted us clear. Immediately we sat down with a bump and roared with laughter. We had to scramble back on the raft as quickly as possible and calm the last two who had not been out yet, for they thought we had all gone stark staring mad.

It was ourselves and our proud vessel which made such a completely hopeless, lunatic impression on us the first time we saw the whole thing at a distance. We had never before had an outside view of ourselves in the open sea. The logs of timber disappeared behind the smallest waves, and, when we saw anything at all, it was the low cabin with the wide door-way and the bristly roof of leaves that bobbed up from among the seas. The raft looked exactly like an old Norwegian hay-loft lying helpless, drifting about in the open sea—a warped hayloft full of sunburned bearded ruffians. If anyone had come paddling after us at sea in a bathtub, we should have felt the same spontaneous urge to laughter. Even an ordinary swell rolled halfway up the cabin wall and looked as if it would pour in unhindered through the wide open door in which the bearded fellows lay gaping. But then the crazy craft came up to the surface again, and the vagabonds lay there as dry, shaggy, and intact as before. If a higher sea came racing by, cabin and sail and the whole mast might disappear behind the mountain of water, but just as certainly the cabin with its vagabonds would be there again next moment. The situation looked bad, and we could not realize that things had gone so well on board the zany craft.

Next time we rowed out to have a good laugh at ourselves we nearly had a disaster. The wind and sea were higher than we supposed, and the *Kon-Tiki* was cleaving a path for her-self over the swell much more quickly than we realized. We in the dinghy had to row for our lives out in the open sea in an attempt to regain the unmanageable raft, which could not stop and wait and could not possibly turn around and come back. Even when the boys on board the *Kon-Tiki* got the sail down, the wind got such a grip on the bamboo cabin

that the raft drifted away to westward as fast as we could
splash after her in the dancing rubber dinghy with its tiny
toy oars. There was only one thought in the head of every
man—we must not be separated. Those were horrible minutes
we spent out on the sea before we got hold of the runaway
raft and crawled on board to the others, home again.

From that day it was strictly forbidden to go out in the rubber dinghy without having a long line made fast to the bow,
so that those who remained on board could haul the dinghy
in if necessary. We never went far away from the raft, there-
after, except when the wind was light and the Pacific curving
itself in a gentle swell. But we had these conditions when
the raft was halfway to Polynesia and the ocean, all dominat-
ing, arched itself round the globe toward every point of the
compass. Then we could safely leave the Kon-Tiki and row
away into the blue space between sky and sea.

When we saw the silhouette of our craft grow smaller and
smaller in the distance, and the big sail at last shrunken to a
vague black square on the horizon, a sensation of loneliness
sometimes crept over us. The sea curved away under us as
blue upon blue as the sky above, and where they met all the
blue flowed together and became one. It almost seemed as if
we were suspended in space. All our world was empty and
blue; there was no fixed point in it but the tropical sun,
golden and warm, which burned our necks. Then the distant
sail of the lonely raft drew us to it like a magnetic point on
the horizon. We rowed back and crept on board with a feeling
that we had come home again to our own world—on board
and yet on firm, safe ground. And inside the bamboo cabin
we found shade and the scent of bamboos and withered palm
leaves. The sunny blue purity outside was now served to us in
a suitably large dose through the open cabin wall. So we
were accustomed to it and so it was good for a time, till the
great clear blue tempted us out again.

It was most remarkable what a psychological effect the
shaky bamboo cabin had on our minds. It measured eight by
fourteen feet, and to diminish the pressure of wind and sea
it was built low so that we could not stand upright under
the ridge of the roof. Walls and roof were made of strong

bamboo canes, lashed together and guyed, and covered with a tough wickerwork of split bamboos. The green and yellow bars, with fringes of foliage hanging down from the roof, were restful to the eye as a white cabin wall never could have been, and, despite the fact that the bamboo wall on the starboard side was open for one third of its length and roof and walls let in sun and moon, this primitive lair gave us a greater feeling of security than white-painted bulkheads and closed portholes would have given in the same circumstances.

We tried to find an explanation for this curious fact and came to the following conclusion. Our consciousness was totally unaccustomed to associating a palm-covered bamboo dwelling with sea travel. There was no natural harmony between the great rolling ocean and the drafty palm hut which was floating about among the seas. Therefore, either the hut would seem entirely out of place in among the waves, or the waves would seem entirely out of place round the hut wall. So long as we kept on board, the bamboo hut and its jungle scent were plain reality, and the tossing seas seemed rather visionary. But from the rubber boat, waves and hut exchanged roles.

The fact that the balsa logs always rode the seas like a gull, and let the water right through aft if a wave broke on board, gave us an unshakable confidence in the dry part in the middle of the raft where the cabin was. The longer the voyage lasted, the safer we felt in our cozy lair, and we looked at the white-crested waves that danced past outside our doorway as if they were an impressive movie, conveying no menace to us at all. Even though the gaping wall was only five feet from the un-protected edge of the raft and only a foot and a half above the water line, yet we felt as if we had traveled many miles away from the sea and occupied a jungle dwelling remote from the sea's perils once we had crawled inside the door. There we could lie on our backs and look up at the curious roof which twisted about like boughs in the wind, enjoying the jungle smell of raw wood, bamboos, and withered palm leaves.

Sometimes, too, we went out in the rubber boat to look at ourselves by night. Coal-black seas towered up on all sides,

and a glittering myriad of tropical stars drew a faint reflection
from plankton in the water. The world was simple—stars in
the darkness. Whether it was 1947 B.C. or A.D. suddenly became of no significance. We lived, and that we felt with alert
intensity. We realized that life had been full for men before
the technical age also—in fact, fuller and richer in many ways
than the life of modern man. Time and evolution somehow
ceased to exist; all that was real and that mattered were the
same today as they had always been and would always be. We
were swallowed up in the absolute common measure of history—endless unbroken darkness under a swarm of stars.

Before us in the night the *Kon-Tiki* rose out of the seas to
sink down again behind black masses of water that towered
between her and us. In the moonlight there was a fantastic
atmosphere about the raft. Stout, shining wooden logs fringed
with seaweed, the square pitch-black outline of a Viking
sail, a bristly bamboo hut with the yellow light of a paraffin
lamp aft—the whole suggested a picture from a fairytale rather
than an actual reality. Now and then the raft disappeared
completely behind the black seas; then she rose again and
stood out sharp in silhouette against the stars, while glittering
water poured from the logs.

When we saw the atmosphere about the solitary raft, we
could well see in our mind's eye the whole flotilla of such
vessels, spread in fan formation beyond the horizon to increase the chances of finding land, when the first men made
their way across this sea. The Inca Tupak Yupanqui, who
had brought under his rule both Peru and Ecuador, sailed
across the sea with an armada of many thousand men
on balsa rafts, just before the Spaniards came, to search
for islands which rumor had told of out in the Pacific. He
found two islands, which some think were the Galapagos,
and after eight months' absence he and his numerous paddlers
succeeded in toiling their way back to Ecuador. Kon-Tiki
and his followers had certainly sailed in a similar formation
several hundred years before but, having discovered the
Polynesian islands, they had no reason for trying to struggle
back.

When we jumped on board the raft again, we often sat

down in a circle round the paraffin lamp on the bamboo deck and talked of the seafarers from Peru who had had all these same experiences fifteen hundred years before us. The lamp flung huge shadows of bearded men on the sail, and we thought of the white men with the beards from Peru whom we could follow in mythology and architecture all the way from Mexico to Central America and into the northwestern area of South America as far as Peru. Here this mysterious civilization disappeared, as by the stroke of a magic wand, before the coming of the Incas and reappeared just as suddenly out on the solitary islands in the west which we were now approaching. Were the wandering teachers men of an early civilized race from across the Atlantic, who in times long past, in the same simple manner, had come over with the westerly ocean current and the trade wind from the area of the Canary Islands to the Gulf of Mexico? That was indeed a far shorter distance than the one we were covering, and we no longer believed in the sea as a completely isolating factor.

Many observers have maintained, for weighty reasons, that the great Indian civilizations, from the Aztecs in Mexico to the Incas in Peru, were inspired by sporadic intruders from over the seas in the east, while all the American Indians in general are Asiatic hunting and fishing peoples who in the course of twenty thousand years or more trickled into America from Siberia. It is certainly striking that there is not a trace of gradual development in the high civilizations which once stretched from Mexico to Peru. The deeper the archaeologists dig, the higher the culture, until a definite point is reached at which the old civilizations have clearly arisen without any foundation in the midst of primitive cultures.

And the civilizations have arisen where the current comes in from the Atlantic, in the midst of the desert and jungle regions of Central and South America, instead of in the more temperate regions where civilizations, in both old and modern times, have had easier conditions for their development.

The same cultural distribution is seen in the South Sea islands. It is the island nearest to Peru, Easter Island, which bears the deepest traces of civilization, although the insignificant little island is dry and barren and is the farthest from Asia of all the islands in the Pacific.

When we had completed half our voyage, we had sailed just the distance from Peru to Easter Island and had the legendary island due south of us. We had left land at a chance point in the middle of the coast of Peru to imitate an average raft putting to sea. If we had left the land farther south, nearer Kon-Tiki's ruined city Tiahuanaco, we should have got the same wind but a weaker current, both of which would have carried us in the direction of Easter Island.

When we passed 110° west, we were within the Polynesian ocean area, inasmuch as the Polynesian Easter Island was now nearer Peru than we were. We were on a line with the first outpost of the South Sea islands, the center of the oldest island civilization. And when at night our glowing road guide, the sun, climbed down from the sky and disappeared beyond the sea in the west with his whole spectrum of colors, the gentle trade wind blew life into the stories of the strange mystery of Easter Island. While the night sky smothered all concept of time, we sat and talked and bearded giants' heads were again thrown upon the sail.

But far down south, on Easter Island, stood yet larger giants' heads cut in stone, with bearded chins and white men's features, brooding over the secret of centuries.

Thus they stood when the first Europeans discovered the island in 1722, and thus they had stood twenty-two Polynesian generations earlier, when, according to native tradition, the present inhabitants landed in great canoes and exterminated all men among an earlier population found on the island. The primitive newcomers had arrived from the islands farther west, but the Easter Island traditions claim that the earliest inhabitants, and the true discovers of the island, had come from a distant land *toward the rising sun*. There is no land in this direction but South America. With the early extermination of the unknown local architects the giant stone heads on Easter Island have become one of the foremost symbols of the insoluble mysteries of antiquity. Here and there on the slopes of the treeless island their huge figures have risen to the sky, stone colossi splendidly carved in the shape of men and set up as a single block as high as a normal building of three or four floors. How had the men of old been able to shape, transport, and erect such gigantic stone colossi? As if the problem was not big enough, they had further succeeded in balancing an extra giant block of red stone like a colossal wig on the top of several of the heads, thirty-six feet above the ground. What did it all mean, and what kind of mechanical knowledge had the vanished architects who had mastered problems great enough for the foremost engineers of today?

If we put all the pieces together, the mystery of Easter Island is perhaps not insoluble after all, seen against a background of raftsmen from Peru. The old civilization has left on this island traces which the tooth of time has not been able to destroy.

Easter Island is the top of an ancient extinct volcano. Paved roads laid down by the old civilized inhabitants lead to well-preserved landing places on the coast and show that the water level round the island was exactly the same then as it is today. This is no remains of a sunken continent but a tiny desolate island, which was as small and solitary when it was a vivid cultural center as it is today.

In the eastern corner of this wedge-shaped island lies one of the extinct craters of the Easter Island volcano, and down in the crater lies the sculptors' amazing quarry and workshop. It lies there exactly as the old artists and architects left it hundreds of years ago, when they fled in haste to the eastern extremity of the island where, according to tradition, there was a furious battle which made the present Polynesians victors and rulers of the island, whereas all grown men among the aboriginals were slain and burned in a ditch. The sudden interruption of the artists' work gives a clear cross section of an ordinary working day in the Easter Island crater. The sculptors' stone axes, hard as flint, lie strewn about their working places and show that this advanced people was as ignorant of iron as Kon-Tiki's sculptors were when they were driven in flight from Peru, leaving behind them similar gigantic stone statues on the Andes plateau. In both places the quarry can be found where the legendary white people with beards hewed blocks of stone thirty feet long or more right out of the mountainside with the help of axes of still harder stone. And in both places the gigantic blocks, weighing many tons, were transported for many miles over rough ground before being set up on end as enormous human figures, or raised on top of one another to form mysterious terraces and walls.

Many huge unfinished figures still lie where they were begun, in their niches in the crater wall on Easter Island, and show how the work was carried on in different stages. The largest human figure, which was almost completed when the builders had to flee, was sixty-six feet long; if it had been finished and set up, the head of this stone colossus would have been level with the top of an eight-floor building. Every separate figure was hewn out of a single connected block of stone, and the working niches for sculptors round the lying stone figures show that not many men were at work at the same time on each figure. Lying on their backs with their arms bent and their hands placed on their stomachs, exactly like the stone colossi in South America, the Easter Island figures were completed in every minute detail before they were removed from the workshop and transported to their destinations round about on the island. In the last stage inside the quarry the giant was attached to the cliff side by only a narrow ridge under his back; then this too was hewn away, the giant meanwhile being supported by boulders.

Large quantities of these figures were just dragged down to the bottom of the crater and set up on the slope there. But a number of the largest colossi were transported up and over the wall of the crater, and for many miles round over difficult country, before being set up on a stone platform and having an extra stone colossus of red tuff placed on their heads. This transport in itself may appear to be a complete mystery, but we cannot deny that it took place or that the architects who disappeared from Peru left in the Andes Mountains stone colossi of equal size, which show that they were absolute experts in this line. Even if the monoliths are largest and most numerous on Easter Island, and the sculptors there had acquired an individual style, the same vanished civilization erected similar giant statues in human shape on many of the other Pacific islands, but only on those nearest to America, and everywhere the monoliths were brought to their final site from out-of-the-way quarries. In the Marquesas, I heard legends of how the gigantic stones were maneuvered, and, as these corresponded exactly to the natives' stories of the transport of the stone pillars to the huge portal on Tongatabu, it can be assumed that the same people employed the same method with the columns on Easter Island.

The sculptors' work in the pit took a long time but required only a few experts. The work of transport each time a statue was completed was more quickly done but, on the other hand, required large numbers of men. Little Easter Island was then both rich in fish and thoroughly cultivated, with large plantations of Peruvian sweet potatoes, and experts believe that the island in its great days could have supported a population of seven or eight thousand. About a thousand men were quite enough to haul the huge statues up and over the steep crater wall, while five hundred were sufficient to drag them on further across the island.

Wearproof cables were plaited from bast and vegetable fibers, and, using wooden frames, the multitude dragged the stone colossus over logs and small boulders made slippery with taro roots. That old civilized peoples were masters in making ropes and cables is well known from the South Sea islands and still more from Peru, where the first Europeans found suspension bridges a hundred yards long laid across torrents and gorges by means of plaited cables as thick as a man's waist.

When the stone colossus had arrived at its chosen site and was to be set up on end, the next problem arose. The crowd built a temporary inclined plane of stone and sand and pulled the giant up the less steep side, legs first. When the statue reached the top, it shot over a sharp edge and slid straight down so that the footpiece landed in a ready-dug hole. As the complete inclined plane still stood there, rubbing against the back of the giant's head, they rolled up an extra cylinder of stone and placed it on the top of his head; then the whole temporary plane was removed. Ready-built inclined planes like this stand in several places on Easter Island, waiting for huge figures which have never come. The technique was admirable but in no way mysterious if we cease to underestimate the intelligence of men in ancient times and the amount of time and manpower which they had at their command.

But why did they make these statues? And why was it necessary to go off to another quarry four miles away from the crater workshop to find a special kind of red stone to place on the figure's head? Both in South America and in the Marquesas Islands the whole statue was often of this red stone, and the natives went great distances to get it. Red headdresses for persons of high rank were an important feature both in Polynesia and in Peru.

Let us see first whom the statues represented. When the first Europeans visited the island, they saw mysterious "white men" on shore and, in contrast to what is usual among peoples of this kind, they found men with long flowing beards, the descendants of women and children belonging to the first race on the island, who had been spared by the invaders. The natives themselves declared that some of their ancestors had been white, while others had been brown. They calculated precisely that the last-named had immigrated from elsewhere in Polynesia twenty-two generations before, while the first had come from eastward in large vessels as much as fifty-seven generations back (*i.e.*, *ca.* 400–500 A.D.). The race which came from the east were given the name "long-ears," because they lengthened their ears artificially by hanging weights on the lobes so that they hung down to their shoulders. These were the mysterious "long-ears" who were killed when the "short-ears" came to the island, and all the stone figures on Easter Island had large ears hanging down to their shoulders, as the sculptors themselves had had.

Now the Inca legends in Peru say that the sun-king Kon-Tiki ruled over a white people with beards who were called by the Incas "big-ears," because they had their ears artificially lengthened so that they reached down to their shoulders. The Incas emphasized that it was Kon-Tiki's "big-ears" who had erected the abandoned giant statues in the Andes Mountains before they were exterminated or driven out by the Incas themselves in the battle on an island in Lake Titicaca.

To sum up: Kon-Tiki's white "big-ears" disappeared from Peru westward with ample experience of working on colossal stone statues, and Tiki's white "long-ears" came to Easter Island from eastward skilled in exactly the same art, which they at once took up in full perfection so that not the smallest trace can be found on Easter Island of any development leading up to the masterpieces on the island.

There is often a greater resemblance between the great stone statues in South America and those on certain South Sea islands than there is between the monoliths on the different South Sea islands compared with one another. In the Marquesas Islands and Tahiti such statues were known under the generic name *Tiki*, and they represented ancestors honored in the islands' history who, after their death, had been ranked as gods. And therein undoubtedly may be found the explanation of the curious red stone caps on the Easter Island figures. At the time of the European explorations there existed on all the islands in Polynesia scattered individuals and whole families with reddish hair and fair skins, and the islanders themselves declared that it was these who were descended from the first white people on the islands. On certain islands religious festivals were held, the participators in which colored their skins white and their hair red to resemble their earliest ancestors. At annual ceremonies on Easter Island the chief person of the festival had all his hair cut off so that his head might be painted red. And the colossal red-stone caps on the giant statues on Easter Island were carved in the shape which was typical of the local hair style; they had a round knot on the top, just as the men had their hair tied in a little traditional topknot in the middle of the head.

The statues on Easter Island had long ears because the sculptors themselves had lengthened ears. They had specially chosen red stones as wigs because the sculptors themselves had reddish hair. They had their chins carved pointed and projecting, because the sculptors themselves grew beards. They had the typical physiognomy of the white race with a straight and narrow nose and thin sharp lips, because the sculptors themselves did not belong to the Indonesian race. And when the statues had huge heads and tiny legs, with their hands laid in position on their stomachs, it was because it was just in this way the people were accustomed to make giant statues in South America. The sole decoration of the Easter Island figures is a belt which was always carved round the figure's stomach. The same symbolic belt is found on every single statue in Kon-Tiki's ancient ruins by Lake Titicaca. It is the legendary emblem of the sun-god, the rainbow belt. There was a myth on the island of Mangareva according to which the sun-god had taken off the rainbow which was his magic belt and climbed down it from the sky on to Mangareva to people the island with his white-skinned children. The sun was once regarded as the oldest original ancestor in all these islands, as well as in Peru.

We used to sit on deck under the starry sky and retell Easter Island's strange history, even though our own raft was carrying us straight into the heart of Polynesia so that we should see nothing of that remote island but its name on the map. But so full is Easter Island of traces from the east that even its name can serve as a pointer.

"Easter Island" appears on the map because some chance Dutchman "discovered" the island one Easter Sunday. And we have forgotten that the natives themselves, who already lived there, had more instructive and significant names for their home. This island has no less than three names in Polynesian.

One name is *Te-Pito-te-Henua*, which means "navel of the islands." This poetical name clearly places Easter Island in a special position in regard to the other islands farther westward and is the oldest designation for Easter Island according to the Polynesians themselves. On the eastern side of the island, near the traditional landing place of the first "long-ears," is a carefully tooled sphere of stone which is called the "golden navel" and is in turn regarded as the navel of Easter Island itself. When the poetical Polynesian ancestors carved the island navel on the east coast and selected the island nearest Peru as the navel of their myriad islands further west, it had a symbolic meaning. And when we know that Polynesian tradition refers to the discovery of their islands as the "birth" of their islands, then it is more than suggested that Easter Island of all places was considered the "navel," symbolic of the islands' birthmark and as the connecting link with their original motherland.

Easter Island's second name is Rapa Nui which means "Great Rapa," while Rapa Iti or "Little Rapa" is another island of the same size which lies a very long way west of Easter Island. Now it is the natural practice of all peoples to call their first home "Great——" while the next is called "New ——" or "Little——" even if the places are of the same size. And on Little Rapa the natives have quite correctly maintained traditions that the first inhabitants of the island came from Great Rapa, Easter Island, to the eastward, nearest to America. This points directly to an original immigration from the east.

The third and last name of this key island is *Mata-Kite-Rani*, which means "the eye (which) looks (toward) heaven." At first glance this is puzzling, for the relatively low Easter Island does not look toward heaven any more than the other loftier islands—for example, Tahiti, the Marquesas, or Hawaii. But *Rani*, heaven, had a double meaning to the Polynesians. It was also their ancestors' original homeland, the holy land of the sun-god, Tiki's forsaken mountain kingdom. And it is very significant that they should have called just their easternmost island, of all the thousands of islands in the ocean, "the eye which looks toward heaven." It is all the more striking seeing that the kindred name *Mata-Rani*, which means in Polynesian "the eye of heaven," is an old Peruvian place name, that of a spot on the Pacific coast of Peru opposite Easter Island and right at the foot of Kon-Tiki's old ruined city in the Andes.

The fascination of Easter Island provided us with plenty of subjects of conversation as we sat on deck under the starry sky, feeling ourselves to be participators in the whole prehistoric adventure. We almost felt as if we had done nothing else since Tiki's days but sail about the seas under sun and stars searching for land.

We no longer had the same respect for waves and sea. We

knew them and their relationship to us on the raft. Even the shark had become a part of the everyday picture; we knew it and its usual reactions. We no longer thought of the hand harpoon, and we did not even move away from the side of the raft, if a shark came up alongside. On the contrary, we were more likely to try and grasp its back fin as it glided unperturbed along the logs. This finally developed into a quite new form of sport—tug of war with shark without a line.

We began quite modestly. We caught all too easily more dolphins than we could eat. To keep a popular form of amusement going without wasting food, we hit on comic fishing without a hook for the mutual entertainment of the dolphins and ourselves. We fastened unused flying fish to a string and drew them over the surface of the water. The dolphins shot up to the surface and seized the fish, and then we tugged, each in our own direction, and had a fine circus performance, for if one dolphin let go another came in its place. We had fun, and the dolphins got the fish in the end.

Then we started the same game with the sharks. We had either a bit of fish on the end of a rope or often a bag with scraps from dinner, which we let out on a line. Instead of turning on its back, the shark pushed its snout above the water and swam forward with jaws wide to swallow the morsel. We could not help pulling on the rope just as the shark was going to close its jaws again, and the cheated animal swam on with an unspeakably foolish, patient expression and opened its jaws again for the offal, which jumped out of its mouth every time it tried to swallow it. It ended by the shark's coming right up to the logs and jumping up like a begging dog for the food which hung dangling in a bag above its nose. It was just like feeding a gaping hippopotamus in a zoological gardens, and one day at the end of July, after three months on board the raft, the following entry was made in the diary:

—*We made friends with the shark which followed us today. At dinner we fed it with scraps which we poured right down into its open jaws. It has the effect of a half fierce, half good-natured and friendly dog when it swims alongside us. It cannot be denied that sharks can seem quite pleasant so long as we do not get into their jaws ourselves. At least we find it amusing to have them about us, except when we are bathing.*

One day a bamboo stick, with a bag of sharks' food tied to a string, was lying ready for use on the edge of the raft when a sea came and washed it overboard. The bamboo stick was already lying afloat a couple of hundred yards astern of the raft, when it suddenly rose upright in the water and came rushing after the raft by itself, as if it intended to put itself nicely back in its place again. When the fishing rod came swaying nearer us, we saw a ten-foot shark swimming right under it, while the bamboo stick stuck up out of the waves like a periscope. The shark had swallowed the food bag without biting off the line. The fishing rod soon overtook us, passed us quite quietly, and vanished ahead.

But, even if we gradually came to look upon the shark with quite other eyes, our respect for the five or six rows of razor-sharp teeth which lay in ambush in the huge jaws never disapppeared.

One day Knut had an involuntary swim in company with a shark. No one was ever allowed to swim away from the raft, both on account of the raft's drift and because of sharks. But one day it was extra quiet and we had just pulled on board such sharks as had been following us, so permission was given for a quick dip in the sea. Knut plunged in and had gone quite a long way before he came up to the surface to crawl back. At that moment we saw from the mast a shadow bigger than himself coming up behind him, deeper down. We shouted warnings as quietly as we could so as not to create a panic, and Knut heaved himself toward the side of the raft. But the shadow below belonged to a still better swimmer, which shot up from the depths and gained on Knut. They reached the raft at the same time. While Knut was clambering on board, a six-foot shark glided past right under his stomach and stopped beside the raft. We gave it a dainty dolphin's head to thank it for not having snapped.

Generally it is smell more than sight which excites the sharks' voracity. We have sat with our legs in the water to test them, and they have swum toward us till they were two or three feet away, only quietly to turn their tails toward us again. But, if the water was in the least bloodstained, as it was when we had been cleaning fish, the sharks' fins came to life and they would suddenly collect like bluebottles from a long way off. If we flung out shark's guts, they simply went mad and dashed about in a blind frenzy. They savagely devoured the liver of their own kind and then, if we put a foot into the sea, they came for it like rockets and even dug their teeth into the logs where the foot had been. The mood of a shark may vary immensely, the animal being completely at the mercy of its own emotions.

The last stage in our encounter with sharks was that we began to pull their tails. Pulling animals' tails is held to be an inferior form of sport, but that may be because no one has tried it on a shark. For it was, in truth, a lively form of sport.

To get hold of a shark by the tail we first had to give it a real tidbit. It was ready to stick its head high out of the water to get it. Usually it had its food served dangling in a bag. For, if one has fed a shark directly by hand once, it is no longer amusing. If one feeds dogs or tame bears by hand, they set their teeth into the meat and tear and worry it till they get a bit off or until they get the whole piece for themselves. But, if one holds out a large dolphin at a safe distance from the shark's head, the shark comes up and smacks his jaws together, and, without one's having felt the slightest tug, half the dolphin is suddenly gone and one is left sitting with a tail in one's hand. We had found it a hard job to cut the dolphin in two with knives, but in a fraction of a second the shark, moving its triangular saw teeth quickly sideways, had chopped off the backbone and everything else like a sausage machine.

When the shark turned quietly to go under again, its tail flickered up above the surface and was easy to grasp. The shark's skin was just like sandpaper to hold on to, and inside the upper point of its tail there was an indentation which might have been made solely to allow of a good grip. If we once got a firm grasp there, there was no chance of our grip's not holding. Then we had to give a jerk, before the shark could collect itself, and get as much as possible of the tail pulled in tight over the logs. For a second or two the shark realized nothing, but then it began to wriggle and struggle in a spiritless manner with the fore part of its body, for without the help of its tail a shark cannot get up any speed. The other fins are only apparatus for balancing and steering. After a few desperate jerks, during which we had to keep a tight hold of the tail, the surprised shark became quite crestfallen and apathetic, and, as the loose stomach began to sink down toward the head, the shark at last became completely paralyzed.

When the shark had become quiet and, as it were, hung stiff awaiting developments, it was time for us to haul in with all our might. We seldom got more than the half the heavy fish up out of the water; then the shark too woke up and did the rest itself. With violent jerks it swung its head round and up on to the logs, and then we had to tug with all our might and jump well out of the way, and that pretty quickly, if we wanted to save our legs. For now the shark was in no kindly mood. Jerking itself round in great leaps, it thrashed at the bamboo wall, using its tail as a sledge hammer. Now it no longer spared its iron muscles. The huge jaws were opened wide, and the rows of teeth bit and snapped in the air for anything they could reach. It might happen that the war dance ended in the shark's more or less involuntarily tumbling overboard and disappearing for good after its shameful humiliation, but most often the shark flung itself about at random on the logs aft, till we got a running noose round the root of its tail or till it had ceased to gnash its devilish teeth forever.

The parrot was quite thrilled when we had a shark on deck. It came scurrying out of the bamboo cabin and climbed up the wall at frantic speed till it found itself a good, safe lookout post on the palm-leaf roof, and there it sat shaking its head or fluttered to and fro along the ridge, shrieking with excitement. It had at an early date become an excellent sailor and was always bubbling over with humor and laughter. We reckoned ourselves as seven on board—six of us and the green parrot. The crab Johannes had, after all, to reconcile itself to being regarded as a cold-blooded appendage. At night the parrot crept into its cage under the roof of the bamboo cabin,

but in the daytime it strutted about the deck or hung on to
guy ropes and stays and did the most fascinating acrobatic
exercises.

At the start of the voyage we had turnbuckles on the stays
of the mast but they wore the ropes, so we replaced them
by ordinary running knots. When the stays stretched and
grew slack from sun and wind, all hands had to turn to and
brace up the mast, so that its mangrove wood, as heavy as
iron, should not bump against and cut into the ropes till they
fell down. While we were hauling and pulling, at the most
critical moment the parrot began to call out with its cracked
voice: "Haul! Haul! Ho, ho, ho, ho, ha ha ha!" And if it
made us laugh, it laughed till it shook at its own cleverness
and swung round and round on the stays.

At first the parrot was the bane of our radio operators. They
might be sitting happily absorbed in the radio corner with
their magic earphones on and perhaps in contact with a radio
"ham" in Oklahoma. Then their earphones would suddenly
go dead, and they could not get a sound however much they
coaxed the wires and turned the knobs. The parrot had been
busy and bitten off the wire of the aerial. This was specially
tempting in the early days, when the wire was sent up with
a little balloon. But one day the parrot became seriously ill.
It sat in its cage and moped and touched no food for two
days, while its droppings glittered with golden scraps of
aerial. Then the radio operators repented of their angry words
and the parrot of its misdeeds, and from that day Torstein
and Knut were its chosen friends and the parrot would never
sleep anywhere but in the radio corner. The parrot's mother
tongue was Spanish when it first came on board; Bengt declared it took to talking Spanish with a Norwegian accent
long before it began to imitate Torstein's favorite ejaculations
in full-blooded Norwegian.

We enjoyed the parrot's humor and brilliant colors for two
months, till a big sea came on board from astern while it was
on its way down the stay from the masthead. When we discovered that the parrot had gone overboard, it was too late.
We did not see it. And the Kon-Tiki could not be turned
or stopped; if anything went overboard from the raft, we

had no chance of turning back for it—numerous experiences had shown that.

The loss of the parrot had a depressing effect on our spirits the first evening; we knew that exactly the same thing would happen to ourselves if we fell overboard on a solitary night watch. We tightened up on all the safety regulations, brought into use new life lines for the night watch, and frightened one another out of believing that we were safe because things had gone well in the first two months. One careless step, one thoughtless movement, could send us where the green parrot had gone, even in broad daylight.

We had several times observed the large white shells of cuttlefish eggs, lying floating like ostrich eggs or white skulls on the blue swell. On one solitary occasion we saw a squid lying wriggling underneath. We observed the snow-white balls floating on a level with ourselves and thought at first that it would be an easy matter to row out in the dinghy and get them. We thought the same that time when the rope of the plankton net broke so that the cloth net was left behind alone, floating in our wake. Each time we launched the dinghy, with a rope attached, to row back and pick up the floating object. But we saw to our surprise that the wind and sea held the dinghy off and that the line from the *Kon-Tiki* had so violent a braking effect in the water that we could never row right back to a point we had already left. We might get within a few yards of what we wanted to pick up, but then the whole line was out and the *Kon-Tiki* was pulling us away westward. "Once overboard always overboard" was a lesson that was gradually branded into our consciousness on board. If we wanted to go with the rest, we must hang on till the *Kon-Tiki* ran her bow against land on the other side.

The parrot left a blank in the radio corner, but, when the tropical sun shone out over the Pacific next day, we soon became reconciled to his loss. We hauled in many sharks the next few days, and we constantly found black curved parrots' beaks, or so we thought, among tunnies' heads and other curiosities in the shark's belly. But on closer examination the black beaks always proved to belong to assimilated cuttlefish.

The two radio operators had had a tough job in their corner since the first day they came on board. The very first day, in the Humboldt Current, sea water trickled even from the battery cases so that they had to cover the sensitive radio corner with canvas to save what could be saved in the high seas. And then they had the problem of fitting a long enough aerial on the little raft. They tried to send the aerial up with a kite, but in a gust of wind the kite simply plunged down into a wave crest and disappeared. Then they tried to send it up with a balloon, but the tropical sun burned holes in the balloon so that it collapsed and sank into the sea. And then they had the trouble with the parrot. In addition to all this, we were a fortnight in the Humboldt Current before we came out of a dead zone of the Andes in which the short wave was as dumb and lifeless as the air in an empty soapbox.

But then one night the short wave suddenly broke through, and Torstein's call signal was heard by a chance radio amateur in Los Angeles who was sitting fiddling with his transmitter to establish contact with another amateur in Sweden. The man asked what kind of set we had and, when he got a satisfactory answer to his question, he asked Torstein who he was and where he lived. When he heard that Torstein's abode was a bamboo cabin on a raft in the Pacific, there were several peculiar clickings until Torstein supplied more details. When the man on the air had pulled himself together, he told us that his name was Hal and his wife's name Anna and that she was Swedish by birth and would let our families know we were alive and well.

It was a strange thought for us that evening that a total stranger called Hal, a chance moving-picture operator far away among the swarming population of Los Angeles, was the only person in the world but ourselves who knew where we were and that we were well. From that night onward Hal, alias Harold Kempel, and his friend Frank Cuevas took it in turns to sit up every night and listen for signals from the raft, and Herman received grateful telegrams from the head of the U.S. Weather Bureau for his two daily code reports from an area for which there were extremely few reports and no statistics. Later Knut and Torstein established contact with other radio amateurs almost every night, and these passed on greetings to Norway through a radio "ham" named Egil Berg at Notodden.

When we were just a few days out in mid-ocean, there was too much salt water for the radio corner, and the station stopped working altogether. The operators stood on their heads day and night with screws and soldering irons, and all our distant radio fans thought the raft's days were ended. But then one night the signals LI 2 B burst out into the ether, and in a moment the radio corner was buzzing like a wasp's nest as several hundred American operators seized their keys simultaneously and replied to the call.

Indeed one always felt as if one were sitting down on a wasp's nest if one strayed into the radio operators' domain. It was damp with sea water, which forced its way up along the woodwork everywhere, and, even if there was a piece of raw rubber on the balsa log where the operator sat, one got electric shocks both in the hinder parts and in the finger tips if one touched the Morse key. And, if one of us outsiders tried to steal a pencil from the well-equipped corner, either his hair stood straight up on his head or he drew long sparks from the stump of the pencil. Only Torstein and Knut and the parrot could wriggle their way about in that corner unscathed, and we put up a sheet of cardboard to mark the danger zone for the rest of us.

Late one night Knut was sitting tinkering by lamplight in the radio corner when he suddenly shook me by the leg and said he had been talking to a fellow who lived just outside Oslo and was called Christian Amundsen. This was a bit of an amateur record, for the little short-wave transmitter on board the raft with its 13,990 kilocycles per second did not send out more than 6 watts, about the same strength as a small electric torch. This was August 2, and we had sailed more than sixty degrees round the earth, so that Oslo was at the opposite end of the globe. King Haakon was seventy-five years old the day after, and we sent him a message of congratulations direct from the raft; the day after that Christian was again audible and sent us a reply from the

King, wishing us continued good luck and success on our voyage.

Another episode we remember as an unusual contrast to the rest of the life on the raft. We had two cameras on board, and Erik had with him a parcel of materials for developing photographs on the voyage, so that we could take duplicate snapshots of things that had not come out well. After the whale shark's visit he could contain himself no longer, and one evening he mixed the chemicals and water carefully in exact accordance with the instructions and developed two films. The negatives looked like long-distance photographs— nothing but obscure spots and wrinkles. The film was ruined. We telegraphed to our contacts for advice, but our message was picked up by a radio amateur near Hollywood. He telephoned a laboratory and soon afterward he broke in and told us that our developer was too warm; we must not use water above 60° or the negative would be wrinkled.

We thanked him for his advice and ascertained that the very lowest temperature in our surroundings was that of the ocean current itself, which was nearly 80°. Now Herman was a refrigerating engineer, and I told him by way of a joke to get the temperature of the water down to 60°. He asked to have the use of the little bottle of carbonic acid belonging to the already inflated rubber dinghy, and after some hocuspocus in a kettle covered with a sleeping bag and a woolen vest suddenly there was snow on Herman's stubby beard, and he came in with a big lump of white ice in the kettle.

Erik developed afresh with splendid results.

Even though the ghost words carried through the air by short wave were an unknown luxury in Kon-Tiki's early days, the long ocean waves beneath us were the same as of old and they carried the balsa raft steadily westward as they did then, fifteen hundred years ago.

The weather became a little more unsettled, with scattered rain squalls, after we had entered the area nearer the South Sea islands and the trade wind had changed its direction. It had blown steadily and surely from the southeast until we were a good way over in the Equatorial Current; then it had veered round more and more toward due east. We reached our most northerly position on June 10 with latitude 6° 19′ south. We were then so close up to the Equator that it looked as if we should sail above even the most northerly islands of the Marquesas group and disappear completely in the sea without finding land. But then the trade wind swung round farther, from east to northeast, and drove us in a curve down toward the latitude of the world of islands.

It often happened that wind and sea remained unchanged for days on end, and then we clean forgot whose steering watch it was except at night, when the watch was alone on deck. For, if sea and wind were steady, the steering oar was lashed fast and the Kon-Tiki sail remained filled without our attending to it. Then the night watch could sit quietly in the cabin door and look at the stars. If the constellations changed their position in the sky, it was time for him to go out and see whether it was the steering oar or the wind that had shifted.

It was incredible how easy it was to steer by the stars when we had seen them marching across the vault of the sky for weeks on end. Indeed, there was not much else to look at at night. We knew where we could expect to see the different constellations night after night, and, when we came up toward the Equator, the Great Bear rose so clear of the horizon in the north that we were anxious lest we should catch a glimpse of the Pole Star, which appears when one comes from southward and crosses the Equator. But as the northeasterly trade wind set in, the Great Bear sank again.

The old Polynesians were great navigators. They took bearings by the sun by day and the stars by night. Their knowledge of the heavenly bodies was astonishing. They knew that the earth was round, and they had names for such abstruse conceptions as the Equator and the northern and southern tropics. In Hawaii they cut charts of the ocean on the shells of round bottle gourds, and on certain other islands they made detailed maps of plaited boughs to which shells were attached to mark the islands, while the twigs marked particular currents. The Polynesians knew five planets, which they called wandering stars, and distinguished them from the fixed stars, for which they had nearly two hundred dif-

ferent names. A good navigator in old Polynesia knew well
in what part of the sky the different stars would rise and
where they would be at different times of the night and at
different times of the year. They knew which stars culminated over the different islands, and there were cases in which
an island was named after a star which culminated over it
night after night and year after year.

Apart from the fact that the starry sky lay like a glittering
giant compass revolving from east to west, they understood
that the different stars right over their heads always showed
them how far north or south they were. When the Polynesians
had explored and brought under their sway their present domain, which is the whole of the sea nearest to America, they
maintained traffic between some of the islands for many generations to come. Historical traditons relate that, when the
chiefs from Tahiti visited Hawaii, which lay more than 2,000
sea miles farther north and several degrees farther west, the
helmsman steered first due north by sun and stars, till the
stars right above their heads told them that they were on the
latitude of Hawaii. Then they turned at a right angle and
steered due west till they came so near that birds and clouds
told them where the group of islands lay.

Whence had the Polynesians obtained their vast astronomical knowledge and their calendar, which was calculated with
astonishing thoroughness? Certainly not from Melanesian or
Malayan peoples to the westward. But the same old vanished
civilized race, the "white and bearded men," who had taught
Aztecs, Mayas, and Incas their amazing culture in America,
had evolved a curiously similar calendar and a similar astronomical knowledge which Europe in those times could not
match. In Polynesia, as in Peru, the calendar year had been
so arranged as to begin on the particular day of the year
when the constellation of the Pleiades first appeared above
the horizon, and in both areas this constellation was considered the patron of agriculture.

In Peru, where the continent slopes down toward the
Pacific, there stand to this day in the desert sand the ruins
of an astronomical observatory of great antiquity, a relic of
the same mysterious civilized people which carved stone

colossi, erected pyramids, cultivated sweet potatoes and bottle gourds, and began their year with the rising of the Pleiades. Kon-Tiki knew the movement of the stars when he set sail upon the Pacific Ocean.

On July 2 our night watch could no longer sit in peace studying the night sky. We had a strong wind and nasty sea after several days of light northeasterly breeze. Late in the night we had brilliant moonlight and a quite fresh sailing wind. We measured our speed by counting the seconds we took to pass a chip, flung out ahead on one side of us, and found that we were establishing a speed record. While our average speed was from twelve to eighteen "chips," in the jargon current on board, we were now for a time down to "six chips," and the phosphorescence swirled in a regular wake astern of the raft.

Four men lay snoring in the bamboo cabin while Torstein sat clicking with the Morse key and I was on steering watch. Just before midnight I caught sight of a quite unusual sea which came breaking astern of us right across the whole of my disturbed field of vision. Behind it I could see here and there the foaming crests of two more huge seas like the first, following hard on its heels. If we ourselves had not just passed the place, I should have been convinced that what I saw was high surf flung up over a dangerous shoal. I gave a warning shout, as the first sea came like a long wall sweeping after us in the moonlight, and wrenched the raft into position to take what was coming.

When the first sea reached us, the raft flung her stern up sideways and rose up over the wave back which had just broken, so that it hissed and boiled all along the crest. We rode through the welter of boiling foam which poured along both sides of the raft, while the heavy sea itself rolled by under us. The bow flung itself up last as the wave passed, and we slid, stern first, down into a broad trough of the waves. Immediately after the next wall of water came on and rose up, while we were again lifted hurriedly into the air and the clear water masses broke over us aft as we shot over the edge. As a result the raft was flung right broadside on to the seas, and it was impossible to wrench her round quickly enough.

The next sea came on and rose out of the stripes of foam like a glittering wall which began to fall along its upper edge just as it reached us. When it plunged down, I saw nothing else to do but hang on as tight as I could to a projecting bamboo pole of the cabin roof; there I held my breath while I felt that we were flung sky-high and everything round me carried away in roaring whirlpools of foam. In a second we and the *Kon-Tiki* were above water again and gliding quietly down a gentle wave back on the other side. Then the seas were normal again. The three great wave walls raced on before us, and astern in the moonlight a string of coconuts lay bobbing in the water.

The last wave had given the cabin a violent blow, so that Torstein was flung head over heels into the radio corner and the others woke, scared by the noise, while the water gushed up between the logs and in through the wall. On the port side of the foredeck the bamboo wickerwork was blown open like a small crater, and the diving basket had been knocked flat up in the bow, but everything else was as it had been. Where the three big seas came from, we have never been able to explain with certainty, unless they were due to disturbances on the sea bottom, which are not so uncommon in these regions.

Two days later we had our first storm. It started by the trade wind dying away completely, and the feathery, white trade-wind clouds, which were drifting over our heads up in the topmost blue, being suddenly invaded by a thick black cloud bank which rolled up over the horizon from southward. Then there came gusts of wind from the most unexpected directions, so that it was impossible for the steering watch to keep control. As quickly as we got our stern turned to the new direction of the wind, so that the sail bellied out stiff and safe, just as quickly the gusts came at us from another quarter, squeezed the proud bulge out of the sail, and made it swing round and thrash about to the peril of both crew and cargo. But then the wind suddenly set in to blow straight from the quarter whence the bad weather came, and, as the black clouds rolled over us, the breeze increased to a fresh wind which worked itself up into a real storm.

In the course of an incredibly short time the seas round about us were flung up to a height of fifteen feet, while single crests were hissing twenty and twenty-five feet above the trough of the sea, so that we had them on a level with our masthead when we ourselves were down in the trough. All hands had to scramble about on deck bent double, while the wind shook the bamboo wall and whistled and howled in all the rigging.

To protect the radio corner we stretched canvas over the rear wall and port side of the cabin. All loose cargo was lashed securely, and the sail was hauled down and made fast around the bamboo yard. When the sky clouded over, the sea grew dark and threatening, and in every direction it was white-crested with breaking waves. Long tracks of dead foam lay like stripes to windward down the backs of the long seas; and everywhere, where the wave ridges had broken and plunged down, green patches like wounds lay frothing for a long time in the blue-black sea. The crests blew away as they broke, and the spray stood like salt rain over the sea. When the tropical rain poured over us in horizontal squalls and whipped the surface of the sea, invisible all round us, the water that ran from our hair and beards tasted brackish, while we crawled about the deck naked and frozen, seeing that all the gear was in order to weather the storm.

When the storm rushed up over the horizon and gathered about us for the first time, strained anticipation and anxiety were discernible in our looks. But when it was upon us in earnest, and the *Kon-Tiki* took everything that came her way with ease and buoyancy, the storm became an exciting form of sport, and we all delighted in the fury round about us which the balsa raft mastered so adroitly, always seeing that she herself lay on the wave tops like a cork, while all the main weight of the raging water was always a few inches beneath. The sea had much in common with the mountains in such weather. It was like being out in the wilds in a storm, up on the highest mountain plateaus, naked and gray. Even though we were right in the heart of the tropics, when the raft glided up and down over the smoking waste of sea we always thought of racing downhill among snowdrifts and rock faces.

The steering watch had to keep its eyes open in such weather. When the steepest seas passed under the forward half of the raft, the logs aft rose right out of the water, but the next second they plunged down again to climb up over the next crest. Each time the seas came so close upon one another that the hindmost reached us while the first was still holding the bow in the air. Then the solid sheets of water thundered in over the steering watch in a terrifying welter, but next second the stern went up and the flood disappeared as through the prongs of a fork.

We calculated that in an ordinary calm sea, where there were usually seven seconds between the highest waves, we took in about two hundred tons of water astern in twenty-four hours. But we hardly noticed it because it just flowed in quietly round the bare legs of the steering watch and as quietly disappeared again between the logs. But in a heavy storm more than ten thousand tons of water poured on board astern in the course of twenty-four hours, seeing that loads varying from a few gallons to two or three cubic yards, and occasionally much more, flowed on board every five seconds. It sometimes broke on board with a deafening thunderclap, so that the helmsman stood in water up to his waist and felt as if he were forcing his way against the current in a swift river. The raft seemed to stand trembling for a moment, but then the cruel load that weighed her down astern disappeared overboard again in great cascades.

Herman was out all the time with his anemometer measuring the squalls of gale force, which lasted for twenty-four hours. Then they gradually dropped to a stiff breeze with scattered rain squalls, which continued to keep the seas boiling round us as we tumbled on westward with a good sailing wind. To obtain accurate wind measurements down among the towering seas Herman had, whenever possible, to make his way up to the swaying masthead, where it was all he could do to hold on.

When the weather moderated, it was as though the big fish around us had become completely infuriated. The water round the raft was full of sharks, tunnies, dolphins, and a few dazed bonitos, all wriggling about close under the timber of the raft and in the waves nearest to it. It was a ceaseless life-and-death struggle; the backs of big fishes arched themselves over the water and shot off like rockets, one chasing another in pairs, while the water round the raft was repeatedly tinged with thick blood. The combatants were mainly tunnies and dolphins, and the dolphins came in big shoals which moved much more quickly and alertly than usual. The tunnies were the assailants; often a fish of 150 to 200 pounds would leap high into the air holding a dolphin's bloody head in its mouth. But, even if individual dolphins dashed off with tunnies hard on their heels, the actual shoal of dolphins did not give ground, although there were often several wriggling round with big gaping wounds in their necks. Now and again the sharks, too, seemed to become blind with rage, and we saw them catch and fight with big tunnies, which met in the shark a superior enemy.

Not one single peaceful little pilot fish was to be seen. They had been devoured by the furious tunnies, or they had hidden in the chinks under the raft or fled far away from the battlefield. We dared not put our heads down into the water to see.

I had a nasty shock—and could not help laughing afterward at my own complete bewilderment—when I was aft, obeying a call of nature. We were accustomed to a bit of a swell in the water closet, but it seemed contrary to all reasonable probabilities when I quite unexpectedly received a violent punch astern from something large and cold and very heavy, which came butting up against me like a shark's head in the sea. I was actually on my way up the mast stay, with a feeling that I had a shark hanging on to my hindquarters, before I collected myself. Herman, who was hanging over the steering oar doubled up with laughter, was able to tell me that a huge tunny had delivered a sideways smack at my nakedness with his 160 pounds or so of cold fish. Afterward, when Herman and then Torstein were on watch, the same fish tried to jump on board with the seas from astern, and twice the big fellow was right up on the end of the logs, but each time it flung itself overboard again before we could get a grip of the slippery body.

After that a stout bewildered bonito came right on board with a sea, and with that, and a tunny caught the day before, we decided to fish, to bring order into the sanguinary chaos that surrounded us.

Our diary says:

—*A six-foot shark was hooked first and hauled on board. As soon as the hook was out again, it was swallowed by an eight-foot shark, and we hauled that on board. When the hook came out again, we got a fresh six-foot shark and had hauled it over the edge of the raft when it broke loose and dived. The hook went out again at once, and an eight-foot shark came on to it and gave us a hard tussle. We had its head over the logs when all four steel lines were cut through and the shark dived into the depths. New hook out, and a seven-foot shark was hauled on board. It was now dangerous to stand on the slippery logs aft fishing, because the three sharks kept on throwing up their heads and snapping, long after one would have thought they were dead. We dragged the sharks forward by the tail into a heap on the foredeck, and soon afterward a big tunny was hooked and gave us more of a fight than any shark before we got it on board. It was so fat and heavy that none of us could lift it by the tail.*

The sea was just as full of furious fish backs. Another shark was hooked but broke away just when it was being pulled on board. But then we got a six-foot shark safely on board. After that a five-foot shark, which also came on board. Then we caught yet another six-foot shark and hauled it up. When the hook came out again, we hauled in a seven-foot shark.

Wherever we walked on deck, there were big sharks lying in the way, beating their tails convulsively on the deck or thrashing against the bamboo cabin as they snapped around them. Already tired and worn out when we began to fish after the storm, we became completely befuddled as to which sharks were quite dead, which were still snapping convulsively if we went near them, and which were quite alive and were lying in ambush for us with their green cat's eyes.

When we had nine big sharks lying round us in every direction, we were so weary of hauling on heavy lines and fighting with the twisting and snapping giants that we gave up after five hours' toil.

Next day there were fewer dolphins and tunnies but just as many sharks. We began to fish and haul them in again but soon stopped when we perceived that all the fresh shark's blood that ran off the raft only attracted still more sharks. We threw all the dead sharks overboard and washed the whole deck clean of blood. The bamboo mats were torn by shark teeth and rough sharkskin, and we threw the bloodiest and most torn of them overboard and replaced them with new golden-yellow bamboo mats, several layers of which were lashed fast on the foredeck.

When we turned in on these evenings in our mind's eye we saw greedy, open shark jaws and blood. And the smell of shark meat stuck in our nostrils. We could eat shark—it tasted like haddock if we got the ammoniac out of the pieces by putting them in sea water for twenty-four hours—but bonito and tunny were infinitely better.

That evening, for the first time, I heard one of the fellows say that it would soon be pleasant to be able to stretch oneself out comfortably on the green grass on a palm island; he would be glad to see something other than cold fish and rough sea.

The weather had become quite quiet again, but it was never as constant and dependable as before. Incalculable, violent gusts of wind from time to time brought with them heavy showers, which we were glad to see because a large part of our water supply had begun to go bad and tasted like evil-smelling marsh water. When it was pouring the hardest, we collected water from the cabin roof and stood on deck naked, thoroughly to enjoy the luxury of having the salt washed off with fresh water.

The pilot fish were wriggling along again in their usual places, but whether they were the same old ones which had returned after the blood bath, or whether they were new followers taken over in the heat of the battle, we could not say.

On July 21 the wind suddenly died away again. It was oppressive and absolutely still, and we knew from previous experience what this might mean. And, right enough, after a few violent gusts from east and west and south, the wind freshened up to a breeze from southward, where black, threatening clouds had again rushed up over the horizon. Herman was out with his anemometer all the time, measuring already fifty feet and more per second, when suddenly Torstein's sleeping bag went overboard. And what happened in the next few seconds took a much shorter time than it takes to tell it.

Herman tried to catch the bag as it went, took a rash step, and fell overboard. We heard a faint cry for help amid the noise of the waves, and saw Herman's head and a waving arm as well as some vague green object twirling about in the water near him. He was struggling for life to get back to the raft through the high seas which had lifted him out from the port side. Torstein, who was at the steering oar aft, and I myself, up in the bow, were the first to perceive him, and we went cold with fear. We bellowed "Man overboard!" at the top of our lungs as we rushed to the nearest life-saving gear. The others had not heard Herman's cry because of the noise of the sea, but in a trice there was life and bustle on deck. Herman was an excellent swimmer, and, though we realized at once that his life was at stake, we had a fair hope that he would manage to crawl back to the edge of the raft before it was too late.

Torstein, who was nearest, seized the bamboo drum round which was the line we used for the lifeboat, for this was within his reach. It was the only time on the whole voyage that this line got caught up. Herman was now on a level with the stern of the raft but a few yards away, and his last hope was to crawl to the blade of the steering oar and hang on to it. As he missed the end of the logs, he reached out for the oar blade, but it slipped away from him. And there he lay, just where experience had shown we could get nothing back. While Bengt and I launched the dinghy, Knut and Erik threw out the life belt. Carrying a long line, it hung ready for use on the corner of the cabin roof, but today the wind was so strong that when it was thrown it was simply blown back to the raft. After a few unsuccessful throws Herman was already far astern of the steering oar, swimming desperately to keep up with the raft, while the distance increased with each gust of wind. He realized that henceforth the gap would simply go on increasing, but he set a faint hope on the dinghy which we had now got into the water. Without the line, which acted as a brake, it would perhaps be possible to drive the rubber raft to meet the swimming man, but whether the rubber raft would ever get back to the *Kon-Tiki* was another matter. Nevertheless, three men in a rubber dinghy had some chance; one man in the sea had none.

Then we suddenly saw Knut take off and plunge headfirst into the sea. He had the life belt in one hand and was heaving himself along. Every time Herman's head appeared on a wave back Knut was gone, and every time Knut came up Herman was not there. But then we saw both heads at once; they had swum to meet each other and both were hanging on to the life belt. Knut waved his arm, and, as the rubber raft had meanwhile been hauled on board, all four of us took hold of the line of the life belt and hauled for dear life, with our eyes fixed on the great dark object which was visible just behind the two men. This same mysterious beast in the water was pushing a big greenish-black triangle up above the wave crests; it almost gave Knut a shock when he was on his way over to Herman. Only Herman knew then that the triangle did not belong to a shark or any other sea monster. It was an inflated corner of Torstein's watertight sleeping bag. But the sleeping bag did not remain floating for long after we had hauled the two men safe and sound on board. Whatever dragged the sleeping bag down into the depths had just missed a better prey.

"Glad I wasn't in it," said Torstein and took hold of the steering oar where he had let it go.

But otherwise there were not many wisecracks that evening. We all felt a chill running through nerve and bone for a long time afterward. But the cold shivers were mingled with a warm thankfulness that there were still six of us on board.

We had a lot of nice things to say to Knut that day—Herman and the rest of us, too.

But there was not much time to think about what had already happened, for as the sky grew black over our heads the gusts of wind increased in strength, and before night a new storm was upon us. We finally got the life belt to hang astern of the raft on a long line, so that we had something behind the steering oar toward which to swim if one of us should fall overboard again in a squall. Then it grew pitch dark around us as night fell and hid the raft and the sea. Bouncing wildly up and down in the darkness, we only heard and felt the gale howling in masts and guy ropes, while the gusts pressed with smashing force against the springy bamboo cabin till we thought it would fly overboard. But it was covered with canvas and well guyed. And we felt the *Kon-Tiki* tossing with the foaming seas, while the logs moved up and down with the movement of the waves like the keys of an instrument. We were astonished that cascades of water did not gush up through the wide chinks in the floor, but they only acted as a regular bellows through which damp air rushed up and down.

For five whole days the weather varied between full storm and light gale; the sea was dug up into wide valleys filled with the smoke from foaming gray-blue seas, which seemed to have their backs pressed out long and flat under the onset of the wind. Then on the fifth day the heavens split to show a glimpse of blue, and the malignant, black cloud cover gave place to the ever victorious blue sky as the storm passed on. We had come through the gale with the steering oar smashed and the sail rent; the centerboards hung loose and banged about like crowbars among the logs, because all the ropes which had tightened them up under water were worn through. But we ourselves and the cargo were completely undamaged.

After the two storms the *Kon-Tiki* had become a good deal weaker in the joints. The strain of working over the steep wave backs had stretched all the ropes, and the continuously working logs had made the ropes eat into the balsa wood. We thanked Providence that we had followed the Incas' custom and had not used wire ropes, which would simply have sawed the whole raft into matchwood in the gale. And, if we had used bone-dry, high-floating balsa at the start, the raft would long ago have sunk into the sea under us, saturated with sea water. It was the sap in the fresh logs which served as an impregnation and prevented the water from filtering in through the porous balsa wood.

But now the ropes had become so loose that it was dangerous to let one's foot slip down between two logs, for it could be crushed when they came together violently. Forward and aft, where there was no bamboo deck, we had to give at the knees when we stood with our feet wide apart on two logs at the same time. The logs aft were as slippery as banana leaves with wet seaweed, and, even though we had made a regular path through the greenery where we usually walked and had laid down a broad plank for the steering watch to stand on, it was not easy to keep one's foothold when a sea struck the raft. On the port side one of the nine giants bumped and banged against the crossbeams with dull, wet thuds both by night and by day. There came also new and fearful creakings from the ropes which held the two sloping masts together at the masthead, for the steps of the masts worked about independently of each other, because they rested on two different logs.

We got the steering oar spliced and lashed with long billets of mangrove wood, as hard as iron, and with Erik and Bengt as sailmakers Kon-Tiki soon raised his head again and swelled his breast in a stiff bulge toward Polynesia, while the steering oar danced behind in seas which the fine weather had made soft and gentle. But the centerboards never again became quite what they had been; they did not meet the pressure of the water with their full strength but gave way and hung, dangling loose and unguyed, under the raft. It was useless to try to inspect the ropes on the underside, for they were completely overgrown with seaweed. On taking up the whole bamboo deck we found only three of the main ropes broken; they had been lying crooked and pressed against the cargo, which had worn them away. It was evident that the logs had absorbed a great weight of water but, since the cargo had been lightened, this was roughly canceled out. Most of our provisions and drinking water were already used up, likewise the radio operators' dry batteries.

Nevertheless, after the last storm it was clear enough that we should both float and hold together for the short distance that separated us from the islands ahead. Now quite another problem came into the foreground—how would the voyage end?

The *Kon-Tiki* would slog on inexorably westward until she ran her bow into a solid rock or some other fixed object which would stop her drifting. But our voyage would not be ended until all hands had landed safe and sound on one of the numerous Polynesian islands ahead.

When we came through the last storm, it was quite uncertain where the raft would end up. We were at an equal distance from the Marquesas Islands and the Tuamotu group, and in a position which meant that we could very easily pass right between the two groups of islands without having a glimpse of one of them. The nearest island in the Marquesas group lay 300 sea miles northwest, and the nearest island in the Tuamotu group lay 300 sea miles southwest, while wind and current were uncertain, with their general direction westerly and toward the wide ocean gap between the two island groups.

The island which lay nearest to the northwest was no other than Fatu Hiva, the little jungle-clad mountainous island where I had lived in a hut built on piles on the beach and heard the old man's vivid stories of the ancestral hero Tiki. If the *Kon-Tiki* stood in to that same beach, I should meet many acquaintances, but hardly the old man himself. He must have departed long ago, with a fair hope of meeting the real Tiki again. If the raft headed in toward the mountain ranges of the Marquesas group, I knew the few islands in the group were along way apart and the sea thundered unchecked against perpendicular cliffs where we should have to keep our eyes open while steering for the mouths of the few valleys, which always ended in narrow strips of beach.

If, on the contrary, she headed down toward the coral reefs of the Tuamotu group, there the numerous islands lay close

together and covered a wide space of sea. But this group of
islands is also known as the Low or Dangerous Archipelago,
because the whole formation has been built up entirely by
coral polyps and consists of treacherous submerged reefs and
palm-clad atolls which rise only six or ten feet above the surface of the sea. Dangerous ring-shaped reefs fling themselves
protectingly round every single atoll and are a menace to shipping throughout the area. But, even if coral polyps built the
Tuamotu atolls while the Marquesas Islands are remains of
extinct volcanoes, both groups are inhabited by the same
Polynesian race, and the royal families in both regard Tiki as
their primeval ancestor.

As early as July 3, when we were still 1,000 sea miles from
Polynesia, Nature herself was able to tell us, as she was able
to tell the primitive raftsmen from Peru in their time, that
there really was land ahead somewhere out in the sea. Until
we were a good thousand sea miles out from the coast of
Peru we had noted small flocks of frigate birds. They disappeared at about 100° west, and after that we saw only small
petrels which have their home on the sea. But on July 3
the frigate birds reappeared, at 125° west, and from now onward small flocks of frigate birds were often to be seen, either
high up in the sky or shooting down over the wave crests,
where they snapped up flying fish which had taken to the
air to escape from dolphins. As these birds did not come from
America astern of us, they must have their homes in another country ahead.

On July 16 Nature betrayed herself still more obviously.
On that day we hauled up a nine-foot shark, which threw
up from its stomach a large undigested starfish which it had
recently brought from some coast out here in the ocean.

And the very next day we had the first definite visitor
straight from the islands of Polynesia.

It was a great moment on board when two large boobies
were spotted above the horizon to westward and soon afterward came sailing in over our mast, flying low. With a wing-
spread of five feet they circled round us many times, then
folded their wings and settled on the sea alongside us. Dolphins rushed to the spot at once and wriggled inquisitively

round the great swimming birds, but neither party touched the other. These were the first living messengers that came to bid us welcome to Polynesia. They did not go back in the evening but rested on the sea, and after midnight we still heard them flying in circles round the mast, uttering hoarse cries.

The flying fish which came on board were now of another and much larger species; I recognized them from fishing trips I had taken with the natives along the coast of Fatu Hiva.

For three days and nights we made straight toward Fatu Hiva, but then a strong northeast wind came on and sent us down in the direction of the Tuamotu atolls. We were now blown out of the real South Equatorial Current, and the ocean currents were no longer behaving dependably. One day they were there; another day they were gone. The currents could run like invisible rivers branching out all over the sea. If the current was swift, there was usually more swell and the temperature of the water usually fell one degree. It showed its direction and strength every day by the difference between Erik's calculated and his measured position.

On the threshold of Polynesia the wind said "Pass," having handed us over to a weak branch of the current which, to our alarm, had its course in the direction of the Antarctic. The wind did not become absolutely still—we never experienced that throughout the voyage—and when it was feeble we hoisted every rag we had to collect what little there was. There was not one day on which we moved backward toward America, and our smallest distance in twenty-four hours was 9 sea miles, while our average run for the voyage as a whole was 42½ sea miles in twenty-four hours.

The trade wind, after all, had not the heart to fail us right in the last lap. It reported for duty again and pushed and shoved at the ramshackle craft which was preparing her entry into a new and strange part of the world.

With each day that passed, larger flocks of sea birds came and circled over us aimlessly in all directions. One evening, when the sun was about to sink into the sea, we noticed that the birds had received a violent impetus. They were flying away in a westerly direction without paying any attention to us or the flying fish beneath them. From the masthead we could see that, as they came over, they all flew straight on on exactly the same course. Perhaps they saw something from up above which we did not see. Perhaps they were flying by instinct. In any case they were flying with a plan, straight home to the nearest island, their breeding place.

We twisted the steering oar and set our course exactly in the direction in which the birds had disappeared. Even after it was dark, we heard the cries of stragglers flying over us against the starry sky on exactly the same course as that which we were now following. It was a wonderful night; the moon was nearly full for the third time in the course of the *Kon-Tiki's* voyage.

Next day there were still more birds over us, but we did not need to wait for them to show us our way again in the evening. This time we had detected a curious stationary cloud above the horizon. The other clouds were small feathery wisps of wool which came up in the south and passed across the vault of the sky with the trade wind till they disappeared over the horizon in the west. So I had once come to know the drifting trade-wind clouds on Fatu Hiva, and so we had seen them over us night and day on board the *Kon-Tiki*. But the lonely cloud on the horizon to the southwest did not move; it just rose like a motionless column of smoke while the trade-wind clouds drifted by. The Polynesians knew land lay under such clouds. For, when the tropical sun bakes the hot sand, a stream of warm air is created which rises up and causes its vapor content to condense up in the colder strata of air.

We steered on the cloud till it disappeared after sunset. The wind was steady, and with the steering oar lashed tight the *Kon-Tiki* kept to her course unaided. The steering watch's job was now to sit on the plank at the masthead, shiny with wear, and keep a lookout for anything that indicated land.

There was a deafening screaming of birds over us all that night. And the moon was nearly full.

7 TO THE SOUTH SEA ISLANDS

First Sight of Land—We Drift Away from Puka Puka—
A Festal Day along the Angatau Reef—On the Threshold
of Paradise—The First Natives—The Kon-Tiki Gets a New
Crew—Knut on Shore Leave—A Losing Battle—We Drift
Out to Sea Again—In Dangerous Waters—From Takume to
Raroia—Drifting toward the Witches' Caldron—At the Mercy
of the Breakers—A Shipwreck—Cast Ashore on the Coral
Reef—We Find a Desert Island

ON THE NIGHT BEFORE JULY 30 THERE WAS A
new and strange atmosphere about the *Kon-Tiki.* Perhaps it
was the deafening clamor from all the sea birds over us which
showed that something fresh was brewing. The screaming of
birds with many voices sounded hectic and earthly after the
dead creaking of lifeless ropes, which was all we had heard
above the noise of the sea in the three months we had behind
us. And the moon seemed larger and rounder than ever as it
sailed over the lookout at the masthead. In our fancy it reflected palm tops and warm-blooded romance; it did not shine
with such a yellow light over the cold fishes out at sea.

At six o'clock Bengt came down from the masthead, woke
Herman, and turned in. When Herman clambered up the
creaking, swaying mast, the day had begun to break. Ten
minutes later he was down the rope ladder again and was
shaking me by the leg.

"Come out and have a look at your island!"

His face was radiant and I jumped up, followed by Bengt

who had not quite gone to sleep yet. Hard on one another's heels, we huddled together as high as we could climb, at the point where the masts crossed. There were many birds around us, and a faint violet-blue veil over the sky was reflected in the sea as a last relic of the departing night. But over the whole horizon away to the east a ruddy glow had begun to spread, and far down to the southeast it gradually formed a blood-red background for a faint shadow, like a blue pencil line, drawn for a short way along the edge of the sea.

Land! An island! We devoured it greedily with our eyes and woke the others, who tumbled out drowsily and stared in all directions as if they thought our bow was about to run on to a beach. Screaming sea birds formed a bridge across the sky in the direction of the distant island, which stood out sharper against the horizon as the red background widened and turned gold with the approach of the sun and the full daylight.

Our first thought was that the island did not lie where it should. As the island could not have drifted, the raft must have been caught up in a northward current in the course of the night. We had only to cast one glance over the sea to perceive at once, from the direction of the waves, that we had lost our chance in the darkness. Where we now lay, the wind no longer allowed us to press the raft on a course toward the island. The region round the Tuamotu Archipelago was full of strong, local ocean currents which twisted in all directions as they ran up against land; many of them varied in direction as they met powerful tidal currents flowing in and out over reefs and lagoons.

We laid the steering oar over, but we knew quite well that it was useless. At half-past six the sun rose out of the sea and climbed straight up as it does in the tropics. The island lay some few sea miles away and had the appearance of a quite low strip of forest creeping along the horizon. The trees were crowded close together behind a narrow light-colored beach, which lay so low that it was hidden behind the seas at regular intervals. According to Erik's positions this island was Puka Puka, the first outpost of the Tuamotu group. *Sail-*

ing Directions for Pacific Islands—1940, our two different charts, and Erik's observations gave, in all, four quite different positions for this island, but as there were no other islands in all that neighborhood there could be no doubt that the island we saw was Puka Puka.

No extravagant outbursts were to be heard on board. After the sail had been trimmed and the oar laid over, we all formed a silent group at the masthead or stood on deck staring toward the land which had suddenly cropped up out in the middle of the endless, all-dominating sea. At last we had a visible proof that we had really been moving in all these months; we had not just been lying tumbling about in the center of the same eternal circular horizon. To us it seemed as if the island were mobile and had suddenly entered the circle of blue and empty sea in the center of which we had our permanent abode; as if the island were drifting slowly across our own domain, heading for the eastern horizon. We were all filled with a warm, quiet satisfaction at having actually reached Polynesia, mingled with a faint momentary disappointment at having to submit helplessly to seeing the island lie there like a mirage while we continued our eternal drift across the sea westward.

Just after sunrise a thick black column of smoke rose above the treetops to the left of the middle of the island. We followed it with our eyes and thought to ourselves that the natives were rising and getting their breakfast. We had no idea then that native lookout posts had seen us and were sending up smoke signals to invite us to land. About seven o'clock we scented a faint breath of burned *borao* wood which tickled our salted nostrils. It awoke in me at once slumbering memories of the fire on the beach on Fatu Hiva. Half an hour later we caught the smell of newly cut wood and of forest. The island had now begun to shrink and lay astern of us so that we received flickering wafts of breeze from it. For a quarter of an hour Herman and I clung to the masthead and let the warm smell of leaves and greenery filter in through our nostrils. This was Polynesia—a beautiful, rich smell of dry land after ninety-three salty days down among the waves. Bengt already lay snoring in his sleeping bag again. Erik and Torstein lay on their backs in the cabin meditating, and Knut ran in and out and sniffed the smell of leaves and wrote in his diary.

At half-past eight Puka Puka sank into the sea astern of us, but right on till eleven o'clock we could see, on climbing to the masthead, that there was a faint blue streak above the horizon in the east. Then that too was gone, and a high cumulo-nimbus cloud, rising motionless skyward, was all that showed where Puka Puka lay. The birds disappeared. They kept by preference to windward of the islands so that they had the wind with them when they returned home in the evening with full bellies. The dolphins also had become noticeably scarcer, and there were again only a few pilot fish under the raft.

That night Bengt said he longed for a table and chair, for it was so tiring to lie and turn from back to stomach while reading. Otherwise he was glad we had missed our landing, for he still had three books to read. Torstein suddenly had a desire for an apple, and I myself woke up in the night because I definitely smelled a delicious odor of steak and onions. But it turned out to be only a dirty shirt.

The very next morning we detected two new clouds rising up like the steam from two locomotives below the horizon. The map was able to tell us that the names of the coral islands they came from were Fangahina and Angatau. The cloud over Angatau lay the most favorably for us as the wind was blowing, so we set our course for that, lashed the oar fast, and enjoyed the wonderful peace and freedom of the Pacific. So lovely was life on this fine day on the bamboo deck of the *Kon-Tiki* that we drank in all the impressions in the certainty that the journey would soon be over now, whatever might await us.

For three days and nights we steered on the cloud over Angatau; the weather was brilliant, the oar alone held us on our course, and the current played us no tricks. On the fourth morning Torstein relieved Herman after the 4–6 watch and was told that Herman thought he had seen the outlines of a low island in the moonlight. When the sun rose just afterward, Torstein stuck his head in at the cabin door and shouted:

"Land ahead!"

We all plunged out on deck, and what we saw made us hoist all our flags. First the Norwegian aft, then the French at the masthead because we were heading for a French colony. Soon the raft's entire collection of flags was fluttering in the fresh trade wind—the American, British, Peruvian, and Swedish flags besides the flag of the Explorers Club—so there was no doubt on board that now the *Kon-Tiki* was dressed. The island was ideally placed this time, right in our own course and a little farther away from us than Puka Puka had been when it cropped up at sunrise four days before. As the sun rose straight up over the sky astern of us, we could see a clear green glimmer high up toward the misty sky over the island. It was the reflection of the still, green lagoon on the inside of the surrounding reef. Some of the low atolls throw up mirages of this kind for many thousand feet into the air, so that they show their position to primitive seafarers many days before the island itself is visible above the horizon.

About ten o'clock we took charge of the steering oar ourselves; we must now decide toward which part of the island we should steer. We could already distinguish individual treetops from the others and could see rows of tree trunks shining in the sun, which stood out against the background of dense shadowy foliage.

We knew that somewhere between us and the island there was a dangerous submerged shoal, lying in ambush for anything that approached the innocent island. This reef lay right under the deep, free roll of the swell from the east, and, as the huge masses of water lost their balance above the shoal, they wavered skyward and plunged down, thundering and foaming, over the sharp coral reef. Many vessels have been caught in the terrible suction against the submerged reefs in the Tuamotu group and have been smashed to pieces against the coral.

From the sea we saw nothing of this insidious trap. We sailed in, following the direction of the waves, and saw only the curved shining back of sea after sea disappearing toward the island. Both the reef and the whole frothing witches' dance over it were hidden behind rising rows of broad wave backs ahead of us. But along both ends of the island where we saw the beach in profile, both north and south, we saw that a few hundred yards from land the sea was one white boiling mass flinging itself high into the air.

We laid our course so as to graze the outside of the witches' kitchen off the southern point of the island, hoping, when we got there, to be able to steer along the atoll till we came round the point on the lee side or till we touched, before we drifted past, a place where it was so shallow that we could stop our drift with a makeshift anchor and wait till the wind changed and placed us under the lee of the island.

About noon we could see through the glass that the vegetation on shore consisted of young green coconut palms, which stood with their tops close together over a waving hedge of luxuriant undergrowth in the foreground. On the beach in front of them a number of large coral blocks lay strewn about on the bright sand. Otherwise there was no sign of life, apart from white birds sailing over the palm tufts.

At two o'clock we had come so close that we began to sail along the island, just outside the baffling reef. As we gradually approached, we heard the roar of the breakers like a steady waterfall against the reef, and soon they sounded like an endless express train running parallel with us a few hundred yards from our starboard side. Now, too, we could see the white spray which was occasionally flung high into the air behind the curly, breaking wave backs just in there where the "train" was roaring along.

Two men at the same time stood turning the steering oar; they were behind the bamboo cabin and so had no view ahead whatever. Erik, as navigator, stood on the top of the kitchen box and gave directions to the two men at the heavy oar. Our plan was to keep as close in to the dangerous reef as was safe. We kept a continuous lookout from the masthead for a gap or opening in the reef where we could try to slip the raft through. The current was now driving us along the whole length of the reef and played us no tricks. The

loose centerboards allowed us to steer at an angle of about
20° to the wind on both sides, and the wind was blowing
along the reef.

While Erik directed our zigzag course and took his loops
as near the reef as was advisable in view of the suction, Herman and I went out in the rubber dinghy at the end of a
rope. When the raft was on the inward tack, we swung after
her on the rope and came so close to the thundering reef
that we caught a glimpse of the glass-green wall of water that
was rolling away from us and saw how, when the seas sucked
themselves back, the naked reef exposed itself, resembling a
torn-up barricade of rusty iron ore. As far as we could see
along the coast there was no gap or passage. So Erik trimmed
the sail by tightening the port and loosening the starboard
sheets, and the helmsman followed with the steering oar, so
that the *Kon-Tiki* turned her nose out again and tumbled
away from the danger zone till her next drive inward.

Each time the *Kon-Tiki* stood in toward the reef and
swung out again, we two who were in tow in the dinghy sat
with our hearts in our mouths, for each time we came so close
in that we felt the beat of the seas becoming nervous as it
rose higher and fiercer. And each time we were convinced
that this time Erik had gone too far, that this time there was
no hope of getting the *Kon-Tiki* out again clear of the breakers which drew us in toward the devilish red reef. But each
time Erik got clear with a smart maneuver, and the *Kon-Tiki*
ran safely out into the open sea again, well out of the clutch
of the suction. All the time we were gliding along the island,
so close that we saw every detail on shore; yet the heavenly
beauty there was inaccessible to us because of the frothing
moat that lay between.

About three o'clock the forest of palms ashore opened, and
through a wide gap we saw right into a blue glassy lagoon.
But the surrounding reef lay as compact as ever, gnashing
its blood-red teeth ominously in the foam. There was no passage, and the palm forest closed again as we plodded on along
the island with the wind at our backs. Later the palm forest
became thinner and thinner and gave us a view into the interior of the coral island. This consisted of the fairest, bright-

est salt-water lagoon, like a great silent tarn, surrounded by swaying coconut palms and shining bathing beaches. The seductive, green palm island itself formed a broad, soft ring of sand round the hospitable lagoon, and a second ring ran round the whole island—the rust-red sword which defended the gates of heaven.

All day we zigzagged along Angatau and had its beauty at close quarters, just outside the cabin door. The sun beat down on all the palms, and all was Paradise and joy on the island within. As our maneuvers gradually became a matter of routine, Erik got out his guitar and stood on deck in a huge Peruvian sun hat playing and singing sentimental South Sea songs, while Bengt served an excellent dinner on the edge of the raft. We opened an old coconut from Peru and drank to the young fresh nuts which hung on the trees inside. The whole atmosphere—the peace over the bright, green palm forest which stood deep-rooted and beckoned toward us, the peace over the white birds that sailed round the palm tops, the peace over the glassy lagoon and the soft sand beach, and the viciousness of the red reef, the cannonading and roll of drums in the air—all made an overwhelming impression on the six of us who had come in from the sea. An impression which can never be effaced from our memories. There was no doubt that now we had reached the other side; we should never see a more genuine South Sea island. Landing or no landing, we had nonetheless reached Polynesia; the expanse of sea lay behind us for all time.

It happened that this festal day off Angatau was the ninety-seventh day on board. Strangely enough, it was ninety-seven days that we had estimated in New York as the absolute minimum time in which, in theoretically ideal conditions, we could reach the nearest islands of Polynesia.

About five o'clock we passed two palm-roofed huts which lay among the trees on shore. There was no smoke and no sign of life.

At half-past five we stood in toward the reef again; we had sailed along the whole south coast and were getting near the west end of the island, and must have a last look round in the hope of finding a passage before we passed. The sun now stood so low that it blinded us when we looked ahead, but we saw a little rainbow in the air where the sea broke against the reef a few hundred yards beyond the last point of the island. This now lay as a silhouette ahead of us. On the beach inside we detected a cluster of motionless black spots. Suddenly one of them moved slowly down toward the water, while several of the others made off at full speed up to the edge of the woods. They were people! We steered along the reef as close in as we dared; the wind had died down so that we felt we were within an inch of getting under the lee of the island. Now we saw a canoe being launched, and two individuals jumped on board and paddled off on the other side of the reef. Farther down they turned the boat's head out, and we saw the canoe lifted high in the air by the seas as it shot through a passage in the reef and came straight out toward us.

The opening in the reef, then, was down there; there was our only hope. Now, too, we could see the whole village lying in among the palm trunks. But the shadows were already growing long.

The two men in the canoe waved. We waved back eagerly, and they increased their speed. It was a Polynesian outrigger canoe; two brown figures in singlets sat paddling, facing ahead. Now there would be fresh language difficulties. I alone of those on board remembered a few words of Marquesan from my stay on Fatu Hiva, but Polynesian is a difficult language to keep up, for lack of practice in our northern countries.

We felt some relief, therefore, when the canoe bumped against the raft's side and the two men leaped on board, for one of them grinned all over his face and held out a brown hand, exclaiming in English:

"Good night!"

"Good night," I replied in astonishment. "Do you speak English?"

The man grinned again and nodded.

"Good night," he said. "Good night."

This was his entire vocabulary in foreign languages, and thereby he scored heavily over his more modest friend, who just stood in the background and grinned, much impressed, at his experienced comrade.

"Angatau?" I asked, pointing toward the island.

"H'angatau," the man nodded affirmatively.

Erik nodded proudly. He had been right; we were where the sun had told him that we were.

"*Maimai hee iuta,*" I tried.

According to my knowledge acquired on Fatu Hiva this should mean approximately, "Want to go to land."

They both pointed toward the invisible passage in the reef, and we laid the oar over and decided to take our chance.

At that moment fresher gusts of wind came from the interior of the island. A small rain cloud lay over the lagoon. The wind threatened to force us away from the reef, and we saw that the *Kon-Tiki* was not answering the steering oar at a wide enough angle to be able to reach the mouth of the opening in the reef. We tried to find bottom, but the anchor rope was not long enough. Now we had to have resort to the paddles, and pretty quickly, too, before the wind got a fair hold of us. We hauled down the sail at top speed and each of us got out his big paddle.

I wanted to give an extra paddle to each of the two natives, who stood enjoying the cigarettes they had been given on board. They only shook their heads vigorously, pointed out the course, and looked confused. I made signs that we must all paddle and repeated the words, "Want to go to land!" Then the most advanced of the two bent down, made a cranking motion in the air with his right hand, and said:

Brrrrrrrrr-l

There was no doubt whatever that he wanted us to start the engine. They thought they were standing on the deck of a curiously deep loaded boat. We took them aft and made them feel under the logs to show them that we had no propeller or screw. They were dumbfounded and, putting out their cigarettes, flung themselves down on the side of the raft where we sat—four men on each outside log, dipping our paddles into the water. At the same time the sun sank straight into the sea behind the point, and the gusts of wind from the interior of the island freshened. It did not look as if we were moving an inch. The natives looked frightened, jumped back into the canoe, and disappeared. It grew dark, and we were alone once more, paddling desperately so as not to drift out to sea again.

As darkness fell over the island, four canoes came dancing out from behind the reef, and soon there was a crowd of Polynesians on board, all wanting to shake hands and get cigarettes. With these fellows on board, who had local knowledge, there was no danger. They would not let us go out to sea again and out of sight, so we should be ashore that evening!

We quickly had ropes made fast from the sterns of all the canoes to the bow of the *Kon-Tiki*, and the four sturdy outrigger canoes spread out in fan formation, like a dog team, ahead of the wooden raft. Knut jumped into the dinghy and found a place as draft dog in among the canoes, and we others, with paddles, posted ourselves on the two outside logs of the *Kon-Tiki*. And so began, for the first time, a struggle against the east wind which had been at our back for so long.

It was now pitch dark until the moon rose, and there was a fresh wind. On land the inhabitants of the village had collected brushwood and lighted a big fire to show us the direction of the passage through the reef. The thundering from the reef surrounded us in the darkness like a ceaselessly roaring waterfall, and at·first the noise grew louder and louder.

We could not see the team that was pulling us in the canoes ahead, but we heard them singing exhilarating war songs in Polynesian at the top of their lungs. We could hear that Knut was with them, for every time the Polynesian music died away we heard Knut's solitary voice singing Norwegian folk songs in the midst of the Polynesians' chorus. To complete the chaos we on board the raft chimed in with "Tom Brown's baby had a pimple on his nose," and both white and brown men heaved at their paddles with laughter and song.

We were overflowing with high spirits. Ninety-seven days. Arrived in Polynesia. There would be a feast in the village that evening. The natives cheered and bellowed and shouted. There was a landing on Angatau only once a year, when the copra schooner came from Tahiti to fetch coconut kernels. So there would indeed be a feast round the fire on land that evening.

But the angry wind blew stubbornly. We toiled till every limb ached. We held our ground, but the fire did not come any nearer and the thunder from the reef was just the same as before. Gradually the singing died away. All grew still. It was all and more the men could do to row. The fire did not move; it only danced up and down as we fell and rose with the seas. Three hours passed, and it was now nine o'clock. Gradually we began to lose ground. We were tired.

We made the natives understand that we needed more help from land. They explained to us that there were plenty of people ashore, but they had only these four seagoing canoes in the whole island.

Then Knut appeared out of the darkness with the dinghy. He had an idea; he could row in in the rubber dinghy and fetch more natives. Five or six men could sit crowded together in the dinghy at a pinch.

This was too risky. Knut had no local knowledge; he would never be able to feel his way forward to the opening in the coral reef in that pitch-black darkness. He then proposed to take with him the leader of the natives, who could show him the way. I did not think this plan a safe one, either, for the native had no experience in maneuvering a clumsy rubber dinghy through the narrow and dangerous passage. But I asked Knut to fetch the leader, who was sitting paddling in the darkness ahead of us, so that we might hear what he thought of the situation. It was clear enough that we were no longer able to prevent ourselves from drifting astern.

Knut disappeared into the darkness to find the leader. When some time had passed and Knut had not returned with the leader, we shouted for them but received no answer except from a cackling chorus of Polynesians ahead. Knut had vanished into the darkness. At that moment we understood what had happened. In all the bustle, noise, and turmoil Knut had misunderstood his instructions and rowed shoreward with the leader. All our shouting was useless, for where Knut now was all other sounds were drowned by the thunder all along the barrier.

We quickly got hold of a Morse lamp, and a man climbed up to the masthead and signaled, "Come back. Come back."

But no one came back.

With two men away and one continuously signaling at the masthead our drift astern increased, and the rest of us had begun to grow really tired. We threw marks overboard and saw that we were moving slowly but surely the wrong way. The fire grew smaller and the noise from the breakers less. And the farther we emerged from under the lee of the palm forest, the firmer hold of us the eternal east wind took. We felt it again now; it was almost as it had been out at sea. We gradually realized that all hope had gone—we were drifting out to sea. But we must not slacken our paddling. We must put the brake on the drift astern with all our might till Knut was safe on board again.

Five minutes went. Ten minutes. Half an hour. The fire grew smaller; now and then it disappeared altogether when we ourselves slid down into the trough of the sea. The breakers became a distant murmur. Now the moon rose; we could just see the glimmer of its disk behind the palm tops on land, but the sky seemed misty and half clouded over. We heard the natives beginning to murmur and exchange words. Suddenly we noticed that one of the canoes had cast off its rope into the sea and disappeared. The men in the other three canoes were tired and frightened and were no longer pulling their full weight. The *Kon-Tiki* went on drifting out over the open sea.

Soon the three remaining ropes slackened and the three canoes bumped against the side of the raft. One of the natives came on board and said quietly with a jerk of his head:

"*Iuta* (To land)."

He looked anxiously at the fire, which now disappeared for long periods at a time and only flashed out now and again like a spark. We were drifting fast. The breakers were silent; only the sea roared as it used to, and all the ropes on board the *Kon-Tiki* creaked and groaned.

We plied the natives with cigarettes, and I hurriedly

scrawled a note which they were to take with them and give to Knut if they found him. It ran:

"Take two natives with you in a canoe with the dinghy in tow. Do NOT come back in the dinghy alone."

We counted on the helpful islanders being willing to take Knut with them in a canoe, assuming they thought it advisable to put to sea at all; if they did not think it advisable, it would be madness for Knut to venture out on to the ocean in the dinghy in the hope of overtaking the runaway raft.

The natives took the scrap of paper, jumped into the canoes, and disappeared into the night. The last we heard was the shrill voice of our first friend out in the darkness calling politely:

"Good night!"

There was a murmur of appreciation from the less accomplished linguists, and then all was as silent, as free from sounds from without, as when we were 2,000 sea miles from the nearest land.

It was useless for us four to do anything more with the paddles out here in the open sea, under the full pressure of the wind, but we continued the light signals from the masthead. We dared not send "Come back" any longer; we now sent out only regular flashes. It was pitch dark. The moon appeared only through occasional rifts in the bank of clouds. It must have been Angatau's cumulo-nimbus cloud which was hanging over us.

At ten o'clock we gave up the last faint hope of seeing Knut again. We sat down in silence on the edge of the raft and munched a few biscuits, while we took turns flashing signals from the masthead, which seemed just a naked projection without the broad *Kon-Tiki* sail.

We decided to keep the lamp-signaling going all night, so long as we did not know where Knut was. We refused to believe that he had been caught by the breakers. Knut always landed on his feet, whether it was heavy water or breakers; he was alive all right. Only it was so damnable to have him stuck down among Polynesians on an out-of-the-way island in the Pacific. An accursed business! After all that long voyage all we could do was to nip in and land a man on a

remote South Sea island and sail off again. No sooner had
the first Polynesians come smiling on board than they had to
clear out headlong to escape being themselves caught up in
the *Kon-Tiki's* wild, incontinent rush westward. It was the
devil of a situation. And the ropes were creaking horribly
that night. Not one of us showed a sign of wanting to sleep.

It was half-past ten. Bengt was coming down to be relieved at the swaying masthead. Then we all started. We had
heard voices clearly, out on the sea in the darkness. There it
was again. It was Polynesians talking. We shouted into the
black night with all the strength of our lungs. They shouted
back, and—there was Knut's voice among the rest! We were
mad with excitement. Our tiredness had gone; the whole
thundercloud had lifted. What did it matter if we drifted
away from Angatau? There were other islands in the sea.
Now the nine balsa logs, so fond of travel, could drift where
they liked, so long as all six of us were assembled on board
again.

Three outrigger canoes emerged from the darkness, riding
over the swell, and Knut was the first man to jump across to
the dear old *Kon-Tiki*, followed by six brown men. There
was little time for explanations; the natives must have pres-
ents and be off on their adventurous journey back to the
island. Without seeing light or land, and with hardly any
stars, they had to find their course by paddling against wind
and sea till they saw the light from the fire. We rewarded
them amply with provisions, cigarettes, and other gifts, and
each of them shook us heartily by the hand in a last farewell.

They were clearly anxious on our account; they pointed
westward, indicating that we were heading toward dangerous reefs. The leader had tears in his eyes and kissed me
tenderly on the chin, which made me thank Providence for
my beard. Then they crept into the canoes, and we six com-
rades were left on the raft, together and alone.

We left the raft to her own devices and listened to Knut's
story.

Knut had in good faith made for land in the dinghy with
the native leader on board. The native himself was sitting

at the little oars and rowing toward the opening in the reef, when Knut to his surprise saw the light signals from the *Kon-Tiki* asking him to come back. He made signs to the rower to turn, but the native refused to obey. Then Knut took hold of the oars himself, but the native tore his hands away, and with the reef thundering round them it was no use starting a fight. They had bounded right in through the opening in the reef and gone on inside it, until they were lifted right up on to a solid coral block on the island itself. A crowd of natives caught hold of the dinghy and dragged it high up on the shore, and Knut stood alone under the palm trees surrounded by a huge crowd of natives chattering away in an unknown lingo. Brown, barelegged men, women, and children of all ages flocked round him and felt the material of his shirt and trousers. They themselves wore ragged old European clothes, but there were no white men on the island.

Knut got hold of some of the smartest fellows and made signs to them that they should go out in the dinghy with him. Then a big fat man came waddling up who Knut presumed must be the chief, for he had an old uniform cap on his head and talked in a loud, authoritative voice. All made way for him. Knut explained both in Norwegian and in English that he needed men and must get back to the raft before we others drifted away. The chief beamed and understood nothing, and Knut, despite his most vehement protests, was pushed over to the village by the whole shouting crowd. There he was received by dogs and pigs and pretty South Sea girls who came along carrying fresh fruit. It was clear that the natives were prepared to make Knut's stay as agreeable as possible, but Knut was not to be enticed; he thought sadly of the raft which was vanishing westward. The natives' intention was obvious. They badly wanted our company, and they knew that there were a lot of good things on board white men's ships. If they could keep Knut ashore, the rest of us and the queer boat would certainly come in also. No vessel would leave a white man behind on such an out-of-the-way island as Angatau.

After more curious experiences Knut got away and hurried down to the dinghy, surrounded by admirers of both sexes.

His international speech and gesticulations could no longer be misunderstood; they realized that he must and would return to the odd craft out in the night, which was in such a hurry that she had to go on at once.

Then the natives tried a trick; they indicated by signs that the rest of us were coming ashore on the other side of the point. Knut was puzzled for a few minutes, but then loud voices were heard down on the beach, where women and children were tending the flickering fire. The three canoes had come back, and the men brought Knut the note. He was in a desperate situation. Here were instructions not to row out on the sea alone, and all the natives absolutely refused to go with him.

There followed a high-pitched, noisy argument among all the natives. Those who had been out and seen the raft understood perfectly well that it was of little use to keep Knut back in the hope of getting the rest of us ashore. The end of it was that Knut's promises and threats in international accents induced the crews of three canoes to accompany him out to sea in pursuit of the *Kon-Tiki*. They put out to sea in the tropical night with the dinghy dancing along in tow, while the natives stood motionless by the dying fire and watched their new blond friend disappear as quickly as he had come.

Knut and his companions could see the faint light signals from the raft far out to sea when the swell lifted the canoes. The long, slim Polynesian canoes, stiffened by pointed side floats, cut through the water like knives, but it seemed an eternity to Knut before he felt the thick round logs of the *Kon-Tiki* under his feet again.

"Have a good time ashore?" Torstein asked enviously.

"Oho, you just should have seen the hula girls!" Knut teased him.

We left the sail down and the oar inboard, and all six of us crept into the bamboo cabin and slept like boulders on the beach at Angatau.

For three days we drifted across the sea without a sight of land.

We were drifting straight toward the ominous Takume

and Raroia reefs, which together blocked up forty to fifty miles of the sea ahead of us. We made desperate efforts to steer clear, to the north of these dangerous reefs, and things seemed to be going well till one night the watch came hurrying in and called us all out.

The wind had changed. We were heading straight for the Takume reef. It had begun to rain, and there was no visibility at all. The reef could not be far off.

In the middle of night we held a council of war. It was a question of saving our lives now. To get past on the north side was now hopeless; we must try to get through on the south side instead. We trimmed the sail, laid the oar over, and began a dangerous piece of sailing with the uncertain north wind behind us. If the east wind came back before we had passed the whole façade of the fifty-mile-long reefs, we should be hurled in among the breakers, at their mercy.

We agreed on all that should be done if shipwreck was imminent. We would stay on board the *Kon-Tiki* at all costs. We would not climb up the mast, from which we should be shaken down like rotten fruit, but would cling tight to the stays of the mast when the seas poured over us. We laid the rubber raft loose on the deck and made fast to it a small watertight radio transmitter, a small quantity of provisions, water bottles, and medical stores. This would be washed ashore independently of us if we ourselves should get over the reef safe but empty-handed. In the stern of the *Kon-Tiki* we made fast a long rope with a float which also would be washed ashore, so that we could try to pull in the raft if she were stranded out on the reef. And so we crept into bed and left the watch to the helmsman out in the rain.

As long as the north wind held, we glided slowly but surely down along the façade of the coral reefs which lay in ambush below the horizon. But then one afternoon the wind died away, and when it returned it had gone round into the east. According to Erik's position we were already so far down that we now had some hope of steering clear of the southernmost point of the Raroia reef. We would try to get round it and into shelter before going on to other reefs beyond it.

When night came, we had been a hundred days at sea

Late in the night I woke, feeling restless and uneasy. There
was something unusual in the movement of the waves. The
Kon-Tiki's motion was a little different from what it usually
was in such conditions. We had become sensitive to changes
in the rhythm of the logs. I thought at once of suction from
a coast, which was drawing near, and was continually out on
deck and up the mast. Nothing but sea was visible. But I
could get no quiet sleep. Time passed.

At dawn, just before six, Torstein came hurrying down
from the masthead. He could see a whole line of small palm-
clad islands far ahead. Before doing anything else we laid
the oar over to southward as far as we could. What Torstein
had seen must be the small coral islands which lay strewn
like pearls on a string behind the Raroia reef. A northward
current must have caught us.

At half-past seven palm-clad islets had appeared in a row
all along the horizon to westward. The southernmost lay
roughly ahead of our bow, and thence there were islands
and clumps of palms all along the horizon on our starboard
side till they disappeared as dots away to northward. The
nearest were four or five sea miles away.

A survey from the masthead showed that, even if our bow
pointed toward the bottom island in the chain, our drift sideways was so great that we were not advancing in the direction
in which our bow pointed. We were drifting diagonally right
in toward the reef. With fixed centerboards we should still
have had some hope of steering clear. But sharks were following close astern, so that it was impossible to dive under the
raft and tighten up the loose centerboards with fresh guy
ropes.

We saw that we had now only a few hours more on board
the Kon-Tiki. They must be used in preparation for our inevitable wreck on the coral reef. Every man learned what he
had to do when the moment came; each one of us knew
where his own limited sphere of responsibility lay, so that
we should not fly round treading on one another's toes when
the time came and seconds counted. The Kon-Tiki pitched
up and down, up and down, as the wind forced us in. There
was no doubt that here was the turmoil of the waves created

by the reef—some waves advancing while others were hurled back after beating vainly against the surrounding wall.

We were still under full sail in the hope of even now being able to steer clear. As we gradually drifted nearer, half sideways, we saw from the mast how the whole string of palm-clad isles was connected with a coral reef, part above and part under water, which lay like a mole where the sea was white with foam and leaped high into the air. The Raroia atoll is oval in shape and has a diameter of twenty-five miles, not counting the adjoining reefs of Takume. The whole of its longer side faces the sea to eastward, where we came pitching in. The reef itself, which runs in one line from horizon to horizon, is only a few hundred yards clear, and behind it idyllic islets lie in a string round the still lagoon inside.

It was with mixed feelings that we saw the blue Pacific being ruthlessly torn up and hurled into the air all along the horizon ahead of us. I knew what awaited us; I had visited the Tuamotu group before and had stood safe on land looking out over the immense spectacle in the east, where the surf from the open Pacific broke in over the reef. New reefs and islands kept on gradually appearing to southward. We must be lying off the middle of the façade of the coral wall.

On board the *Kon-Tiki* all preparations for the end of the voyage were being made. Everything of value was carried into the cabin and lashed fast. Documents and papers were packed into watertight bags, along with films and other things which would not stand a dip in the sea. The whole bamboo cabin was covered with canvas, and especially strong ropes were lashed across it. When we saw that all hope was gone, we opened up the bamboo deck and cut off with machete knives all the ropes which held the centerboards down. It was a hard job to get the centerboards drawn up, because they were all thickly covered with stout barnacles. With the centerboards up the draught of our vessel was no deeper than to the bottom of the timber logs, and we would therefore be more easily washed in over the reef. With no centerboards and with the sail down, the raft lay completely sideways on and was entirely at the mercy of wind and sea.

We tied the longest rope we had to the homemade anchor

and made it fast to the step of the port mast, so that the *Kon-Tiki* would go into the surf stern first when the anchor was thrown overboard. The anchor itself consisted of empty water cans filled with used radio batteries and heavy scrap, and solid mangrove-wood sticks projected from it, set cross-wise.

Order number one, which came first and last, was: Hold on to the raft! Whatever happened, we must hang on tight on board and let the nine great logs take the pressure from the reef. We ourselves had more than enough to do to withstand the weight of the water. If we jumped overboard, we should become helpless victims of the suction which would fling us in and out over the sharp corals. The rubber raft would cap-size in the steep seas or, heavily loaded with us in it, it would be torn to ribbons against the reef. But the wooden logs would sooner or later be cast ashore, and we with them, if we only managed to hold fast.

Next, all hands were told to put on their shoes for the first time in a hundred days and to have their life belts ready. The last precaution, however, was not of much value, for if a man fell overboard he would be battered to death, not drowned. We had time, too, to put our passports and such few dollars as we had left into our pockets. But it was not lack of time that was troubling us.

Those were anxious hours in which we lay drifting help-lessly sideways, step after step, in toward the reef. It was no-ticeably quiet on board; we all crept in and out from cabin to bamboo deck, silent or laconic, and carried on with our jobs. Our serious faces showed that no one was in doubt as to what awaited us, and the absence of nervousness showed that we had all gradually acquired an unshakable confidence in the raft. If it had brought us across the sea, it would also manage to bring us ashore alive.

Inside the cabin there was a complete chaos of provision cartons and cargo, lashed fast. Torstein had barely found room for himself in the radio corner, where he had got the shortwave transmitter working. We were now over 4,000 sea miles from our old base at Callao, where the Peruvian Naval War School had maintained regular contact with us, and still farther from Hal and Frank and the other radio amateurs in the United States. But, as chance willed, we had on the previous day got in touch with a capable radio "ham" who had a set on Rarotonga in the Cook Islands, and the operators, quite contrary to all our usual practice, had arranged for an extra contact with him early in the morning. All the time we were drifting closer and closer in to the reef, Torstein was sitting tapping his key and calling Rarotonga.

Entries in the *Kon-Tiki's* log ran:

—8:15: *We are slowly approaching land. We can now make out with the naked eye the separate palm trees inside on the starboard side.*

—8:45: *The wind has veered into a still more unfavorable quarter for us, so we have no hope of getting clear. No nervousness on board, but hectic preparations on deck. There is something lying on the reef ahead of us which looks like the wreck of a sailing vessel, but it may be only a heap of driftwood.*

—9:45: *The wind is taking us straight toward the last island but one we see behind the reef. We can now see the whole coral reef clearly; here it is built up like a white and red speckled wall which barely sticks up out of the water as a belt in front of all the islands. All along the reef white foaming surf is flung up toward the sky. Bengt is just serving up a good hot meal, the last before the great action!*

It is a wreck lying in there on the reef. We are so close now that we can see right across the shining lagoon behind the reef and see the outlines of other islands on the other side of the lagoon.

As this was written, the dull drone of the surf came near again; it came from the whole reef and filled the air like thrilling rolls of the drum, heralding the exciting last act of the *Kon-Tiki*.

—9:50: *Very close now. Drifting along the reef. Only a hundred yards or so away. Torstein is talking to the man on Rarotonga. All clear. Must pack up log now. All in good spirits; it looks bad, but we shall make it!*

A few minutes later the anchor rushed overboard and caught hold of the bottom, so that the *Kon Tiki* swung around and turned her stern inward toward the breakers. It held us for a few valuable minutes, while Torstein sat hammering like mad on the key. He had got Rarotonga now. The breakers thundered in the air and the sea rose and fell furiously. All hands were at work on deck, and now Torstein got his message through. He said we were drifting toward the Raroia reef. He asked Rarotonga to listen in on the same wave length every hour. If we were silent for more than thirty-six hours, Rarotonga must let the Norwegian Embassy in Washington know. Torstein's last words were:

"O.K. Fifty yards left. Here we go. Good-by."

Then he closed down the station, Knut sealed up the papers, and both crawled out on deck as fast as they could to join the rest of us, for it was clear now that the anchor was giving way.

The swell grew heavier and heavier, with deep troughs between the waves, and we felt the raft being swung up and down, up and down, higher and higher.

Again the order was shouted: "Hold on, never mind about the cargo, hold on!"

We were now so near the waterfall inside that we no longer heard the steady continuous roar from all along the reef. We now heard only a separate boom each time the nearest breaker crashed down on the rocks.

All hands stood in readiness, each clinging fast to the rope he thought the most secure. Only Erik crept into the cabin at the last moment; there was one part of the program he had not yet carried out—he had not found his shoes!

No one stood aft, for it was there the shock from the reef would come. Nor were the two firm stays which ran from the masthead down to the stern safe. For if the mast fell they would be left hanging overboard, over the reef. Herman, Bengt, and Torstein had climbed up on some boxes which were lashed fast forward of the cabin wall, and, while Herman clung on to the guy ropes from the ridge of the roof, the other two held on to the ropes from the masthead by which the sail at other times was hauled up. Knut and I chose the stay running from the bow up to the masthead, for, if mast and cabin and everything else went overboard, we thought the rope from the bow would nevertheless remain lying inboard, as we were now head on to the seas.

When we realized that the seas had got hold of us, the anchor rope was cut and we were off. A sea rose straight up under us, and we felt the *Kon-Tiki* being lifted up in the air. The great moment had come; we were riding on the wave back at breathless speed, our ramshackle craft creaking and groaning as she quivered under us. The excitement made one's blood boil. I remember that, having no other inspiration, I waved my arm and bellowed "Hurrah!" at the top of my lungs; it afforded a certain relief and could do no harm anyway. The others certainly thought I had gone mad, but they all beamed and grinned enthusiastically. On we ran with the seas rushing in behind us; this was the *Kon-Tiki's* baptism of fire. All must and would go well.

But our elation was soon dampened. A new sea rose high up astern of us like a glittering, green glass wall. As we sank down it came rolling after us, and, in the same second in which I saw it high above me, I felt a violent blow and was submerged under floods of water. I felt the suction through my whole body, with such great power that I had to strain every single muscle in my frame and think of one thing only —hold on, hold on! I think that in such a desperate situation the arms will be torn off before the brain consents to let go, evident as the outcome is. Then I felt that the mountain of water was passing on and relaxing its devilish grip of my body. When the whole mountain had rushed on, with an ear-splitting roaring and crashing, I saw Knut again hanging on beside me, doubled up into a ball. Seen from behind, the great sea was almost flat and gray. As it rushed on, it swept over the ridge of the cabin roof which projected from the water, and there hung the three others, pressed against the cabin roof as the water passed over them.

We were still afloat.

In an instant I renewed my hold, with arms and legs bent round the strong rope. Knut let himself down and with a tiger's leap joined the others on the boxes, where the cabin took the strain. I heard reassuring exclamations from them, but at the same time I saw a new green wall rise up and

come towering toward us. I shouted a warning and made
myself as small and hard as I could where I hung. In an
instant hell was over us again, and the *Kon-Tiki* disappeared
completely under the masses of water. The sea tugged and
pulled with all the force it could bring to bear at the poor
little bundles of human bodies. The second sea rushed over
us, to be followed by a third like it.

Then I heard a triumphant shout from Knut, who was
now hanging on to the rope ladder:

"Look at the raft—she's holding!"

After three seas only the double mast and the cabin had
been knocked a bit crooked. Again we had a feeling of triumph over the elements, and the elation of victory gave us
new strength.

Then I saw the next sea come towering up, higher than
all the rest, and again I bellowed a warning aft to the others
as I climbed up the stay, as high as I could get in a hurry,
and hung on fast. Then I myself disappeared sideways into
the midst of the green wall which towered high over us. The
others, who were farther aft and saw me disappear first, estimated the height of the wall of water at twenty-five feet,
while the foaming crest passed by fifteen feet above the part
of the glassy wall into which I had vanished. Then the great
wave reached them, and we had all one single thought—hold
on, hold on, hold, hold, hold!

We must have hit the reef that time. I myself felt only the
strain on the stay, which seemed to bend and slacken jerkily.
But whether the bumps came from above or below I could
not tell, hanging there. The whole submersion lasted only
seconds, but it demanded more endurance than we usually
have in our bodies. There is greater strength in the human
mechanism than that of the muscles alone. I determined that,
if I was to die, I would die in this position, like a knot on
the stay. The sea thundered on, over and past, and as it
roared by it revealed a hideous sight. The *Kon-Tiki* was
wholly changed, as by the stroke of a magic wand. The
vessel we knew from weeks and months at sea was no more;
in a few seconds our pleasant world had become a shattered
wreck.

I saw only one man on board besides myself. He lay pressed flat across the ridge of the cabin roof, face downward with his arms stretched out on both sides, while the cabin itself was crushed in, like a house of cards, toward the stern and toward the starboard side. The motionless figure was Herman. There was no other sign of life, while the hill of water thundered by, in across the reef. The hardwood mast on the starboard side was broken like a match, and the upper stump, in its fall, had smashed right through the cabin roof, so that the mast and all its gear slanted at a low angle over the reef on the starboard side. Astern, the steering block was twisted round lengthways and the crossbeam broken, while the steering oar was smashed to splinters. The splashboards at the bow were broken like cigar boxes, and the whole deck was torn up and pasted like wet paper against the forward wall of the cabin, along with boxes, cans, canvas, and other cargo. Bamboo sticks and rope ends stuck up everywhere, and the general effect was of complete chaos.

I felt cold fear run through my whole body. What was the good of my holding on? If I lost one single man here, in the run in, the whole thing would be ruined, and for the moment there was only one human figure to be seen after the last buffet. In that second Torstein's hunched-up form appeared outside the raft. He was hanging like a monkey in the ropes from the masthead and managed to get on to the logs again, where he crawled up on to the debris forward of the cabin. Herman, too, now turned his head and gave me a forced grin of encouragement, but did not move. I bellowed in the faint hope of locating the others and heard Bengt's calm voice call out that all hands were aboard. They were lying holding on to the ropes behind the tangled barricade which the tough plaiting from the bamboo deck had built up.

All this happened in the course of a few seconds, while the *Kon-Tiki* was being drawn out of the witches' caldron by the backwash, and a fresh sea came rolling over her. For the last time I bellowed "Hang on!" at the top of my lungs amid the uproar, and that was all I myself did; I hung on and disappeared in the masses of water which rushed over and

past in those endless two or three seconds. That was enough
for me. I saw the ends of the logs knocking and bumping
against a sharp step in the coral reef without going over it.
Then we were sucked out again. I also saw the two men who
lay stretched out across the ridge of the cabin roof, but none
of us smiled any longer. Behind the chaos of bamboo I heard a
calm voice call out:

"This won't do."

I myself felt equally discouraged. As the masthead sank
farther and farther out over the starboard side, I found myself hanging on to a slack line outside the raft. The next sea
came. When it had gone by I was dead tired, and my only
thought was to get up on to the logs and lie behind the barricade. When the backwash retreated, I saw for the first time
the rugged red reef naked beneath us and perceived Torstein
standing, bent double, on gleaming red corals, holding on to
a bunch of rope ends from the mast. Knut, standing aft, was
about to jump. I shouted that we must all keep on the logs,
and Torstein, who had been washed overboard by the pressure of water, sprang up again like a cat.

Two or three more seas rolled over us with diminishing
force, and what happened then I do not remember, except
that water foamed in and out and I myself sank lower and
lower toward the red reef over which we were being lifted in.
Then only crests of foam full of salt spray came whirling in,
and I was able to work my way in on to the raft, where we
all made for the after end of the logs which was highest up
on the reef.

At the same moment Knut crouched down and sprang up
on to the reef with the line which lay clear astern. While
the backwash was running out, he waded through the whirling water some thirty yards in and stood safely at the end of
the line when the next sea foamed in toward him, died down,
and ran back from the flat reef like a broad stream.

Then Erik came crawling out of the collapsed cabin, with
his shoes on. If we had all done as he did, we should have
got off cheaply. As the cabin had not been washed overboard
but had been pressed down pretty flat under the canvas, Erik
lay quietly stretched out among the cargo and heard the peals

of thunder crashing above him while the collapsed bamboo walls curved downward. Bengt had had a slight concussion when the mast fell but had managed to crawl under the wrecked cabin alongside Erik. We should all of us have been lying there if we had realized in advance how firmly the countless lashings and plaited bamboo sheets would hang on to the main logs under the pressure of the water.

Erik was now standing ready on the logs aft, and when the sea retired he, too, jumped up on to the reef. It was Herman's turn next, and then Bengt's. Each time the raft was pushed a bit farther in, and, when Torstein's turn and my own came, the raft already lay so far in on the reef that there was no longer any ground for abandoning her. All hands began the work of salvage.

We were now twenty yards away from that devilish step up on the reef, and it was there and beyond it that the breakers came rolling after one another in long lines. The coral polyps had taken care to build the atoll so high that only the very tops of the breakers were able to send a fresh stream of sea water past us and into the lagoon, which abounded in fish. Here inside was the corals' own world, and they disported themselves in the strangest shapes and colors.

A long way in on the reef the others found the rubber raft, lying drifting and quite waterlogged. They emptied it and dragged it back to the wreck, and we loaded it to the full with the most important equipment, like the radio set, provisions, and water bottles. We dragged all this in across the reef and piled it up on the top of a huge block of coral, which lay alone on the inside of the reef like a large meteorite. Then we went back to the wreck for fresh loads. We could never know what the sea would be up to when the tidal currents got to work around us.

In the shallow water inside the reef we saw something bright shining in the sun. When we waded over to pick it up, to our astonishment we saw two empty tins. This was not exactly what we had expected to find there, and we were still more surprised when we saw that the little boxes were quite bright and newly opened and stamped "Pineapple," with the same inscription as that on the new field rations we ourselves were testing for the quartermaster. They were indeed two of our own pineapple tins which we had thrown overboard after our last meal on board the *Kon-Tiki*. We had followed close behind them up on the reef.

We were standing on sharp, rugged coral blocks, and on the uneven bottom we wadded now ankle-deep, now chest-deep, according to the channels and stream beds in the reef. Anemones and corals gave the whole reef the appearance of a rock garden covered with mosses and cactus and fossilized plants, red and green and yellow and white. There was no color that was not represented, either in corals or algae or in shells and sea slugs and fantastic fish, which were wriggling about everywhere. In the deeper channels small sharks about four feet long came sneaking up to us in the crystal-clear water. But we had only to smack the water with the palms of our hands for them to turn about and keep at a distance.

Where we had stranded, we had only pools of water and wet patches of coral about us; farther in lay the calm blue lagoon. The tide was going out, and we continually saw more corals sticking up out of the water round us, while the surf which thundered without interruption along the reef sank down, as it were, a floor lower. What would happen there on the narrow reef when the tide began to flow again was uncertain. We must get away.

The reef stretched like a half-submerged fortress wall up to the north and down to the south. In the extreme south was a long island densely covered with tall palm forest. And just above us to the north, only 600 or 700 yards away, lay another but considerably smaller palm island. It lay inside the reef, with palm tops rising into the sky and snow-white sandy beaches running out into the still lagoon. The whole island looked like a bulging green basket of flowers, or a little bit of concentrated paradise.

This island we chose.

Herman stood beside me beaming all over his bearded face. He did not say a word, only stretched out his hand and laughed quietly. The *Kon-Tiki* still lay far out on the reef with the spray flying over her. She was a wreck, but an honorable wreck. Everything above deck was smashed up, but the nine balsa logs from the Quevedo forest in Ecuador were as intact as ever. They had saved our lives. The sea had claimed but little of the cargo, and none of what we had stowed inside the cabin. We ourselves had stripped the raft of everything of real value, which now lay in safety on the top of the great sun-smitten rock inside the reef.

Since I had jumped off the raft, I had genuinely missed the sight of all the pilot fish wriggling in front of our bow. Now the great balsa logs lay up on the reef in six inches of water, and brown sea slugs lay writhing under the bows. The pilot fish were gone. The dolphins were gone. Only unknown flat fish with peacock patterns and blunt tails wriggled inquisitively in and out between the logs. We had arrived in a new world. Johannes had left his hole. He had doubtless found another lurking place here.

I took a last look round on board the wreck and caught sight of a little baby palm in a flattened basket. It projected from an eye in a coconut to a length of eighteen inches, and two roots stuck out below. I waded in toward the island with the nut in my hand. A little way ahead I saw Knut wading happily landward with a model of the raft, which he had made with much labor on the voyage, under his arm. We soon passed Bengt. He was a splendid steward. With a lump on his forehead and sea water dripping from his beard, he was walking bent double pushing a box, which danced along before him every time the breakers outside sent a stream over into the lagoon. He lifted the lid proudly. It was the kitchen box, and in it were the primus and cooking utensils in good order.

I shall never forget that wade across the reef toward the heavenly palm island that grew larger as it came to meet us. When I reached the sunny sand beach, I slipped off my shoes and thrust my bare toes down into the warm, bone-dry sand. It was as though I enjoyed the sight of every footprint which dug itself into the virgin sand beach that led up to the palm trunks. Soon the palm tops closed over my head, and I went on, right in toward the center of the tiny island. Green coconuts hung under the palm tufts, and some luxuriant bushes were thickly covered with snow-white blossoms, which smelled so sweet and seductive that I felt quite faint. In the interior of the island two quite tame terns flew about my shoulders. They were as white and light as wisps of cloud. Small lizards shot away from my feet, and the most important inhabitants of the island were large blood-red hermit crabs which lumbered along in every direction with stolen snail shells as large as eggs adhering to their soft hinder parts.

I was completely overwhelmed. I sank down on my knees and thrust my fingers deep down into the dry warm sand.

The voyage was over. We were all alive. We had run ashore on a small uninhabited South Sea island. And what an island! Torstein came in, flung away a sack, threw himself flat on his back and looked up at the palm tops and the white birds, light as down, which circled noiselessly just above us. Soon we were all six lying there. Herman, always energetic, climbed up a small palm and pulled down a cluster of large green coconuts. We cut off their soft tops with our machete knives, as if they were eggs, and poured down our throats the most delicious refreshing drink in the world—sweet, cold milk from young and seedless palm fruit. On the reef outside resounded the monotonous drum beats from the guard at the gates of paradise.

"Purgatory was a bit damp," said Bengt, "but heaven is more or less as I'd imagined it."

We stretched ourselves luxuriously on the ground and smiled up at the white trade-wind clouds drifting by westward up above the palm tops. Now we were no longer following them helplessly; now we lay on a fixed, motionless island, in Polynesia.

And as we lay and stretched ourselves, the breakers outside us rumbled like a train, to and fro, to and fro, all along the horizon.

Bengt was right; this was heaven.

8 AMONG POLYNESIANS

A Robinson Crusoe Touch—Fear of Relief—All Well,
Kon-Tiki!—Other Wrecks—Uninhabited Islands—Fight with
Marine Eels—Natives Find Us—Ghosts on the Reef—
Envoy to the Chief—The Chief Visits Us—The Kon-Tiki
Is Recognized—A High Tide—Our Craft's Overland
Cruise—Only Four on the Island—Natives Fetch Us—
Reception in the Village— Forefathers from the Sunrise—
Hula Feast—Medicine Men on the Air—We Become Royalty
—Another Shipwreck—The "Tamara" Salvages the "Maoae"—
To Tahiti—Meeting on the Quay—A Royal Stay—Six
Wreaths

OUR LITTLE ISLAND WAS UNINHABITED. WE
soon got to know every palm clump and every beach, for
the island was barely two hundred yards across. The highest
point was less than six feet above the lagoon.

Over our heads, in the palm tops, there hung great clusters
of green coconut husks, which insulated their contents of
cold coconut milk from the tropical sun, so we should not
be thirsty in the first weeks. There were also ripe coconuts, a
swarm of hermit crabs, and all sorts of fish in the lagoon;
we should be well off.

On the north side of the island we found the remnants of
an old, unpainted wooden cross, half buried in the coral sand.
Here there was the view northward along the reef to the
stripped wreck, which we had first seen closer in as we drifted
by on the way to our stranding. Still farther northward we

saw in a bluish haze the palm tufts of another small island. The island to southward, on which the trees grew thickly, was much closer. We saw no sign of life there, either, but for the time we had other matters to think about.

Robinson Crusoe Hesselberg came limping up in his big straw hat with his arms full of crawling hermit crabs. Knut set fire to some dry wood, and soon we had crab and coconut milk with coffee for dessert.

"Feels all right being ashore, doesn't it, boys?" Knut asked delightedly.

He had himself enjoyed this feeling once before on the voyage, at Angatau. As he spoke, he stumbled and poured half a kettle of boiling water over Bengt's bare feet. We were all of us a bit unsteady the first day ashore, after 101 days on board the raft, and would suddenly begin reeling about among the palm trunks because we had put out a foot to counter a sea that did not come.

When Bengt handed over to us our respective mess utensils, Erik grinned broadly. I remember that, after the last meal on board, I had leaned over the side of the raft and washed up as usual, while Erik looked in across the reef, saying: "I don't think I shall bother to wash up today." When he found his things in the kitchen box, they were as clean as mine.

After the meal and a good stretch on the ground we set about putting together the soaked radio apparatus; we must do it quickly so that Torstein and Knut might get on the air before the man on Rarotonga sent out a report of our sad end.

Most of the radio equipment had already been brought ashore, and among the things which lay drifting on the reef Bengt found a box, on which he laid hands. He jumped high into the air from an electric shock; there was no doubt that the contents belonged to the radio section. While the operators unscrewed, coupled, and put together, we others set about pitching camp.

Out on the wreck we found the heavy waterlogged sail and dragged it ashore. We stretched it between two big palms in a little opening, looking on to the lagoon, and supported two other corners with bamboo sticks which came drifting in from the wreck. A thick hedge of wild flowering bushes forced the sail together so that we had a roof and three walls and, moreover, a clear view of the shining lagoon, while our nostrils were filled with an insinuating scent of blossoms. It was good to be here. We all laughed quietly and enjoyed our ease; we each made our beds of fresh palm leaves, pulling up loose branches of coral which stuck up inconveniently out of the sand. Before night fell we had a very pleasant rest, and over our heads we saw the big bearded face of good old Kon-Tiki. No longer did he swell out his breast with the east wind behind him. He now lay motionless on his back looking up at the stars which came twinkling out over Polynesia.

On the bushes round us hung wet flags and sleeping bags, and soaked articles lay on the sand to dry. Another day on this island of sunshine and everything would be nicely dry. Even the radio boys had to give it up until the sun had a chance of drying the inside of their apparatus next day. We took the sleeping bags down from the trees and turned in, disputing boastfully as to who had the driest bag. Bengt won, for his did not squelch when he turned over. Heavens, how good it was to be able to sleep!

When we woke next morning at sunrise, the sail was bent down and full of rain water as pure as crystal. Bengt took charge of this asset and then ambled down to the lagoon and jerked ashore some curious breakfast fish which he decoyed into channels in the sand.

That night Herman had had pains in the neck and back where he had injured himself before the start from Lima, and Erik had a return of his vanished lumbago. Otherwise we had come out of the trip over the reef astonishingly lightly, with scratches and small wounds, except for Bengt who had had a blow on the forehead when the mast fell and had a slight concussion. I myself looked most peculiar, with my arms and legs bruised blue black all over by the pressure against the rope.

But none of us was in such a bad state that the sparkling clear lagoon did not entice him to a brisk swim before breakfast. It was an immense lagoon. Far out it was blue and rip-

pled by the trade wind, and it was so wide that we could
only just see the tops of a row of misty, blue palm islands
which marked the curve of the atoll on the other side. But
here, in the lee of the islands, the trade wind rustled peacefully in the fringed palm tops, making them stir and sway,
while the lagoon lay like a motionless mirror below and reflected all their beauty. The bitter salt water was so pure and
clear that gaily colored corals in nine feet of water seemed
so near the surface that we thought we should cut our toes
on them in swimming. And the water abounded in beautiful varieties of colorful fish. It was a marvelous world in
which to disport oneself. The water was just cold enough to
be refreshing, and the air was pleasantly warm and dry from
the sun. But we must get ashore again quickly today;
Rarotonga would broadcast alarming news if nothing had
been heard from the raft at the end of the day.

Coils and radio parts lay drying in the tropical sun on slabs
of coral, and Torstein and Knut coupled and screwed. The
whole day passed, and the atmosphere grew more and more
hectic. The rest of us abandoned all other jobs and crowded
round the radio in the hope of being able to give assistance.
We must be on the air before 10 P.M. Then the thirty-six
hours' time limit would be up, and the radio amateur on
Rarotonga would send out appeals for airplane and relief expeditions.

Noon came, afternoon came, and the sun set. If only the
man on Rarotonga would contain himself! Seven o'clock,
eight, nine. The tension was at breaking point. Not a sign of
life in the transmitter, but the receiver, an NC-173, began
to liven up somewhere at the bottom of the scale and we
heard faint music. But not on the amateur wave length. It
was eating its way up, however; perhaps it was a wet coil
which was drying inward from one end. The transmitter was
still stone-dead—short circuits and sparks everywhere.

There was less than an hour left. This would never do.
The regular transmitter was given up, and a little sabotage
transmitter from wartime was tried again. We had tested it
several times before in the course of the day, but without
result. Now perhaps it had become a little drier. All the bat-

teries were completely ruined, and we got power by cranking a tiny hand generator. It was heavy, and we four who
were laymen in radio matters took turns all day long sitting
and turning the infernal thing.

The thirty-six hours would soon be up. I remember someone whispering "Seven minutes more," "Five minutes more,"
and then no one would look at his watch again. The transmitter was as dumb as ever, but the receiver was sputtering
upward toward the right wave length. Suddenly it crackled
on the Rarotonga man's frequency, and we gathered that he
was in full contact with the telegraph station in Tahiti. Soon
afterward we picked up the following fragment of a message
sent out from Rarotonga:

"- - - no plane this side of Samoa. I am quite sure - - -."

Then it died away again. The tension was unbearable.
What was brewing out there? Had they already begun to
send out plane and rescue expeditions? Now, no doubt, messages concerning us were going over the air in every direction.

The two operators worked feverishly. The sweat trickled
from their faces as freely as it did from ours who sat turning
the handle. Power began slowly to come into the transmitter's
aerial, and Torstein pointed ecstatically to an arrow which
swung slowly up over a scale when he held the Morse key
down. Now it was coming!

We turned the handle madly while Torstein called Rarotonga. No one heard us. Once more. Now the receiver was
working again, but Rarotonga did not hear us. We called
Hal and Frank at Los Angeles and the Naval School at Lima,
but no one heard us.

Then Torstein sent out a CQ message: that is to say, he
called all the stations in the world which could hear us on
our special amateur wave length.

That was of some use. Now a faint voice out in the ether
began to call us slowly. We called again and said that we
heard him. Then the slow voice out in the ether said:

"My name is Paul—I live in Colorado. What is your name
and where do you live?"

This was a radio amateur. Torstein seized the key, while
we turned the handle, and replied:

"This is the *Kon-Tiki*. We are stranded on a desert island in the Pacific."

Paul did not believe the message. He thought it was a radio amateur in the next street pulling his leg, and he did not come on the air again. We tore our hair in desperation. Here were we, sitting under the palm tops on a starry night on a desert island, and no one even believed what we said.

Torstein did not give up; he was at the key again sending "All well, all well, all well," unceasingly. We must at all costs stop all this rescue machinery from starting out across the Pacific.

Then we heard, rather faintly, in the receiver:

"If all's well, why worry?"

Then all was quiet in the ether. That was all.

We could have leaped into the air and shaken down all the coconuts for sheer desperation, and heaven knows what we should have done if both Rarotonga and good old Hal had not suddenly heard us. Hal wept for delight, he said, at hearing LI 2 B again. All the tension stopped immediately; we were once more alone and undisturbed on our South Sea island and turned in, worn out, on our beds of palm leaves.

Next day we took it easy and enjoyed life to the full. Some bathed, others fished or went out exploring on the reef in search of curious marine creatures, while the most energetic cleared up in camp and made our surroundings pleasant. Out on the point which looked toward the *Kon-Tiki* we dug a hole on the edge of the trees, lined it with leaves, and planted in it the sprouting coconut from Peru. A cairn of corals was erected beside it, opposite the place where the *Kon-Tiki* had run ashore.

The *Kon-Tiki* had been washed still farther in during the night and lay almost dry in a few pools of water, squeezed in among a group of big coral blocks a long way through the reef.

After a thorough baking in the warm sand Erik and Herman were in fine fettle again and were anxious to go southward along the reef in the hope of getting over to the large island which lay down there. I warned them more against eels than against sharks, and each of them stuck his long machete knife into his belt. I knew the coral reef was the habitat of a frightful eel with long poisonous teeth which could easily tear off a man's leg. They wriggle to the attack with lightning rapidity and are the terror of the natives, who are not afraid to swim round a shark.

The two men were able to wade over long stretches of the reef to southward, but there were occasional channels of deeper water running this way and that where they had to jump in and swim. They reached the big island safely and waded ashore. The island, long and narrow and covered with palm forest, ran farther south between sunny beaches under the shelter of the reef. The two continued along the island till they came to the southern point. From here the reef, covered with white foam, ran on southward to other distant islands. They found the wreck of a big ship down there; she had four masts and lay on the shore cut in two. She was an old Spanish sailing vessel which had been loaded with rails, and rusty rails lay scattered all along the reef. They returned along the other side of the island but did not find so much as a track in the sand.

On the way back across the reef they were continually coming upon curious fish and were trying to catch some of them when they were suddenly attacked by no fewer than eight large eels. They saw them coming in the clear water and jumped up on to a large coral block, round and under which the eels writhed. The slimy brutes were as thick as a man's calf and speckled green and black like poisonous snakes, with small heads, malignant snake eyes, and teeth an inch long and as sharp as an awl. The men hacked with their machete knives at the little swaying heads which came writhing toward them; they cut the head off one and another was injured. The blood in the sea attracted a whole flock of young blue sharks which attacked the dead and injured eels, while Erik and Herman were able to jump over to another block of coral and get away.

On the same day I was wading in toward the island when something, with a lightning movement, caught hold of my ankle on both sides and held on tight. It was a cuttlefish. It was not large, but it was a horrible feeling to have the cold

gripping arms about one's limb and to exchange looks with
the evil little eyes in the bluish-red, beaked sack which constituted the body. I jerked in my foot as hard as I could, and
the squid, which was barely three feet long, followed it without letting go. It must have been the bandage on my foot
which attracted it. I dragged myself in jerks toward the beach
with the disgusting carcass hanging on to my foot. Only when
I reached the edge of the dry sand did it let go and retreat
slowly through the shallow water, with arms outstretched
and eyes directed shoreward, as though ready for a new attack if I wanted one. When I threw a few lumps of coral at
it, it darted away.

Our various experiences out on the reef only added a spice
to our heavenly existence on the island within. But we could
not spend all our lives here, and we must begin to think about
how we should get back to the outer world. After a week
the *Kon-Tiki* had bumped her way in to the middle of the
reef, where she lay stuck fast on dry land. The great logs
had pushed away and broken off large slabs of coral in the
effort to force their way forward to the lagoon, but now the
wooden raft lay immovable, and all our pulling and all our
pushing were equally unavailing. If we could only get the
wreck into the lagoon, we could always splice the mast and
rig her sufficiently to be able to sail with the wind across the
friendly lagoon and see what we found on the other side.
If any of the islands were inhabited, it must be some of those
which lay along the horizon away in the east, where the atoll
turned its façade toward the lee side.

The days passed.

Then one morning some of the fellows came tearing up
and said they had seen a white sail on the lagoon. From up
among the palm trunks we could see a tiny speck which was
curiously white against the opal-blue lagoon. It was evidently
a sail close to land on the other side. We could see that it
was tacking. Soon another appeared.

They grew in size, as the morning went on, and came
nearer. They came straight toward us. We hoisted the French
flag on a palm tree and waved our own Norwegian flag on a
pole. One of the sails was now so near that we could see

that it belonged to a Polynesian outrigger canoe. The rig was of more recent type. Two brown figures stood on board gazing at us. We waved. They waved back and sailed straight in on to the shallows.

"*Ia-ora-na*," we greeted them in Polynesian.

"*Ia-ora-na*," they shouted back in chorus, and one jumped out and dragged his canoe after him as he came wading over the sandy shallows straight toward us.

The two men had white men's clothes but brown men's bodies. They were barelegged, well built, and wore homemade straw hats to protect them from the sun. They landed and approached us rather uncertainly, but, when we smiled and shook hands with them in turn, they beamed on us with rows of pearly teeth which said more than words.

Our Polynesian greeting had astonished and encouraged the two canoers in exactly the same way as we ourselves had been deceived when their kinsman off Angatau had called out "Good night," and they reeled off a long rhapsody in Polynesian before they realized that their outpourings were going wide of the mark. Then they had nothing more to say but giggled amiably and pointed to the other canoe which was approaching.

There were three men in this, and, when they waded ashore and greeted us, it appeared that one of them could talk a little French. We learned that there was a native village on one of the islands across the lagoon, and from it the Polynesians had seen our fire several nights earlier. Now there was only one passage leading in through the Raroia reef to the circle of islands around the lagoon, and, as this passage ran right past the village, no one could approach these islands inside the reef without being seen by the inhabitants of the village. The old people in the village, therefore, had come to the conclusion that the light they saw on the reef to eastward could not be the work of men but must be something supernatural. This had quenched in them all desire to go across and see for themselves. But then part of a box had come drifting across the lagoon, and on it some signs were painted. Two of the natives, who had been on Tahiti and learned the alphabet, had deciphered the inscription and read TIKI in

big black letters on the slab of wood. Then there was no
longer any doubt that there were ghosts on the reef, for Tiki
was the long-dead founder of their own race—they all knew
that. But then tinned bread, cigarettes, cocoa, and a box with
an old shoe in it came drifting across the lagoon. Now they all
realized that there had been a shipwreck on the eastern side
of the reef, and the chief sent out two canoes to search for
the survivors whose fire they had seen on the island.

Urged on by the others, the brown man who spoke French
asked why the slab of wood that drifted across the lagoon
had "Tiki" on it. We explained that "Kon-Tiki" was on all our
equipment and that it was the name of the vessel in which
we had come.

Our new friends were loud in their astonishment when
they heard that all on board had been saved, when the vessel
stranded, and that the flattened wreck out on the reef was
actually the craft in which we had come. They wanted to
put us all into the canoes at once and take us across to the
village. We thanked them and refused, as we wanted to stay
till we had got the Kon-Tiki off the reef. They looked aghast
at the flat contraption out on the reef; surely we could not
dream of getting that collapsed hull afloat again! Finally the
spokesman said emphatically that we must go with them; the
chief had given them strict orders not to return without us.

We then decided that one of us should go with the natives
as envoy to the chief and should then come back and report
to us on the conditions on the other island. We would not
let the raft remain on the reef and could not abandon all the
equipment on our little island. Bengt went with the natives.
The two canoes were pushed off from the sand and soon
disappeared westward with a fair wind.

Next day the horizon swarmed with white sails. Now, it
seemed, the natives were coming to fetch us with all the craft
they had.

The whole convoy tacked across toward us, and, when they
came near, we saw our good friend Bengt waving his hat in
the first canoe, surrounded by brown figures. He shouted
to us that the chief himself was with him, and the five of us

formed up respectfully down on the beach where they were wading ashore.

Bengt presented us to the chief with great ceremony. The chief's name, Bengt said, was Tepiuraiarii Teriifaatau, but he would understand whom we meant if we called him Teka. We called him Teka.

Teka was a tall, slender Polynesian with uncommonly intelligent eyes. He was an important person, a descendant of the old royal line in Tahiti, and was chief of both the Raroia and the Takume islands. He had been to school in Tahiti, so that he spoke French and could both read and write. He told me that the capital of Norway was called Christiania and asked if I knew Bing Crosby. He also told us that only three foreign vessels had called at Raroia in the last ten years, but that the village was visited several times a year by the native copra schooner from Tahiti, which brought merchandise and took away coconut kernels in exchange. They had been expecting the schooner for some weeks now, so she might come at any time.

Bengt's report, summarized, was that there was no school, radio, or any white men on Raroia, but that the 127 Polynesians in the village had done all they could to make us comfortable there and had prepared a great reception for us when we came over.

The chief's first request was to see the boat which had brought us ashore on the reef alive. We waded out toward the *Kon-Tiki* with a string of natives after us. When we drew near, the natives suddenly stopped and uttered loud exclamations, all talking at once. We could now see the logs of the *Kon-Tiki* plainly, and one of the natives burst out:

"That's not a boat, it's a *pae-pae!*"

"*Pae-pae!*" they all repeated in chorus.

They splashed out across the reef at a gallop and clambered up on to the *Kon-Tiki*. They scrambled about everywhere like excited children, feeling the logs, the bamboo plaiting, and the ropes. The chief was in as high spirits as the others; he came back and repeated with an inquiring expression:

"The *Tiki* isn't a boat, she's a *pae-pae.*"

Pae-pae is the Polynesian word for "raft" and "platform," and on Easter Island it is also the word used for the natives' canoes. The chief told us that such *pae-pae* no longer existed, but that the oldest men in the village could relate old traditions of them. The natives all outshouted one another in admiration for the great balsa logs, but they turned up their noses at the ropes. Ropes like that did not last many months in salt water and sun. They showed us with pride the lashings on their own outriggers; they had plaited them themselves of coconut hemp, and such ropes remained as good as new for five years at sea.

When we waded back to our little island, it was named Fenua Kon-Tiki, or Kon-Tiki Island. This was a name we could all pronounce, but our brown friends had a hard job trying to pronounce our short Nordic Christian names. They were delighted when I said they could call me Terai Mateata, for the great chief in Tahiti had given me that name when adopting me as his "son" the first time I was in those parts.

The natives brought out fowls and eggs and breadfruit from the canoes, while others speared big fish in the lagoon with three-pronged spears, and we had a feast round the campfire. We had to narrate all our experiences with the *pae-pae* at sea, and they wanted to hear about the whale shark again and again. And every time we came to the point at which Erik rammed the harpoon into its skull, they uttered the same cries of excitement. They recognized at once every single fish of which we showed them sketches and promptly gave us the names in Polynesian. But they had never seen or heard of the whale shark or the *Gempylus*.

When the evening came, we turned on the radio, to the great delight of the whole assemblage. Church music was most to their taste until, to our own astonishment, we picked up real hula music from America. Then the liveliest of them began to wriggle with their arms curved over their heads, and soon the whole company sprang up on their haunches and danced the hula-hula in time with the music. When night came, all camped round a fire on the beach. It was as much of an adventure to the natives as it was to us.

When we awoke next morning, they were already up and

frying newly caught fish, while six freshly opened coconut shells stood ready for us to quench our morning thirst.

The reef was thundering more than usual that day; the wind had increased in strength, and the surf was whipping high into the air out there behind the wreck.

"The *Tiki* will come in today," said the chief, pointing to the wreck. "There'll be a high tide."

About eleven o'clock the water began to flow past us into the lagoon. The lagoon began to fill like a big basin, and the water rose all round the island. Later in the day the real inflow from the sea came. The water came rolling in, terrace after terrace, and more and more of the reef sank below the surface of the sea. The masses of water rolled forward along both sides of the island. They tore away large coral blocks and dug up great sandbanks which disappeared like flour before the wind, while others were built up. Loose bamboos from the wreck came sailing past us, and the *Kon-Tiki* began to move. Everything that was lying along the beach had to be carried up into the interior of the island so that it might not be caught by the tide. Soon only the highest stones on the reef were visible, and all the beaches round our island had gone, while the water flowed up toward the herbage of the pancake island. This was eerie. It looked as if the whole sea was invading us. The *Kon-Tiki* swung right round and drifted until she was caught by some other coral blocks.

The natives flung themselves into the water and swam and waded through the eddies till, moving from bank to bank, they reached the raft. Knut and Erik followed. Ropes lay ready on board the raft, and, when she rolled over the last coral blocks and broke loose from the reef, the natives jumped overboard and tried to hold her. They did not know the *Kon-Tiki* and her ungovernable urge to push on westward; so they were towed along helplessly with her. She was soon moving at a good speed right across the reef and into the lagoon. She became slightly at a loss when she reached quieter water and seemed to be looking round as though to obtain a survey of further possibilities. Before she began to move again and discovered the exit across the lagoon, the natives had already succeeded in getting the end of the rope around a

palm on land. And there the Kon-Tiki hung, tied up fast in
the lagoon. The craft that went over land and water had
made her way across the barricade and into the lagoon in
the interior of Raroia.

With inspiring war cries, to which "ke-ke-te-huru-huru"
formed an animating refrain, we hauled the Kon-Tiki by our
combined efforts in to the shore of the island of her own
name. The tide reached a point four feet above normal high
water. We had thought the whole island was going to disappear before our eyes.

The wind-whipped waves were breaking all over the lagoon, and we could not get much of our equipment into the
narrow, wet canoes. The natives had to get back to the village in a hurry, and Bengt and Herman went with them to
see a small boy who lay dying in a hut in the village. The
boy had an abscess on his head, and we had penicillin.

Next day we four were alone on Kon-Tiki Island. The east
wind was now so strong that the natives could not come
across the lagoon, which was studded with sharp coral formations and shoals. The tide, which had somewhat receded,
flowed in again fiercely, in long, rushing step formations.

Next day it was quieter again. We were now able to dive
under the Kon-Tiki and ascertain that the nine logs were
intact, even if the reef had planed an inch or two off the
bottom. The cordage lay so deep in its grooves that only
four of the numerous ropes had been cut by the corals. We
set about clearing up on board. Our proud vessel looked
better when the mess had been removed from the deck, the
cabin pulled out again like a concertina, and the mast spliced
and set upright.

In the course of the day the sails appeared on the horizon
again; the natives were coming to fetch us and the rest of the
cargo. Herman and Bengt were with them, and they told us
that the natives had prepared great festivities in the village.
When we got over to the other island, we must not leave the
canoes till the chief himself had indicated that we might do
so.

We ran across the lagoon, which here was seven miles
wide, before a fresh breeze. It was with real sorrow that we

saw the familiar palms on Kon-Tiki Island waving us good-by as they changed into a clump and shrank into one small indefinable island like all the others along the eastern reef. But ahead of us larger islands were broadening out. And on one of them we saw a jetty and smoke rising from huts among the palm trunks.

The village looked quite dead; not a soul was to be seen. What was brewing now? Down on the beach, behind a jetty of coral blocks, stood two solitary figures, one tall and thin and one big and stout as a barrel. As we came in, we saluted them both. They were the chief Teka and the vice-chief Tupuhoe. We all fell for Tupuhoe's broad hearty smile. Teka was a clear brain and a diplomat, but Tupuhoe was a pure child of nature and a sterling fellow, with a humor and a primitive force the like of which one meets but rarely. With his powerful body and kingly features he was exactly what one expects a Polynesian chief to be. Tupuhoe was, indeed, the real chief on the island, but Teka had gradually acquired the supreme position because he could speak French and count and write, so that the village was not cheated when the schooner came from Tahiti to fetch copra.

Teka explained that we were to march together up to the meetinghouse in the village, and when all the boys had come ashore we set off thither in ceremonial procession, Herman first with the flag waving on a harpoon shaft, and then I myself between the two chiefs.

The village bore obvious marks of the copra trade with Tahiti; both planks and corrugated iron had been imported in the schooner. While some huts were built in a picturesque old-fashioned style, with twigs and plaited palm leaves, others were knocked together with nails and planks as small tropical bungalows. A large house built of planks, standing alone among the palms, was the new village meetinghouse; there we six whites were to stay. We marched in with the flag by a small back door and out on to a broad flight of steps before the façade. Before us in the square stood everyone in the village who could walk or crawl—women and children, old and young. All were intensely serious; even our cheerful

friends from Kon-Tiki Island stood drawn up among the
others and did not give us a sign of recognition.

When we had all come out on the steps, the whole assembly opened their mouths simultaneously and joined in singing—the "Marseillaise"! Teka, who knew the words, led the
singing, and it went fairly well in spite of a few old women
getting stuck up on the high notes. They had been training
hard for this. The French and Norwegian flags were hoisted
in front of the steps, and this ended the official reception by
the chief Teka. He retired quietly into the background, and
now stout Tupuhoe sprang forward and became master of
the ceremonies. Tupuhoe gave a quick sign, on which the
whole assembly burst into a new song. This time it went
better, for the tune was composed by themselves and the
words, too, were in their language—and sing their own hula
they could. The melody was so fascinating, in all its touching
simplicity, that we felt a tingling down our backs as the
South Sea came roaring toward us. A few individuals led
the singing and the whole choir joined in regularly; there
were variations in the melody, though the words were always the same:

"Good day, Terai Mateata and your men, who have come
across the sea on a *pae-pae* to us on Raroia; yes, good day,
may you remain long among us and share memories with us
so that we can always be together, even when you go away
to a far land. Good day."

We had to ask them to sing the song over again, and more
and more life came into the whole assembly as they began to
feel less constrained. Then Tupuhoe asked me to say a few
words to the people as to why we had come across the sea on
a *pae-pae*; they had all been counting on this. I was to speak
in French, and Teka would translate bit by bit.

It was an uneducated but highly intelligent gathering of
brown people that stood waiting for me to speak. I told them
that I had been among their kinsmen out here in the South
Sea islands before, and that I had heard of their first chief,
Tiki, who had brought their forefathers out to the islands
from a mysterious country whose whereabouts on one knew
any longer. But in a distant land called Peru, I said, a mighty

chief had once ruled whose name was Tiki. The people called him Kon-Tiki, or Sun-Tiki, because he said he was descended from the sun. Tiki and a number of followers had at last disappeared from their country on big *pae-paes;* therefore we six thought that he was the same Tiki who had come to those islands. As nobody would believe that a *pae-pae* could make the voyage across the sea, we ourselves had set out from Peru on a *pae-pae,* and here we were, so it could be done.

When the little speech was translated by Teka, Tupuhoe was all fire and flame and sprang forward in front of the assembly in a kind of ecstasy. He rumbled away in Polynesian, flung out his arms, pointed to heaven and us, and in his flood of speech constantly repeated the word Tiki. He talked so fast that it was impossible to follow the thread of what he said, but the whole assembly swallowed every word and was visibly excited. Teka, on the contrary, looked quite embarrassed when he had to translate.

Tupuhoe had said that his father and grandfather, and his fathers before him, had told of Tiki and had said that Tiki was their first chief who was now in heaven. But then the white men came and said that the traditions of their ancestors were lies. Tiki had never existed. He was not in heaven at all, for Jehovah was there. Tiki was a heathen god, and they must not believe in him any longer. But now we six had come to them across the sea on a *pae-pae.* We were the first whites who had admitted that their fathers had spoken the truth. Tiki had lived, he had been real, but now he was dead and in heaven.

Horrified at the thought of upsetting the missionaries' work, I had to hurry forward and explain that Tiki had lived, that was sure and certain, and now he was dead. But whether he was in heaven or in hell today only Jehovah knew, for Jehovah was in heaven while Tiki himself had been a mortal man, a great chief like Teka and Tupuhoe, perhaps still greater.

This produced both cheerfulness and contentment among the brown men, and the nodding and mumbling among them showed clearly that the explanation had fallen on good

soil. Tiki had lived—that was the main thing. If he was in
hell now, no one was any the worse for it but himself; on
the contrary, Tupuhoe suggested, perhaps it increased the
chances of seeing him again.

Three old men pushed forward and wanted to shake hands
with us. There was no doubt that it was they who had kept
the memories of Tiki alive among the people, and the chief
told us that one of the old men knew an immense number of
traditions and historical ballads from his forefathers' time. I
asked the old man if there was, in the traditions, any hint of
the direction from which Tiki had come. No, none of the old
men could remember having heard that. But after long and
careful reflection the oldest of the three said that Tiki had
with him a near relation who was called Maui, and in the
ballad of Maui it was said that he had come to the islands
from Pura and *pura* was the word for the part of the sky
where the sun rose. If Maui had come from Pura, the old
man said, Tiki had no doubt come from the same place, and
we six on the *pae-pae* had also come from *pura*—that was
sure enough.

I told the brown men that on a lonely island near Easter
Island, called Mangareva, the people had never learned the
use of canoes and had continued to use big *pae-paes* at sea
right down to our time. This the old men did not know, but
they knew that their forefathers also had used big *pae-paes*.
However, they had gradually gone out of use, and now they
had nothing but the name and traditions left. In really ancient times they had been called *rongo-rongo*, the oldest man
said, but that was a word which no longer existed in the
language. *Rongo-rongo* were mentioned in the most ancient
legends.

This name was interesting, for Rongo—on certain islands
pronounced "Lono"—was the name of one of the Polynesians' best-known legendary ancestors. He was expressly described as white and fair-haired. When Captain Cook first
came to Hawaii, he was received with open arms by the
islanders because they thought he was their white kinsman
Rongo, who, after an absence of generations, had come back
from their ancestors' homeland in his big sailing ship. And

on Easter Island the word *"rongo-rongo"* was the designation
for the mysterious hieroglyphs the secret of which was lost
with the last "long-ears" who could write.

While the old men wanted to discuss Tiki and *rongo-
rongo*, the young ones wanted to hear about the whale shark
and the voyage across the sea. But the food was waiting,
and Teka was tired of interpreting.

Now the whole village was allowed to come up and shake
hands with each of us. The men mumbled *"ia-ora-na"* and
almost shook our hands out of joint, while the girls squirmed
forward and greeted us coquettishly yet shyly and the old
women babbled and cackled and pointed to our beards and
the color of our skin. Friendliness beamed from every face,
so it was quite immaterial that there was a hubbub of linguistic confusion. If they said something incomprehensible to
us in Polynesian, we gave them tit for tat in Norwegian. We
had the greatest fun together. The first native word we all
learned was the word for "like," and when, moreover, one
could point to what one liked and count on getting it at
once, it was all very simple. If one wrinkled one's nose when
"like" was said, it meant "don't like," and on this basis we
got along pretty well.

As soon as we had become acquainted with the 127 inhabitants of the village, a long table was laid for the two chiefs
and the six of us, and the village girls come round bearing
the most delicious dishes. While some arranged the table,
others came and hung plaited wreaths of flowers round our
necks and smaller wreaths round our heads. These exhaled
a lingering scent and were cool and refreshing in the heat.
And so a feast of welcome began which did not end till we
left the island weeks after. Our eyes opened wide and our
mouths watered, for the tables were loaded with roast suckling pigs, chickens, roast ducks, fresh lobsters, Polynesian
fish dishes, breadfruit, papaya, and coconut milk. While we
attacked the dishes, we were entertained by the crowd singing hula songs, while young girls danced round the table.

The boys laughed and thoroughly enjoyed themselves,
each of us looking more absurd than the next as we sat and
gorged like starving men, with flowing beards and wreaths

of flowers in our hair. The two chiefs were enjoying life
as wholeheartedly as ourselves.

After the meal there was hula dancing on a grand scale.
The village wanted to show us their local folk dances. While
we six and Teka and Tupuhoe were each given stools in
the orchestra, two guitar players advanced, squatted down,
and began to strum real South Sea melodies. Two ranks of
dancing men and women, with rustling skirts of palm leaves
round their hips, came gliding and wriggling forward
through the ring of spectators who squatted and sang. They
had a lively and spirited leading singer in a luxuriantly fat
vahine, who had had one arm bitten off by a shark. At first
the dancers seemed a little self-conscious and nervous, but
when they saw that the white men from the *pae-pae* did not
turn up their noses at their ancestors' folk dances, the dancing became more and more animated. Some of the older
people joined in; they had a splendid rhythm and could
dance dances which were obviously no longer in common
use. As the sun sank into the Pacific, the dancing under the
palm trees became livelier and livelier, and the applause of
the spectators more and more spontaneous. They had forgotten that we who sat watching them were six strangers; we
were now six of their own people, enjoying ourselves with
them.

The repertory was endless; one fascinating display followed another. Finally a crowd of young men squatted down
in a close ring just in front of us, and at a sign from Tupuhoe
they began to beat time rhythmically on the ground with the
palms of their hands. First slowly, then more quickly, and
the rhythm grew more and more perfect when a drummer
suddenly joined in and accompanied them, beating at a
furious pace with two sticks on a bone-dry, hollowed block
of wood which emitted a sharp, intense sound. When the
rhythm reached the desired degree of animation, the singing
began, and suddenly a hula girl with a wreath of flowers
round her neck and flowers behind one ear leaped into the
ring. She kept time to the music with bare feet and bent
knees, swaying rhythmically at the hips and curving her
arms above her head in true Polynesian style. She danced

splendidly, and soon the whole assembly were beating time with their hands. Another girl leaped into the ring, and after her another. They moved with incredible suppleness in perfect rhythm, gliding round one another in the dance like graceful shadows. The dull beating of hands on the ground, the singing, and the cheerful wooden drum increased their tempo faster and faster and the dance grew wilder and wilder, while the spectators howled and clapped in perfect rhythm.

This was the South Seas life as the old days had known it. The stars twinkled and the palms waved. The night was mild and long and full of the scent of flowers and the song of crickets. Tupuhoe beamed and slapped me on the shoulder.

"*Maitai?*" he asked.

"Yes, *maitai,*" I replied.

"*Maitai?*" he asked all the others.

"*Maitai,*" they all replied emphatically, and they all really meant it.

"*Maitai,*" Tupuhoe nodded, pointing to himself; he too was enjoying himself now.

Even Teka thought it was a very good feast; it was the first time white men had been present at their dances on Raroia, he said. Faster and faster, faster and faster, went the rolls of the drums, the clapping, singing, and dancing. Now one of the girl dancers ceased to move round the ring and remained on the same spot, performing a wriggling dance at a terrific tempo with her arms stretched out toward Herman. Herman snickered behind his beard; he did not quite know how to take it.

"Be a good sport," I whispered. "You're a good dancer."

To the boundless delight of the crowd Herman sprang into the ring and, half crouching, tackled all the difficult wriggling movements of the hula. The jubilation was unbounded. Soon Bengt and Torstein leaped into the dance, striving till the perspiration streamed down their faces to keep up with the tempo, which rose and rose to a furious pace till the drum alone was beating in one prolonged drone and the three real hula dancers quivering in time like aspen

leaves. Then they sank down in the finales and the drumbeats
ceased abruptly.

Now the evening was ours. There was no end to the
enthusiasm.

The next item on the program was the bird dance, which
was one of the oldest ceremonies on Raroia. Men and women
in two ranks jumped forward in a rhythmic dance, imitating
flocks of birds following a leader. The dance leader had the
title of chief of the birds and performed curious maneuvers
without actually joining in the dance. When the dance was
over, Tupuhoe explained that it had been performed in
honor of the raft and would now be repeated , but the dance
leader would be relieved by myself. As the dance leader's
main task appeared to me to consist in uttering wild howls,
hopping around on his haunches, wriggling his backside,
and waving his hands over his head, I pulled the wreath of
flowers well down over my head and marched out into the
arena. While I was curving myself in the dance, I saw old
Tupuhoe laughing till he nearly fell off his stool, and the
music grew feeble because the singers and players followed
Tupuhoe's example.

Now everyone wanted to dance, old and young alike, and
soon the drummer and earth-beaters were there again, giving
the lead to a fiery hula-hula dance. First the hula girls sprang
into the ring and started the dance at a tempo that grew wilder
and wilder, and then we were invited to dance in turn, while
more and more men and women followed, stamping and
writhing along, faster and faster.

But Erik could not be made to stir. The drafts and damp on
board the raft had revived his vanished lumbago and he sat
like an old yacht skipper, stiff and bearded, puffing at his
pipe. He would not be moved by the hula girls who tried to
lure him into the arena. He had put on a pair of wide sheepskin trousers which he had worn at night in the coldest spells
in the Humboldt Current, and, sitting under the palms with
his big beard, body bare to the waist, and sheepskin breeches,
he was a faithful copy of Robinson Crusoe. One pretty girl
after another tried to ingratiate herself, but in vain. He only

sat gravely puffing his pipe, with the wreath of flowers in his bushy hair.

Then a well-developed matron with powerful muscles entered the arena, executed a few more or less graceful hula steps, and then marched determinedly toward Erik. He looked alarmed, but the amazon smiled ingratiatingly, caught him resolutely by the arm, and pulled him off of his stool. Erik's comic pair of breeches had the sheep's wool inside and the skin outside, and they had a rent behind so that a white spot of wool stuck out like a rabbit's tail. Erik followed most reluctantly and limped into the ring with his pipe in one hand and the other pressed against the spot where his lumbago hurt him. When he tried to jump round, he had to let go of his trousers to save his wreath which was threatening to fall off, and then, with the wreath on one side, he had to catch hold of his trousers again, which were coming down of their own weight. The stout dame who was hobbling round in the hula in front of him was just as funny, and tears of laughter trickled down our beards. Soon all the others who were in the ring stopped, and salvos of laughter rang through the palm grove as Hula Erik and the female heavyweight circled gracefully round. At last even they had to stop, because both singers and musicians had more than they could do to hold their sides for laughter at the comic sight.

The feast went on till broad daylight, when we were allowed to have a little pause, after again shaking hands with every one of the 127. We shook hands with every one of them every morning and every evening throughout our stay on the island. Six beds were scraped together from all the huts in the village and placed side by side along the wall in the meetinghouse, and in these we slept in a row like the seven little dwarfs in the fairy story, with sweet-smelling wreaths of flowers hanging above our heads.

Next day the boy of six who had an abscess on his head seemed to be in a bad way. He had a temperature of 106°, and the abscess was as large as a man's fist and throbbed painfully.

Teka declared that they had lost a number of children in this way and that, if none of us could do any doctoring, the boy had not many days to live. We had bottles of penicillin in a new tablet form, but we did not know what dose a small child could stand. If the boy died under our treatment, it might have serious consequences for all of us.

Knut and Torstein got the radio out again and slung up an aerial between the tallest coconut palms. When evening came they got in touch again with our unseen friends, Hal and Frank, sitting in their rooms at home in Los Angeles. Frank called a doctor on the telephone, and we signaled with the Morse key all the boy's symptoms and a list of what we had available in our medical chest. Frank passed on the doctor's reply, and that night we went off to the hut where little Haumata lay tossing in a fever with half the village weeping and making a noise about him.

Herman and Knut were to do the doctoring, while we others had more than enough to do to keep the villagers outside. The mother became hysterical when we came with a sharp knife and asked for boiling water. All the hair was shaved off the boy's head and the abscess was opened. The pus squirted up almost to the roof, and several of the natives forced their way in in a state of fury and had to be turned out. It was a grave moment. When the abscess was drained and sterilized, the boy's head was bound up and we began the penicillin cure. For two days and nights, while the fever was at its maximum, the boy was treated every four hours, and the abscess was kept open. And each evening the doctor in Los Angeles was consulted. Then the boy's temperature fell suddenly, the pus was replaced by plasma which was allowed to heal, and the boy was beaming and wanting to look at pictures from the white man's strange world where there were motorcars and cows and houses with several floors.

A week later Haumata was playing on the beach with the other children, his head bound up in a big bandage which he was soon allowed to take off.

When this had gone well, there was no end to the maladies which cropped up in the village. Toothache and gastric troubles were everywhere, and both old and young had boils in one place or another. We referred the patients to Dr. Knut and Dr. Herman, who ordered diets and emptied the medicine chest of pills and ointments. Some were cured and none became worse, and, when the medicine chest was empty, we made oatmeal porridge and cocoa, which were admirably efficacious with hysterical women.

We had not been among our brown admirers for many days before the festivities culminated in a fresh ceremony. We were to be adopted as citizens of Raroia and receive Polynesian names. I myself was no longer to be Terai Mateata; I could be called that in Tahiti, but not here among them.

Six stools were placed for us in the middle of the square, and the whole village was out early to get good places in the circle round. Teka sat solemnly among them; he was chief all right, but not where old local ceremonies were concerned. Then Tupuhoe took over.

All sat waiting, silent and profoundly serious, while portly Tupuhoe approached solemnly and slowly with his stout knotted stick. He was conscious of the gravity of the moment, and the eyes of all were upon him as he came up, deep in thought, and took up his position in front of us. He was the born chief—a brilliant speaker and actor.

He turned to the chief singers, drummers, and dance leaders, pointed at them in turn with his knotted stick, and gave them curt orders in low, measured tones. Then he turned to us again, and suddenly opened his great eyes wide, so that the large white eyeballs shone as bright as the teeth in his expressive copper-brown face. He raised the knotted stick and, the words streaming from his lips in an uninterrupted flow, he recited ancient rituals which none but the oldest members understood, because they were in an old forgotten dialect.

Then he told us, with Teka as interpreter, that Tikaroa was the name of the first king who had established himself on the island, and that he had reigned over this same atoll from north to south, from east to west, and up into the sky above men's heads.

While the whole choir joined in the old ballad about King Tikaroa, Tupuhoe laid his great hand on my chest and, turning to the audience, said that he was naming me Varoa Tikaroa, or Tikaroa's Spirit.

When the song died away, it was the turn of Herman and Bengt. They had the big brown hand laid upon their chests in turn and received the names Tupuhoe-Itetahua and Topa-kino. These were the names of two old-time heros who had fought a savage sea monster and killed it at the entrance to the Raroia reef.

The drummer delivered a few vigorous rolls, and two robust men with knotted-up loincloths and a long spear in each hand sprang forward. They broke into a march in double-quick time, with their knees raised to their chests and their spears pointing upward, and turned their heads from side to side. At a fresh beat of the drum they leaped into the air and, in perfect rhythm, began a ceremonial battle in the purest ballet style. The whole thing was short and swift and represented the heroes' fight with the sea monster. Then Torstein was named with song and ceremony; he was called Maroake, after a former king in the present village, and Erik and Knut received the names of Tane-Matarau and Tefaunui after two navigators and sea heroes of the past. The long monotonous recitation which accompanied their naming was delivered at breakneck speed and with a continuous flow of words, the incredible rapidity of which was calculated both to impress and amuse.

The ceremony was over. Once more there were white and bearded chiefs among the Polynesian people on Raroia. Two ranks of male and female dancers came forward in plaited straw skirts with swaying bast crowns on their heads. They danced forward to us and transferred the crowns from their own heads to ours; we had rustling straw skirts put round our waists, and the festivities continued.

One night the flower-clad radio operators got into touch with the radio amateur on Rarotonga, who passed on a message to us from Tahiti. It was a cordial welcome from the governor of the French Pacific colonies.

On instructions from Paris he had sent the government schooner "Tamara" to fetch us to Tahiti, so we should not have to wait for the uncertain arrival of the copra schooner. Tahiti was the central point of the French colonies and the only island which had contact with the world in general. We should have to go via Tahiti to get the regular boat home to our own world.

The festivities continued on Raroia. One night some strange hoots were heard from out at sea, and lookout men came down from the palm tops and reported that a vessel was lying at the entrance to the lagoon. We ran through the palm forest and down to the beach on the lee side. Here we looked out over the sea in the opposite direction to that from which we had come. There were much smaller breakers on this side, which lay under the shelter of the entire atoll and the reef.

Just outside the entrance to the lagoon we saw the lights of a vessel. Since the night was clear and starry, we could distinguish the outlines of a broad-beamed schooner with two masts. Was this the governor's ship which was coming for us? Why did she not come in?

The natives grew more and more uneasy. Now we too saw what was happening. The vessel had a heavy list and threatened to capsize. She was aground on an invisible coral reef under the surface.

Torstein got hold of a light and signaled:

"Quel bateau?"

" 'Maoae,' " was flashed back.

The "Maoae" was the copra schooner which ran between the islands. She was on her way to Raroia to fetch copra. There was a Polynesian captain and crew on board, and they knew the reefs inside out. But the current out of the lagoon was treacherous in darkness. It was lucky that the schooner lay under the lee of the island and that the weather was quiet. The list of the "Maoae" became heavier and heavier, and the crew took to the boat. Strong ropes were made fast to her mastheads and rowed in to the land, where the natives fastened them round coconut palms to prevent the schooner from capsizing. The crew, with other ropes, stationed themselves off the opening in the reef in their boat, in the hope of rowing the "Maoae" off when the tidal current ran out of the lagoon. The people of the village launched all their canoes and set out to salvage the cargo. There were ninety tons of valuable copra on board. Load after load of sacks of

copra was transferred from the rolling schooner and brought
on to dry land.

At high water the "Maoae" was still aground, bumping
and rolling against the corals until she sprang a leak. When
day broke she was lying in a worse position on the reef than
ever. The crew could do nothing; it was useless to try to
haul the heavy 150-ton schooner off the reef with her own
boat and the canoes. If she continued to lie bumping where
she was, she would knock herself to pieces, and, if the
weather changed, she would be lifted in by the suction and
be a total loss in the surf which beat against the atoll.

The "Maoae" had no radio, but we had. But it would be
impossible to get a salvage vessel from Tahiti until the
"Maoae" would have had ample time to roll herself into
wreckage. Yet for the second time that month Raroia reef
was balked of its prey.

About noon the same day the schooner "Tamara" came in
sight on the horizon to westward. She had been sent to fetch
us from Raroia, and those on board were not a little astonished when they saw, instead of a raft, the two masts of a
large schooner lying and rolling helplessly on the reef.

On board the "Tamara" was the French administrator of
the Tuamotu and Tubuai groups, M. Frédéric Ahnne, whom
the governor had sent with the vessel from Tahiti to meet
us. There were also a French movie photographer and a
French telegrapher on board, but the captain and crew were
Polynesian. M. Ahnne himself had been born in Tahiti of
French parents and was a splendid seaman. He took over
the command of the vessel with the consent of the Tahitian
captain, who was delighted to be freed from the responsibility
in those dangerous waters. While the "Tamara" was avoiding
a myriad of submerged reefs and eddies, stout hawsers were
stretched between the two schooners and M. Ahnne began
his skillful and dangerous evolutions, while the tide threatened to drag both vessels on to the same coral bank.

At high tide the "Maoae" came off the reef, and the "Tamara" towed her out into deep water. But now water poured
through the hull of the "Maoae," and she had to be hauled
with all speed on to the shallows in the lagoon. For three

days the "Maoae" lay off the village in a sinking condition, with all pumps going day and night. The best pearl divers among our friends on the island went down with lead plates and nails and stopped the worst leaks, so that the "Maoae" could be escorted by the "Tamara" to the dockyard in Tahiti with her pumps working.

When the "Maoae" was ready to be escorted, M. Ahnne maneuvered the "Tamara" between the coral shallows in the lagoon and across to Kon-Tiki Island. The raft was taken in tow, and then he set his course back to the opening with the *Kon-Tiki* in tow and the "Maoae" so close behind that the crew could be taken off if the leaks got the upper hand out at sea.

Our farewell to Raroia was more than sad. Everyone who could walk or crawl was down on the jetty, playing and singing our favorite tunes as the ship's boat took us out to the "Tamara."

Tupuhoe bulked large in the center, holding little Haumata by the hand. Haumata was crying, and tears trickled down the cheeks of the powerful chief. There was not a dry eye on the jetty, but they kept the singing and music going long, long after the breakers from the reef drowned all other sounds in our ears.

Those faithful souls who stood on the jetty singing were losing six friends. We who stood mute at the rail of the "Tamara" till the jetty was hidden by the palms and the palms sank into the sea were losing 127. We still heard the strange music with our inner ear:

"—and share memories with us so that we can always be together, even when you go away to a far land. Good day."

Four days later Tahiti rose out of the sea. Not like a string of pearls with palm tufts. As wild jagged blue mountains flung skyward, with wisps of cloud like wreaths round the peaks.

As we gradually approached, the blue mountains showed green slopes. Green upon green, the lush vegetation of the south rolled down over rust-red hills and cliffs, till it plunged down into deep ravines and valleys running out toward the sea. When the coast came near, we saw slender palms stand-

ing close packed up all the valleys and all along the coast
behind a golden beach. Tahiti was built by old volcanoes.
They were dead now and the coral polyps had slung their
protecting reef about the island so that the sea could not
erode it away.

Early one morning we headed through an opening in the
reef into the harbor of Papeete. Before us lay church spires
and red roofs half hidden by the foliage of giant trees and
palm tops. Papeete was the capital of Tahiti, the only town
in French Oceania. It was a city of pleasure, the seat of government, and the center of all traffic in the eastern Pacific.

When we came into the harbor, the population of Tahiti
stood waiting, packed tight like a gaily colored living wall.
News spreads like the wind in Tahiti, and the *pae-pae* which
had come from America was something everyone wanted to
see.

The *Kon-Tiki* was given the place of honor alongside the
shore promenade, the mayor of Papeete welcomed us, and a
little Polynesian girl presented us with an enormous wheel of
Tahitian wild flowers on behalf of the Polynesian Society.
Then young girls came forward and hung sweet-smelling
white wreaths of flowers round our necks as a welcome to
Tahiti, the pearl of the South Seas.

There was one particular face I was looking for in the
multitude, that of my old adoptive father in Tahiti, the chief
Teriieroo, head of the seventeen native chiefs on the island.
He was not missing. Big and bulky, and as bright and alive
as in the old days, he emerged from the crowd calling, "Terai
Mateata!" and beaming all over his broad face. He had become an old man, but he was the same impressive chieftainly
figure.

"You come late," he said smiling, "but you come with good
news. Your *pae-pae* has in truth brought blue sky (*terai mateata*) to Tahiti, for now we know where our fathers came
from."

There was a reception at the governor's palace and a party
at the town hall, and invitations poured in from every corner
of the hospitable island.

As in former days, a great feast was given by the chief Teriieroo at his house in the Papeno Valley which I knew so well, and, as Raroia was not Tahiti, there was a new ceremony at which Tahitian names were given those who had none before.

Those were carefree days under sun and drifting clouds. We bathed in the lagoon, climbed in the mountains, and danced the hula on the grass under the palms. The days passed and became weeks. It seemed as if the weeks would become months before a ship came which could take us home to the duties that awaited us.

Then came a message from Norway saying that Lars Christensen had ordered the 4,000-tonner "Thor I" to proceed from Samoa to Tahiti to pick up the expedition and take it to America.

Early one morning the big Norwegian steamer glided into Papeete harbor, and the *Kon-Tiki* was towed out by a French naval craft to the side of her large compatriot, which swung out a huge iron arm and lifted her small kinsman up on to her deck. Loud blasts of the ship's siren echoed over the palm-clad island. Brown and white people thronged the quay of Papeete and poured on board with farewell gifts and wreaths of flowers. We stood at the rail stretching out our necks like giraffes to get our chins free from the ever growing load of flowers.

"If you wish to come back to Tahiti," Chief Teriieroo cried as the whistle sounded over the island for the last time, "you must throw a wreath out into the lagoon when the boat goes!"

The ropes were cast off, the engines roared, and the propeller whipped the water green as we slid sideways away from the quay.

Soon the red roofs disappeared behind the palms, and the palms were swallowed up in the blue of the mountains which sank like shadows into the Pacific.

Waves were breaking out on the blue sea. We could no longer reach down to them. White trade-wind clouds drifted across the blue sky. We were no longer traveling their way. We were defying Nature now. We were going back to the twentieth century which lay so far, far away.

But the six of us on deck, standing beside our nine dear balsa logs, were grateful to be all alive. And in the lagoon at Tahiti six white wreaths lay alone, washing in and out, in and out, with the wavelets on the beach.

PUBLISHER'S NOTE

Mr. Heyerdahl's manuscript, "Polynesia and America: A Study of Prehistoric Relations", mentioned in the first two chapters of KON-TIKI as presenting the author's scientific arguments in favor of his migration theory, has now been published by Rand McNally & Company under the title, AMERICAN INDIANS IN THE PACIFIC: THE THEORY BEHIND THE KON-TIKI EXPEDITION.

Index